BLACK SCHOLES

Algorithmic Options Trading with Rust

Hayden Van Der Post

Reactive Publishing

CONTENTS

CHAPTER 1: INTRODUCTION TO OPTIONS AND RUST

I n the financial markets, options are versatile instruments that provide significant strategic flexibility. They offer the holder the right, but not the obligation, to buy or sell an underlying asset at a predetermined price within a specific timeframe. This functionality allows investors to hedge risks, speculate on future price movements, or generate income. To fully harness the potential of options, it is essential to understand the fundamentals of call and put options, their characteristics, and their strategic applications.

Call Options: The Right to Buy

A call option grants the holder the right to purchase the underlying asset at the strike price before the option's expiry. This type of option is particularly beneficial when an investor anticipates a rise in the asset's price. The key elements of a call option include the underlying asset, the strike price, and the expiration date.

Key Characteristics

-Underlying Asset: The asset that the option pertains to, such as a stock, index, or commodity.

-Strike Price: The price at which the holder can buy the asset.

-Expiration Date: The date by which the option must be exercised.

Example Scenario

Consider an investor holding a call option for a stock with a strike price of $100, expiring in one month. If the stock's market price rises to $120 before the option expires, the holder can exercise the option to buy the stock at the strike price of $100. The investor can then sell the stock at the current market price of $120, realizing a profit, excluding the premium paid for the option.

In this scenario, the profit from exercising the call option is calculated as:

$$\text{Profit} = (\text{Market Price} - \text{Strike Price}) - \text{Premium Paid}$$

$$\text{Profit} = (120 - 100) - \text{Premium Paid}$$

Strategic Applications

-Speculation: Investors use call options to speculate on the upward movement of asset prices with limited risk. The maximum loss is limited to the premium paid for the option.

-Hedging: Call options can hedge against short positions. If an investor has sold a stock short, a call option can protect against potential losses if the stock price rises.

-Income Generation: Writing call options (selling call options) against owned stocks can generate income through the premiums received. This strategy, known as covered call writing, is common among income-focused investors.

Put Options: The Right to Sell

Conversely, a put option provides the holder the right to sell the underlying asset at the strike price before the expiration date. Put options are advantageous when an investor expects a decline in the asset's price. The essential elements of a put option are similar to those of a call option: the underlying asset, the strike price, and the expiration date.

Key Characteristics

-Underlying Asset: The asset subject to the option.

-Strike Price: The price at which the holder can sell the asset.

-Expiration Date: The date by which the option must be exercised.

Example Scenario

Imagine an investor holds a put option for a stock with a strike price of $100, expiring in one month. If the stock's market price falls to $80 before the expiration, the holder can exercise the option to sell the stock at the strike price of $100. This allows the investor to sell the stock at a higher price than the current market value, realizing a profit, excluding the premium paid for the option.

In this case, the profit from exercising the put option is calculated as:

\[\text{Profit} = (\text{Strike Price} - \text{Market Price}) - \text{Premium Paid} \]

\[\text{Profit} = (100 - 80) - \text{Premium Paid} \]

Strategic Applications

-Speculation: Investors use put options to speculate on the decline in asset prices. The maximum loss is limited to the premium paid for the option.

-Hedging: Put options can provide insurance against long positions. If an investor owns a stock, a put option can protect against potential losses if the stock price falls.

-Portfolio Protection: Put options are often used to protect the overall portfolio value during market downturns. This strategy, known as portfolio insurance, is crucial for risk management.

Pricing and Volatility Considerations

The value of call and put options depends on several factors, including the price of the underlying asset, the strike price, the time to expiration, interest rates, and volatility. The Black-Scholes model, which will be discussed in subsequent sections, is a widely-used framework for pricing options by incorporating these variables.

Intrinsic Value vs. Extrinsic Value

-Intrinsic Value: The difference between the underlying asset's current price and the option's strike price. For call options, it is the amount by which the asset's price exceeds the strike price. For put options, it is the amount by which the strike price exceeds the asset's price.

-Extrinsic Value: Also known as the time value, it represents the additional value based on the time remaining until expiration and the asset's volatility. The longer the time to expiration and the higher the volatility, the greater the extrinsic value.

The Role of Volatility

Volatility plays a crucial role in options pricing. Higher volatility increases the likelihood of the option finishing in the money, thereby increasing its premium. Conversely, lower volatility lowers the option premium as the chances of significant price movements decrease.

Mastering the basics of call and put options is foundational for any financial professional or trader looking to leverage these instruments effectively. Understanding the mechanics, key characteristics, and strategic applications of options provides a solid groundwork for more advanced topics, such as options pricing models and algorithmic trading strategies. As we transition to deeper dives into the Black-Scholes model and its implementation in Rust, this knowledge will be essential for grasping the intricate dynamics that drive the financial markets.

A Modern Approach to Systems Programming

In the ever-evolving landscape of programming languages, Rust has emerged as a powerful contender, redefining efficiency and safety in systems programming. Created by Graydon Hoare and backed by Mozilla Research, Rust aims to provide a safer alternative to languages like C and C++ without compromising on performance. What sets Rust apart is its unique approach to memory management, known as ownership, which ensures memory safety without needing a garbage collector.

The Need for Rust in Financial Applications

The financial industry demands high-performance computing with minimal risk of errors, especially in algorithmic trading where milliseconds can mean millions. Rust's design principles align perfectly with these requirements. Unlike traditional languages, Rust offers both high-level abstractions and low-level control, making it an ideal choice for performance-critical applications. Its memory safety features prevent common bugs that can lead to costly errors in financial software, providing a robust framework for building reliable trading systems.

Key Features of Rust

Memory Safety

Rust's ownership system ensures that memory errors such as null pointer dereferencing and buffer overflows are caught at compile time. This system revolves around three key concepts: ownership, borrowing, and lifetimes. These concepts work together to ensure that each piece of data has a single owner at a time, preventing data races and ensuring thread safety.

Example:

```rust
fn main() {
let s1 = String::from("Hello");
let s2 = s1; // s1 is no longer valid after this point
println!("{}", s2); // This works
// println!("{}", s1); // This will cause a compile-time error
}
```

In this example, once `s1` is assigned to `s2`, `s1` is no longer accessible, preventing potential memory errors.

Performance and Concurrency

Rust provides high-level abstractions without sacrificing low-level control. It allows for fine-tuned performance optimizations and supports zero-cost abstractions, which means the abstractions you write in Rust get compiled down to as efficient code as if you had written it in assembly.

Concurrency is also a strong suit of Rust. The language's ownership model extends to concurrent programming, preventing data races at compile time. This makes it easier to write safe and efficient multithreaded code, which is crucial for high-frequency trading applications.

Example:

```rust
use std::thread;

fn main() {
let handle = thread::spawn(|| {
for i in 1..10 {
println!("Hello from thread: {}", i);
}
});

for i in 1..5 {
println!("Hello from main: {}", i);
}

handle.join().unwrap();
}
```

This code snippet demonstrates creating and joining a thread, showcasing Rust's straightforward approach to concurrency.

Rich Type System and Pattern Matching

Rust's type system is both expressive and safe, allowing for robust error handling and pattern matching. Enums in Rust can hold multiple data types, and the match expression provides powerful pattern-matching capabilities, simplifying complex decision-making processes.

Example:

```rust
enum Option<T> {
Some(T),
None,
}

fn main() {
let number = Some(5);

match number {
Some(n) => println!("Number is: {}", n),
None => println!("No number found"),
}
}
```

In this example, Rust's enum and match features are used to handle optional values safely and concisely.

Ecosystem and Community

Rust has a thriving ecosystem and a supportive community, contributing to its rapid adoption. The Cargo package manager simplifies the process of managing dependencies, building projects, and running tests. Additionally, the Rust community is known for its commitment to inclusivity and collaboration, providing extensive documentation and resources for developers of all skill levels.

Example:

``` rust
[dependencies]
serde = "1.0"
serde_json = "1.0"
```

Adding dependencies in a Cargo.toml file is straightforward, allowing for easy integration of third-party libraries.

Setting Up the Rust Environment

Getting started with Rust is a streamlined process, thanks to its robust toolchain and clear documentation. Here's a step-by-step guide to setting up the Rust environment on your machine:

1.Installation: Rustup, the official installer for Rust, simplifies the installation process. You can install Rust by running the following command:

``` sh
curl --proto '=https' --tlsv1.2 -sSf https://sh.rustup.rs | sh
```

2.Verifying Installation: After the installation, verify that Rust is correctly installed by running:

``` sh
```

rustc --version

` ` `

3.Setting Up a New Project: Cargo, Rust's package manager, makes it easy to create new projects. Use the following command to create a new project:

` ` `sh

cargo new my_project

cd my_project

` ` `

4.Building and Running: To build and run your project, use Cargo commands:

` ` `sh

cargo build

cargo run

` ` `

5.Adding Dependencies: Modify the `Cargo.toml` file to add dependencies for your project. For example, to add the `serde` and `serde_json` libraries for serialization, update the `[dependencies]` section as follows:

` ` `toml

[dependencies]

serde = "1.0"

serde_json = "1.0"

```
```
```

Then, run:

```sh
cargo build
```

6. Writing Your First Rust Program: Edit the `src/main.rs` file to include your Rust code. Here's a simple "Hello, World!" program:

```rust
fn main() {
println!("Hello, world!");
}
```

7. Running Tests: Rust's built-in testing framework allows you to write and run tests seamlessly. Create a test in `src/lib.rs`:

```rust
#[cfg(test)]
mod tests {
#[test]
fn it_works() {
assert_eq!(2 + 2, 4);
}
```
```

```
}
```

Run the tests using:

```sh
cargo test
```

Rust stands out as a modern programming language designed to meet the demands of high-performance and safe systems programming. Its unique features, such as memory safety, concurrency support, and a rich ecosystem, make it an excellent choice for financial applications. Understanding Rust's fundamentals and setting up the development environment is the first step towards leveraging its capabilities for algorithmic options trading. As we delve deeper into Rust's advanced features and their applications in the financial domain, you'll appreciate the advantages it brings to the table, laying a solid foundation for building sophisticated trading algorithms.

Setting up the Rust Environment

Installation

The Rust programming environment is built around several key components: the Rust compiler (`rustc`), the package manager (`Cargo`), and the installer (`rustup`). These tools work together seamlessly to provide a robust development experience.

1.Install Rustup: Rustup is the recommended way to install Rust because it manages both the installation and updating of Rust, along with its toolchains. To install Rustup, run the following command in your terminal:

```sh
curl --proto '=https' --tlsv1.2 -sSf https://sh.rustup.rs | sh
```

2.Follow Instructions: The command above will download and run the Rustup installation script. Follow the on-screen instructions to complete the installation. This script installs the latest stable version of Rust, along with Cargo, the Rust package manager.

3.Add `~/.cargo/bin` to PATH: The installation process should automatically add Rust's binary directory to your system's PATH environment variable. If it doesn't, you can manually add it by editing your shell's configuration file (e.g., `.bashrc`, `.zshrc`) and adding the following line:

```sh
export PATH="$HOME/.cargo/bin:$PATH"
```

4.Verify Installation: After installation, verify that Rust is correctly installed by running:

```sh
rustc --version
```

cargo --version

``` ` ` ` ```

If both commands return version numbers, your installation is successful.

Setting Up a New Project

Once Rust is installed, you can start creating projects using Cargo. Cargo is more than just a package manager; it handles project creation, building, running, and managing dependencies.

1.Create a New Project: To create a new Rust project, use the `cargo new` command, followed by the project name. For example:

``` ` ` ` sh```

cargo new my_project

``` ` ` ` ```

This command creates a new directory called `my_project`, containing a simple "Hello, World!" Rust application.

2.Navigate to Project Directory: Move into the newly created project directory:

``` ` ` ` sh```

cd my_project

``` ` ` ` ```
```

3.Project Structure: The project directory will have the following structure:

```
my_project
├── Cargo.toml
└── src
└── main.rs
```

The `Cargo.toml` file is where you manage your project's metadata and dependencies. The `src` directory contains the source code, starting with `main.rs`.

Building and Running Your Project

Building and running a Rust project is straightforward with Cargo.

1.Build the Project: To compile the project, use the `cargo build` command:

```sh
cargo build
```

This command compiles the project and places the executable in the `target/debug` directory.

2.Run the Project: To run the compiled project, use the `cargo run` command:

```sh
cargo run
```

This command combines the build and run steps into one. You'll see the output of your program in the terminal. For the default project, it will display:

```
Hello, world!
```

3.Release Build: For an optimized build suitable for production, use the `--release` flag with the build command:

```sh
cargo build --release
```

The optimized executable will be placed in the `target/release` directory.

Managing Dependencies

Rust's ecosystem is rich with libraries, known as "crates,"

that you can leverage to extend your project's functionality. Managing these dependencies is done through the `Cargo.toml` file.

1.Adding Dependencies: To add a dependency, simply edit the `Cargo.toml` file and include the desired crate in the `[dependencies]` section. For example, to add the `serde` crate for serialization and deserialization, update the file as follows:

```toml
[dependencies]
serde = "1.0"
```

2.Building with Dependencies: After adding a dependency, run `cargo build` to download and compile the crate. Cargo fetches the crate from the central repository, `crates.io`, and integrates it into your project.

3.Using Dependencies: You can now use the crate in your code. For instance, to use `serde` for JSON serialization, add the following to your `src/main.rs`:

```rust
use serde::{Serialize, Deserialize};

#[derive(Serialize, Deserialize)]
struct MyStruct {
name: String,
```

```rust
age: u8,
}

fn main() {
let instance = MyStruct {
name: String::from("Alice"),
age: 30,
};

let json = serde_json::to_string(&instance).unwrap();
println!("{}", json);
}
```

Testing Your Code

Rust comes with a built-in test framework to help you write and run tests efficiently. Writing tests ensures that your code works as expected and helps catch bugs early.

1.Creating Tests: Tests are typically placed in a `tests` module within the same file as the code being tested. Here's an example of a simple test in `src/main.rs`:

```rust
#[cfg(test)]
mod tests {
#[test]
```

```
fn it_works() {
assert_eq!(2 + 2, 4);
}

#[test]
#[should_panic]
fn it_fails() {
assert_eq!(2 + 2, 5);
}
}
```
` ` `

2.Running Tests: To run the tests, use the `cargo test` command:

```sh
cargo test
```
` ` `

This command compiles the tests and runs them, displaying the results in the terminal.

1.4b.6 Setting Up Your Development Environment

To streamline your development workflow, consider integrating your Rust environment with an Integrated Development Environment (IDE) or text editor that supports Rust.

1.Visual Studio Code: VS Code is a popular choice with robust Rust support. Install the `rust-analyzer` extension for features like code completion, linting, and debugging.

```sh
code --install-extension rust-lang.rust
```

2.IntelliJ IDEA: Another powerful IDE for Rust development is IntelliJ IDEA with the Rust plugin. Download and install the plugin from the JetBrains plugin repository.

3.Configuring the Editor: Configure your editor to format code on save and provide real-time feedback on errors and warnings through `rustfmt` and `clippy`. Add the following configurations:

- For VS Code, add to `settings.json`:

```json
"rust-analyzer.checkOnSave.command": "clippy",
"editor.formatOnSave": true
```

- For IntelliJ IDEA, configure Rust settings to use `clippy` and `rustfmt`.

Setting up the Rust environment is your gateway to developing high-performance and reliable software. From installation to project creation, dependency management, and testing, Rust provides a streamlined process that emphasizes safety and efficiency. Integrating Rust with your preferred development tools further enhances your productivity, enabling you to focus on building sophisticated financial applications. As you advance through this book, you'll see how this robust environment serves as a foundation for implementing complex algorithms and trading strategies, leveraging Rust's full potential to revolutionize your approach to algorithmic options trading.

The Evolution of Algorithmic Trading

Algorithmic trading has its roots in the early 1970s when the New York Stock Exchange (NYSE) introduced the Designated Order Turnaround (DOT) system. This system allowed brokers to send orders electronically rather than making physical trades on the exchange floor. Over time, advancements in technology and data processing capabilities have propelled algo trading to the forefront of modern finance.

In the 1990s, the rise of electronic communication networks (ECNs) and the introduction of decimalization, which allowed stock prices to be quoted in cents rather than fractions, further accelerated the adoption of algorithmic trading. The ability to process vast amounts of data in real-time and execute trades within milliseconds has fundamentally changed the landscape of financial markets.

Key Concepts in Algorithmic Trading

To grasp the intricacies of algorithmic trading, it's essential to understand the key concepts that underpin this field:

1.Algorithms: At its core, algorithmic trading relies on mathematical models and algorithms to make trading decisions. These algorithms analyze market data, identify trading opportunities, and execute trades automatically, according to predefined rules.

2.Latency: Latency refers to the delay between the initiation and execution of a trade. Lower latency is critical in algorithmic trading, where milliseconds can make the difference between profit and loss. High-frequency trading (HFT) is a subset of algorithmic trading that prioritizes ultra-low latency to capitalize on fleeting market inefficiencies.

3.Order Types: Algorithmic trading employs various order types, including market orders, limit orders, and stop orders. Each order type serves a specific purpose, such as executing trades at current market prices or setting conditions for trade execution.

4.Execution Strategies: Execution strategies determine how trades are placed in the market. Common strategies include time-weighted average price (TWAP), volume-weighted average price (VWAP), and implementation shortfall. These strategies aim to minimize the impact of large trades on market prices and optimize execution costs.

5.Backtesting: Before deploying an algorithm in live trading, it is crucial to backtest it using historical market data. Backtesting helps evaluate the algorithm's performance, identify potential flaws, and refine trading strategies.

Benefits of Algorithmic Trading

Algorithmic trading offers several advantages over traditional manual trading methods:

1.Speed and Efficiency: Algorithms can process vast amounts of data and execute trades faster than human traders, ensuring timely responses to market movements.

2.Precision: Algorithms operate based on predefined rules, eliminating the risk of human error and emotional biases that can affect trading decisions.

3.Cost Reduction: By automating trading processes, algo trading reduces transaction costs associated with manual trading, such as brokerage fees and slippage.

4.Scalability: Algorithms can handle multiple trading strategies simultaneously, allowing traders to diversify their portfolios and manage risk more effectively.

5.Consistency: Algorithms consistently apply trading rules and strategies, ensuring a disciplined approach to trading that is not influenced by market noise or psychological factors.

Challenges and Risks

Despite its benefits, algorithmic trading also presents certain challenges and risks:

1.Technical Failures: Algorithmic trading systems rely heavily on technology, and technical failures such as software bugs, hardware malfunctions, or connectivity issues can lead to significant trading losses.

2.Market Impact: Large orders executed by algorithms can impact market prices, causing adverse price movements and potentially triggering regulatory scrutiny.

3.Overfitting: Backtested algorithms may perform well on historical data but fail in live markets due to overfitting, where the algorithm is too closely tailored to past data and not robust enough to handle future market conditions.

4.Regulatory Compliance: Algorithmic trading is subject to regulatory oversight, and traders must ensure compliance with market regulations and reporting requirements to avoid legal and financial penalties.

Types of Algorithmic Trading Strategies

Algorithmic trading encompasses a wide range of strategies, each designed to exploit specific market conditions and opportunities:

1.Trend Following: Trend-following algorithms identify and capitalize on market trends by entering positions in the direction of the prevailing trend. These strategies can be based on technical indicators such as moving averages, momentum, and relative strength index (RSI).

2.Arbitrage: Arbitrage algorithms seek to profit from price discrepancies between correlated assets or markets. Examples include statistical arbitrage, index arbitrage, and cross-market arbitrage.

3.Market Making: Market-making algorithms provide liquidity by continuously quoting bid and ask prices for a particular asset. These algorithms profit from the bid-ask spread while managing inventory and minimizing risk.

4.Mean Reversion: Mean reversion algorithms are based on the idea that asset prices tend to revert to their historical averages. These strategies identify overbought or oversold conditions and take positions anticipating a return to the mean.

5.Statistical Arbitrage: Statistical arbitrage strategies use statistical methods to identify and exploit pricing inefficiencies between related securities. These strategies often involve pairs trading, where long and short positions are taken in two correlated assets.

6.Machine Learning: Machine learning algorithms leverage advanced data analysis techniques to identify patterns and make predictions based on historical data. These algorithms can adapt and improve over time, enhancing their effectiveness in dynamic market conditions.

Algorithmic Trading in Practice

In practice, algorithmic trading involves several key steps:

1.Strategy Development: The first step is to develop a trading strategy based on sound financial principles and quantitative analysis. This involves defining entry and exit rules, risk management parameters, and execution strategies.

2.Backtesting: Once the strategy is developed, it is backtested using historical market data to evaluate its performance and make necessary adjustments. Backtesting helps identify potential flaws and optimize the strategy for better results.

3.Optimization: After backtesting, the strategy is optimized by fine-tuning parameters and incorporating additional factors to improve performance and robustness.

4.Paper Trading: Before deploying the strategy in live markets, it is tested in a simulated trading environment, known as paper trading. This allows traders to assess the strategy's performance in real-time without risking actual capital.

5.Live Trading: Once the strategy has been validated through backtesting and paper trading, it is deployed in live markets. Continuous monitoring and periodic adjustments are essential to ensure the strategy remains effective under changing market conditions.

The Role of Rust in Algorithmic Trading

Rust's unique features make it an ideal choice for developing high-performance algorithmic trading systems:

1.Memory Safety: Rust's strong emphasis on memory safety helps prevent common programming errors such as null pointer dereferencing and buffer overflows, which can lead to crashes and vulnerabilities in trading systems.

2.Concurrency: Rust's ownership model and concurrency

primitives enable the development of highly parallel and concurrent trading algorithms, allowing for efficient utilization of multi-core processors.

3.Performance: Rust's performance is comparable to low-level languages like C and C++, making it suitable for high-frequency trading applications that require ultra-low latency and real-time processing.

4.Ecosystem: Rust's growing ecosystem of libraries and tools, known as crates, provides a wealth of resources for building and integrating various components of a trading system, from data ingestion to order execution.

5.Developer Productivity: Rust's combination of modern syntax, powerful abstractions, and robust tooling enhances developer productivity, enabling the rapid development and deployment of trading algorithms.

Algorithmic trading represents the intersection of finance and technology, leveraging the power of algorithms to execute trades with speed, precision, and efficiency. By understanding the fundamental concepts, benefits, challenges, and strategies of algorithmic trading, you are better equipped to develop sophisticated trading algorithms using Rust. As we progress through this book, you will learn how to implement these strategies in Rust, harnessing its unique features to create high-performance trading systems that can thrive in the fast-paced world of financial markets.

Intersection of Finance and Technology

The interplay between finance and technology has created

a dynamic and transformative field known as FinTech. This sector leverages technological innovations to disrupt and enhance traditional financial services, providing efficiency, transparency, and accessibility like never before. To fully grasp the implications of this intersection, we need to delve into its evolution, the driving technologies, and their impact on financial markets.

The Evolution of FinTech

The concept of FinTech isn't new; it dates back to the late 19th century when the telegraph was used for transferring financial information. However, the term "FinTech" gained prominence in the 21st century, characterized by the rapid evolution of digital technologies and the internet.

The 1990s and early 2000s marked significant milestones, with the advent of online banking and electronic trading platforms. The dot-com boom saw the emergence of numerous tech-driven financial services, although not all survived the subsequent crash. Nonetheless, this era laid the groundwork for today's FinTech landscape.

The 2008 financial crisis was another pivotal moment. It exposed the inefficiencies and vulnerabilities of the traditional financial system, prompting a wave of innovation aimed at making financial services more robust, user-friendly, and inclusive. Startups began to challenge incumbents by offering digital solutions for payments, lending, investment, and more.

Core Technologies Driving FinTech

Several key technologies underpin the FinTech revolution,

reshaping the way financial services are delivered:

1.Blockchain and Cryptocurrencies: Blockchain technology, with its decentralized and immutable ledger, revolutionized the notion of trust in financial transactions. Cryptocurrencies like Bitcoin and Ethereum have introduced new paradigms for value transfer and storage, challenging traditional currencies and payment systems.

2.Artificial Intelligence (AI) and Machine Learning (ML): AI and ML algorithms analyze vast amounts of data to uncover patterns, make predictions, and automate decision-making. These technologies have applications in credit scoring, fraud detection, algorithmic trading, and personalized financial advice.

3.Big Data: The ability to process and analyze massive datasets in real-time has enabled financial institutions to gain deeper insights into market behavior, customer preferences, and risk management. Big data analytics is pivotal in predictive modeling and strategic planning.

4.Cloud Computing: Cloud infrastructure provides scalable and cost-effective solutions for data storage, processing, and application deployment. It allows financial institutions to innovate rapidly, with reduced IT overhead and enhanced collaboration capabilities.

5.Internet of Things (IoT): IoT devices generate a continuous stream of data, which can be harnessed to improve financial services. For instance, telematics data from vehicles can be used for more accurate insurance pricing.

6.Robotic Process Automation (RPA): RPA automates repetitive and rule-based tasks, increasing operational efficiency and reducing human error. It is widely used in processes like KYC (Know Your Customer), compliance, and customer service.

Impact on Financial Markets

The integration of technology into finance has profoundly impacted financial markets in several ways:

1.Increased Market Accessibility: Digital platforms have democratized access to financial markets, enabling retail investors to participate alongside institutional players. Online brokerage services, robo-advisors, and micro-investing apps have made investing more accessible to the masses.

2.Enhanced Efficiency: Automation and electronic trading have significantly reduced transaction costs and execution times. Algorithms can execute trades within milliseconds, optimizing market strategies and enabling high-frequency trading.

3.Improved Transparency and Compliance: Blockchain technology offers unparalleled transparency, providing an auditable trail of transactions. This feature is particularly beneficial for regulatory compliance and reducing the risk of fraud.

4.Disintermediation: FinTech solutions often bypass traditional intermediaries, reducing costs and friction in financial transactions. Peer-to-peer lending platforms, for example, connect borrowers directly with lenders, eliminating the need for banks.

5.Enhanced Customer Experience: FinTech innovations provide more personalized, user-friendly experiences. AI-driven chatbots, mobile banking apps, and digital wallets enhance customer engagement and satisfaction.

6.Risk Management: Advanced analytics and AI improve risk management by providing real-time insights and predictive capabilities. Financial institutions can better assess credit risk, market risk, and operational risk, leading to more informed decision-making.

Challenges

While the intersection of finance and technology presents numerous opportunities, it also poses several challenges:

1.Cybersecurity: The digitalization of financial services increases the risk of cyberattacks. Financial institutions must invest in robust security measures to protect sensitive data and maintain customer trust.

2.Regulatory Compliance: Navigating the complex and evolving regulatory landscape is a significant challenge for FinTech companies. Compliance with laws such as GDPR, PSD2, and AML is critical to operate legally and ethically.

3.Technological Integration: Integrating new technologies with legacy systems can be challenging and costly. Financial institutions must balance innovation with the stability of their existing infrastructure.

4.Talent Acquisition: The demand for skilled professionals in FinTech, particularly in areas like AI, blockchain, and cybersecurity, outstrips supply. Attracting and retaining top talent is crucial for sustained innovation.

5.Market Volatility: The rapid pace of technological change and market dynamics can lead to volatility and uncertainty. FinTech companies must be agile and adaptable to thrive in this environment.

Despite these challenges, the future of FinTech is bright. The ongoing convergence of finance and technology will continue to drive innovation, create new business models, and enhance the overall efficiency of financial markets.

The Role of Rust in FinTech

Rust, with its unique features, is well-positioned to play a significant role in the FinTech revolution. Its memory safety, concurrency capabilities, and performance make it an ideal choice for developing robust and high-performance financial applications.

1.Safety and Reliability: Rust's emphasis on safety prevents common programming errors that can lead to vulnerabilities and system crashes. This is particularly important in financial applications where reliability and security are paramount.

2.Performance: Rust's performance rivals that of low-level languages like C and C++, making it suitable for high-frequency trading and real-time applications where speed is critical.

3.Concurrency: Rust's ownership model and concurrency support enable the development of highly parallel applications, essential for processing large volumes of financial data and executing complex algorithms.

4.Community and Ecosystem: Rust's growing ecosystem of libraries and tools, along with an active community, provides ample resources for developers to build and integrate financial applications. The availability of crates for data processing, encryption, and networking facilitates rapid development.

5.Adoption in Industry: Several FinTech companies and financial institutions are already leveraging Rust for various applications, from trading systems to blockchain solutions. This adoption trend underscores Rust's potential to become a mainstream language in the FinTech industry.

The intersection of finance and technology has created a fertile ground for innovation, transforming the way financial services are delivered and consumed. FinTech leverages cutting-edge technologies to enhance efficiency, transparency, and accessibility in financial markets. Rust, with its unique features and capabilities, is poised to play a crucial role in this evolution, enabling the development of robust, high-performance financial applications. As we continue our journey through this book, you will learn how to harness the power of Rust to develop sophisticated trading algorithms and financial solutions, positioning yourself at the forefront of the FinTech revolution.

A Brief History of the Black-Scholes Model

The Black-Scholes model occupies a foundational place in the realm of financial engineering, standing as one of the most pivotal advancements in the pricing of options. Its inception marked a watershed moment, transforming the landscape of financial derivatives and earning its creators, Fischer Black, Myron Scholes, and Robert Merton, recognition and accolades, including the Nobel Prize in Economic Sciences awarded to Scholes and Merton in 1997. To appreciate its significance, let's traverse the historical milestones that led to the development of this revolutionary model.

1.7b.1 The Origins of Options Trading

Options trading, in one form or another, dates back to ancient civilizations. Records suggest that the Greeks and Romans engaged in rudimentary forms of options trading. However, it wasn't until the early modern period, particularly in 17th-century Amsterdam, that formalized options contracts began to emerge. The Amsterdam Stock Exchange, established in 1602 by the Dutch East India Company, became a hub for trading various financial instruments, including options.

Fast forward to the 19th and early 20th centuries, options trading started to gain more structure and regulation in the United States. The Chicago Board of Trade (CBOT) introduced standardized options contracts in the 1970s, setting the stage for the development of mathematical models to price these instruments.

1.7b.2 Predecessors to Black-Scholes

Before the Black-Scholes model, several attempts were made

to develop mathematical frameworks for option pricing. One of the earliest efforts was by Louis Bachelier, a French mathematician, who in 1900 presented his dissertation, "Théorie de la spéculation," which introduced the concept of Brownian motion to model stock prices. Although Bachelier's work was ahead of its time, it remained largely unnoticed for several decades.

In the 1950s and 1960s, the field of financial economics began to evolve rapidly. Scholars like Paul Samuelson and Benoit Mandelbrot made significant contributions to the understanding of price movements and market behavior. Samuelson's work on the random walk theory and efficient market hypothesis laid important groundwork for future models.

1.7b.3 The Genesis of the Black-Scholes Model

The collaboration between Fischer Black and Myron Scholes began in the late 1960s. Black, an economist and researcher at Arthur D. Little, was interested in developing a practical model for pricing options. Scholes, a professor at MIT, shared Black's enthusiasm for financial markets and mathematical modeling. Together, they embarked on a journey to create a model that could accurately price European-style options.

A turning point came when Robert Merton, a professor at Harvard, joined the conversation. Merton's expertise in continuous-time finance and his understanding of stochastic processes were instrumental in refining the model. The trio's combined efforts culminated in the development of the Black-Scholes formula, which they published in a seminal paper titled "The Pricing of Options and Corporate Liabilities" in 1973.

1.7b.4 The Black-Scholes Formula

The Black-Scholes formula revolutionized options pricing by providing a closed-form solution for the theoretical value of European call and put options. The formula is given by:

$$ C = S_0 N(d_1) - X e^{-rt} N(d_2) $$

Where:

- C is the price of the call option

- S_0 is the current price of the underlying asset

- X is the strike price of the option

- t is the time to maturity

- r is the risk-free interest rate

- $N(\cdot)$ denotes the cumulative distribution function of the standard normal distribution

- d_1 and d_2 are calculated as follows:

$$ d_1 = \frac{\ln \left(\frac{S_0}{X} \right) + \left(r + \frac{\sigma^2}{2} \right) t}{\sigma \sqrt{t}} $$

$$ d_2 = d_1 - \sigma \sqrt{t} $$

Where σ represents the volatility of the underlying asset.

This model assumes that the price of the underlying asset follows a geometric Brownian motion with constant volatility and that markets are frictionless, with no transaction costs or taxes.

1.7b.5 The Immediate Impact and Adoption

The Black-Scholes model was met with widespread acclaim and quickly became a cornerstone of modern financial theory. Its simplicity and elegance made it an attractive tool for traders, analysts, and academics alike. The Chicago Board Options Exchange (CBOE), which had just opened in 1973, adopted the Black-Scholes model as the standard for pricing options, further solidifying its importance.

The model's introduction also spurred the growth of the options market. Traders now had a reliable method to price options, which led to increased liquidity and the development of more sophisticated trading strategies. Financial institutions began to incorporate the model into their risk management and hedging practices, leveraging its insights to optimize their portfolios.

1.7b.6 Subsequent Developments and Extensions

While the Black-Scholes model was groundbreaking, it wasn't without limitations. Researchers and practitioners have since developed numerous extensions and variations to address these shortcomings. Some of the key advancements include:

1.The Black-Scholes-Merton Model: Robert Merton extended the original model to account for dividends, which are common in real-world financial markets. His contributions further solidified the model's applicability to a broader range of financial instruments.

2.Stochastic Volatility Models: One of the main assumptions of the Black-Scholes model is constant volatility. However, market volatility is often dynamic. Models like the Heston model incorporate stochastic volatility to better capture market behavior.

3.Jump-Diffusion Models: The Black-Scholes model assumes continuous price movements, but real markets can experience sudden jumps. The Merton jump-diffusion model introduces jump processes to account for these discontinuities.

4.Local Volatility Models: These models allow volatility to vary with both the price of the underlying asset and time, providing a more flexible framework for option pricing.

5.Alternative Numerical Methods: While the Black-Scholes formula offers a closed-form solution, complex options and derivatives may require numerical methods like finite difference methods, Monte Carlo simulations, and binomial trees for accurate pricing.

1.7b.7 The Legacy of the Black-Scholes Model

The Black-Scholes model's impact on finance cannot be overstated. It laid the foundation for the field of quantitative finance, inspiring a generation of financial engineers and mathematicians to explore and innovate. The model's principles are now taught in finance and economics programs worldwide, and its applications extend beyond options pricing to areas like risk management, portfolio optimization, and corporate finance.

Moreover, the Black-Scholes model opened the door to the development of more sophisticated financial instruments and derivatives. It provided a common language and framework for understanding and managing financial risk, contributing to the growth and stability of global financial markets.

As we continue to advance in the realm of quantitative finance, the Black-Scholes model remains a testament to the power of mathematical modeling and collaboration. Its legacy endures, reminding us of the profound impact that innovative thinking and rigorous analysis can have on the world of finance.

This detailed exploration of the Black-Scholes model's history sets the stage for understanding its mathematical foundations and practical applications, which we will delve into further in subsequent sections.

The Importance of Rust in Financial Applications

1.8b.1 Performance and Efficiency

At the heart of any high-frequency trading system is the need for speed. Rust's performance is akin to that of C and C++, providing low-level control over hardware while maintaining high-level abstractions for ease of use. This efficiency is crucial in trading environments where algorithms must process vast amounts of data in real-time.

For example, consider a trading algorithm that needs to execute thousands of trades per second. In such a scenario, the overhead associated with garbage collection in languages like Java or Python can introduce latency. Rust's ownership model and deterministic memory management eliminate this overhead, resulting in faster, more predictable execution times.

```rust
// Example: A simple Rust function to calculate the moving average of a data stream
fn moving_average(data: &Vec<f64>, window_size: usize) -> Vec<f64> {
let mut averages = Vec::new();
for i in 0..data.len() - window_size + 1 {
let window = &data[i..i + window_size];
let sum: f64 = window.iter().sum();
averages.push(sum / window_size as f64);
}
averages
}
```

The example above demonstrates a calculation that would be crucial in many financial applications, showcasing Rust's ability to handle computationally intensive tasks with ease.

1.8b.2 Memory Safety

Rust's emphasis on memory safety is a game-changer for financial applications. Memory-related errors such as null pointer dereferencing and buffer overflows can lead to system crashes or, worse, security vulnerabilities. In financial systems, where precision and reliability are paramount, such errors can result in significant financial losses or breaches of sensitive information.

Rust's ownership system enforces strict borrowing rules, ensuring that references to data are always valid. This eradicates an entire class of bugs that plague other systems, enhancing the robustness and reliability of financial software.

```rust
// Example: Demonstrating Rust's ownership system
fn main() {
let data = vec![1, 2, 3, 4, 5];
let avg = calculate_average(&data);
println!("Average: {}", avg);
}

fn calculate_average(data: &Vec<i32>) -> f64 {
let sum: i32 = data.iter().sum();
sum as f64 / data.len() as f64
}
```

In this snippet, Rust guarantees that the `data` reference in `calculate_average` is always valid, preventing common memory errors.

1.8b.3 Concurrency and Parallelism

Financial applications often require the processing of large datasets concurrently. Whether it's backtesting trading strategies on historical data or performing real-time risk analysis, the ability to efficiently handle multiple threads is crucial.

Rust's concurrency model, built around the concept of ownership and borrowing, prevents data races at compile time. This is a significant advantage over languages like C++ and Java, where data races can lead to unpredictable behavior and bugs that are hard to reproduce and fix.

```rust
use std::thread;

fn main() {
let data = vec![1, 2, 3, 4, 5];
let handles: Vec<_> = (0..5).map(|i| {
let data = data.clone();
thread::spawn(move || {
println!("Thread {}: {:?}", i, data);
})
}).collect();
```

```
for handle in handles {
handle.join().unwrap();
}
}
```
` ` `

Here, Rust's ownership and threading model allows the safe and efficient execution of concurrent tasks, crucial for operations like high-frequency trading.

1.8b.4 Reliability and Maintainability

The financial industry demands software that is not only high-performing but also reliable and maintainable. Rust's strict compiler checks and strong type system enforce rigorous safety and correctness standards, leading to code that is easier to maintain and less prone to errors.

Moreover, Rust encourages the use of idiomatic patterns that enhance readability and maintainability. The language's expressive type system and pattern matching capabilities make it easier to write clear, concise code that accurately reflects the underlying financial logic.

` ` `rust

```
// Example: Using pattern matching to handle different trade types
enum TradeType {
Buy,
```

```
Sell,
}

fn execute_trade(trade: TradeType, amount: f64) {
match trade {
TradeType::Buy => println!("Buying {} units", amount),
TradeType::Sell => println!("Selling {} units", amount),
}
}

fn main() {
execute_trade(TradeType::Buy, 100.0);
execute_trade(TradeType::Sell, 50.0);
}
```
```

This example shows how Rust's pattern matching can be used to handle different trade types, making the code more readable and easier to maintain.

1.8b.5 Growing Ecosystem and Community Support

Rust's ecosystem is rapidly expanding, with a growing number of crates (libraries) that provide functionality for a wide range of applications, including finance. The Rust community is known for its welcoming and collaborative nature, offering extensive support through forums, chat channels, and comprehensive documentation.
```

This vibrant ecosystem and community support enable financial developers to leverage existing libraries and tools, accelerating development and reducing the time to market for financial applications.

1.8b.6 Integration with Existing Systems

Financial institutions often have legacy systems written in languages like C++ and Java. One of Rust's strengths is its ability to integrate seamlessly with these existing systems. Through its Foreign Function Interface (FFI), Rust can call functions from other languages and be called from them, facilitating a gradual migration to Rust without the need for a complete system rewrite.

```rust
// Example: Calling a C function from Rust using FFI
extern "C" {
fn sqrt(input: f64) -> f64;
}

fn main() {
let x = 9.0;
unsafe {
println!("The square root of {} is {}", x, sqrt(x));
}
}
```

This interoperability is crucial for financial institutions looking to modernize their technology stack incrementally.

1.8b.7 Security

Security is paramount in financial applications, where dealing with sensitive data and large sums of money is a daily routine. Rust's emphasis on safety extends to security, with features that prevent common vulnerabilities such as buffer overflows and dangling pointers.

Rust also supports various cryptographic libraries and techniques, essential for securing financial transactions and communications. Its strong type system and compile-time checks add an extra layer of security, making it harder for vulnerabilities to slip through.

1.8b.8 Future-Proof and Innovative

Rust is a modern language that continues to evolve, with a strong emphasis on backward compatibility. Its innovative features and active development ensure that it remains at the cutting edge of technology, making it a future-proof choice for financial institutions looking to stay ahead of the curve.

As the financial industry becomes increasingly reliant on technology, the importance of using a language that can keep pace with rapid changes cannot be overstated. Rust's continuous innovation makes it an ideal choice for developing the next generation of financial applications.

Rust offers a unique combination of performance, safety, concurrency, and maintainability that makes it an invaluable tool for financial applications. Its growing ecosystem and strong community support further enhance its appeal, ensuring that developers can leverage the full potential of this powerful language to build robust, efficient, and secure financial systems.

Key Features of Rust for Finance

When it comes to high-stakes financial applications, the choice of programming language can significantly impact performance, safety, and reliability. Rust, a systems programming language known for its speed and memory safety, offers a compelling suite of features tailored to the rigorous demands of financial software. As we delve into the key features of Rust for finance, we will explore how each characteristic can be leveraged to build robust, efficient, and secure financial applications.

Memory Safety Without Garbage Collection

In the realm of finance, where milliseconds can mean millions, performance is paramount. Rust achieves memory safety without the overhead of garbage collection, which is a common feature in languages like Java or C#. This is achieved through Rust's ownership system, which ensures that every piece of data has a single owner, thereby preventing data races and dangling pointers.

```rust
fn calculate_interest(principal: f64, rate: f64, time: f64) -> f64 {
    principal * rate * time
}

fn main() {
    let principal = 1000.0;
    let rate = 0.05;
    let time = 1.0;
    let interest = calculate_interest(principal, rate, time);
    println!("Interest: {}", interest);
}
```

In this example, Rust's ownership model ensures that `principal`, `rate`, and `time` are safely managed within the scope of the `main` function. The absence of a garbage collector means the memory is freed immediately after it goes out of scope, enhancing performance.

Data Integrity with Strong Typing

Financial applications often deal with complex data structures and precise calculations. Rust's strong static typing system helps catch errors at compile time, reducing runtime bugs. This is especially crucial in finance, where errors can have catastrophic consequences.

```rust
struct Stock {
symbol: String,
price: f64,
volume: u32,
}

fn main() {
let s = Stock {
symbol: String::from("AAPL"),
price: 145.32,
volume: 1000,
};
println!("Stock: {}, Price: {}, Volume: {}", s.symbol, s.price, s.volume);
}
```

Here, the `Stock` struct enforces that each stock must have a `symbol`, `price`, and `volume`, ensuring data integrity and consistency throughout the application.

Concurrency and Parallelism

Rust excels in concurrency, a feature that is increasingly vital in financial applications that require the processing of vast amounts of data in real-time. Rust's concurrency model, facilitated by the `std::thread` module, allows developers to write multi-threaded programs that are both safe and efficient.

```rust
use std::thread;

fn main() {
let data = vec![1, 2, 3, 4, 5];
let handles: Vec<_> = data.into_iter().map(|num| {
thread::spawn(move || {
println!("Processing number: {}", num);
})
}).collect();

for handle in handles {
handle.join().unwrap();
}
}
```

By spawning multiple threads to process data concurrently, this example demonstrates how Rust can handle tasks in parallel, making it ideal for high-frequency trading and other time-sensitive financial operations.

Performance and Speed

Rust's performance is comparable to that of C and C++, making it suitable for applications requiring low-latency and high-throughput. Its zero-cost abstractions mean that higher-level abstractions have the same performance as hand-written low-level code, providing both safety and speed.

```rust
fn black_scholes_call_price(s: f64, k: f64, t: f64, r: f64, sigma: f64) -> f64 {
// Black-Scholes formula implementation
let d1 = (s / k).ln() + (r + 0.5 * sigma * sigma) * t;
let d2 = d1 - sigma * (t).sqrt();
s * norm_cdf(d1) - k * (-r * t).exp() * norm_cdf(d2)
}

fn norm_cdf(x: f64) -> f64 {
// Standard normal cumulative density function
(1.0 + (x / (2.0 * std::f64::consts::PI).sqrt()).erf()) / 2.0
}

fn main() {
let call_price = black_scholes_call_price(50.0, 50.0, 1.0, 0.05, 0.2);
println!("Call Price: {}", call_price);
}
```

This code snippet illustrates the implementation of the Black-Scholes formula in Rust, showcasing how its performance can be harnessed for complex financial calculations.

Error Handling

Rust's error handling capabilities are robust and promote writing safe and reliable code. The language uses `Result` and `Option` types to manage recoverable and unrecoverable errors, respectively, ensuring that errors are handled gracefully.

```rust
fn read_price_from_file(filename: &str) -> Result<f64, std::io::Error> {
let content = std::fs::read_to_string(filename)?;
let price: f64 = content.trim().parse().map_err(|_e| {
std::io::Error::new(std::io::ErrorKind::InvalidData, "Invalid price format")
})?;
Ok(price)
}

fn main() {
match read_price_from_file("price.txt") {
Ok(price) => println!("Price: {}", price),
Err(e) => println!("Error reading price: {}", e),
}
}
```

In this example, Rust's error handling ensures that any issues encountered while reading the price from a file are properly managed, preventing the program from crashing unexpectedly.

Ecosystem and Community Support

Rust boasts a thriving ecosystem and active community, which is invaluable for financial developers. The Cargo package manager makes it easy to manage dependencies, and the abundance of crates provides reusable code for various applications.

```toml
[dependencies]
serde = "1.0"
serde_json = "1.0"
```

Adding `serde` and `serde_json` crates to the dependencies in `Cargo.toml`, developers can easily leverage serialization and deserialization functionalities, which are essential for handling financial data.

Rust offers a compelling array of features that make it an excellent choice for financial applications. Its memory safety, strong typing, concurrency model, performance, and robust error handling provide a foundation for developing secure, efficient, and high-performance financial software. As you integrate Rust into your financial systems, you'll find it to be a powerful ally in navigating the complexities of algorithmic options trading and beyond.

Preparing for the Crash Course

Before diving into the intricacies of the Black-Scholes model and Rust programming, it's imperative to establish a solid foundation in both finance and coding. A basic understanding of financial derivatives, particularly options, is essential. Familiarize yourself with concepts such as call and put options, option pricing, volatility, and the Greeks. Numerous online resources, including tutorials, MOOCs, and textbooks, can provide a robust grounding.

Parallelly, ensure your programming skills are up to the mark. Rust, being a systems programming language, has a steeper learning curve compared to languages like Python or JavaScript. It's beneficial to have prior experience in languages such as C or C++, but not mandatory. Rust's ownership model, memory safety features, and concurrency paradigms require a good grasp of programming fundamentals.

Assembling Your Toolkit

Your toolkit for this crash course comprises both software and hardware components. Here's a detailed list of what you'll need:

1. Development Environment:

-Rust Compiler and Cargo: The Rust compiler and Cargo, Rust's package manager, are pivotal. Install them by following the official [Rust installation guide](https://www.rust-lang.org/tools/install).

-IDE or Code Editor: Choose a robust Integrated Development Environment (IDE) like Visual Studio Code or IntelliJ IDEA, enhanced with Rust plugins for syntax highlighting, autocompletion, and debugging.

2. Financial Data Sources:

-API Access: Financial data APIs like Alpha Vantage, IEX Cloud, or Quandl will provide real-time and historical market data.

-Databases: Setting up a database, such as PostgreSQL or SQLite, will be essential for storing and retrieving large datasets efficiently.

3. Computational Tools:

-Mathematical Libraries: Libraries like `nalgebra` for linear algebra operations and `rand` for generating random numbers will be instrumental in implementing financial models.

-Plotting Libraries: Use tools like `plotters` or `gnuplot` for visualizing data and results.

Learning Resources and Community Engagement

Leverage the wealth of learning resources available for both Rust and financial modeling:

1. Documentation and Books:

-Rust Documentation: Rust's official documentation is comprehensive and continually updated. It's an invaluable resource for understanding Rust's syntax and features.

-Financial Modeling Textbooks: Texts such as "Options, Futures, and Other Derivatives" by John C. Hull provide in-depth knowledge on financial instruments and pricing models.

2. Online Courses and Tutorials:

-Rust Programming Courses: Platforms like Udemy, Coursera, and Rust's own [Rustlings](https://github.com/rust-lang/rustlings) provide interactive programming exercises.

-Financial Derivatives MOOCs: Websites like edX and Coursera offer courses on financial derivatives and quantitative finance.

3. Community Forums and Meetups:

-Rust Community: Engage with the Rustacean community through forums like The Rust Programming Language Forum, Reddit, and Discord channels. These platforms offer support, tips, and networking opportunities.

-Finance Meetups: Join local or online meetups focused on quantitative finance and algorithmic trading to exchange ideas and insights with peers.

Structuring Your Learning Path

Organize your learning journey into manageable phases to avoid feeling overwhelmed:

1. Basic Concepts and Syntax:

- Spend the initial weeks understanding Rust's syntax, ownership model, and basic data structures. Simultaneously, revisit the basics of options trading and the Black-Scholes model.

2. Intermediate Application:

- Start implementing simple financial models in Rust. Focus on writing clean, efficient code and handling financial data. Practice reading from APIs and storing data in databases.

3. Advanced Integration:

- Gradually move to more complex implementations, such as calculating the Greeks, backtesting trading strategies, and optimizing algorithms for performance.

4. Real-World Application:

- Apply your knowledge to real-world data. Develop and test full-fledged trading algorithms, stress-test your models, and refine your strategies based on market conditions.

Maintaining a Growth Mindset

Approaching this crash course with the right mindset is crucial. Recognize that both financial modeling and Rust programming are vast fields, and it's natural to encounter challenges and setbacks. Here are some tips to maintain a growth-oriented approach:

1. Patience and Persistence:

- Mastery takes time. Be patient with yourself and persist through complex topics and coding challenges.

2. Continuous Learning:

- The fields of quantitative finance and programming are ever-evolving. Stay updated with the latest trends, tools, and methodologies by reading research papers, attending workshops, and participating in webinars.

3. Practical Application:

- Theory is essential, but practical application solidifies learning. Regularly practice coding, experiment with new financial models, and apply what you learn to real-world scenarios.

Preparing for this crash course is a multi-faceted endeavor, requiring a blend of knowledge acquisition, tool assembly, structured learning, and a resilient mindset. By laying a strong foundation, equipping yourself with the right tools, engaging with the community, and maintaining a growth mindset, you are setting yourself up for success in the demanding yet rewarding world of algorithmic options trading with Rust.

CHAPTER 2: MATHEMATICAL FOUNDATIONS OF BLACK-SCHOLES

The Black-Scholes model, a cornerstone of modern financial theory, revolutionized the way options are priced. However, to fully grasp its applications and limitations, it is crucial to understand the foundational assumptions underlying this model. Each assumption plays a pivotal role in the model's derivation and its practical applicability.

Assumption 1: The Behavior of Stock Prices

At the heart of the Black-Scholes model lies the assumption that stock prices follow a geometric Brownian motion with constant volatility and drift. This implies that price changes are continuous and random, adhering to a log-normal distribution. Mathematically, this can be expressed as:

$$ dS = \mu S \, dt + \sigma S \, dW $$

Where:

- S represents the stock price.

- μ is the constant drift rate.

- σ is the constant volatility.

- dW is a Wiener process, representing the random component.

This assumption ensures that stock prices will never become negative, as a log-normal distribution bounds prices above zero. Furthermore, it implies that the percentage change in stock prices over a small time interval is normally distributed, simplifying the mathematical treatment of price movements.

Assumption 2: No Arbitrage Opportunities

The Black-Scholes model assumes that there are no arbitrage opportunities in the market. Arbitrage involves taking advantage of price differences in different markets or forms to secure a risk-free profit. Under this assumption, the price of the option must be such that no arbitrage opportunities exist. This principle is central to the model and ensures that the pricing of derivatives is coherent with underlying market prices.

To illustrate, consider two portfolios:

1. A portfolio consisting of one European call option and cash.

2. A portfolio consisting of an equivalent position in the underlying asset.

The Black-Scholes model ensures that both portfolios should

provide the same return if arbitrage opportunities are absent. Thus, the model leverages this equilibrium to derive the option pricing formula.

Assumption 3: European Options

The model specifically applies to European-style options, which can only be exercised at expiration. Unlike American options, which can be exercised at any time before or at expiration, European options' restricted exercise time simplifies the mathematical modeling. This assumption limits the model's direct applicability to American options, although extensions and modifications of the Black-Scholes framework exist to handle the flexibility of American options.

Assumption 4: Constant Risk-Free Rate

Another critical assumption is that the risk-free interest rate remains constant over the option's life. The risk-free rate represents the theoretical return on an investment with zero risk, such as government bonds. In practice, this is approximated by the yield on short-term Treasury bills. This assumption allows for the discounting of future cash flows in the options pricing formula.

Mathematically, the constant risk-free rate simplifies the Black-Scholes partial differential equation and ensures that the model remains tractable. Here's the formula within the context of the risk-free rate r:

$$C = S_0 N(d_1) - K e^{-rT} N(d_2)$$

Where:

- C is the price of the call option.

- S_0 is the current stock price.

- K is the strike price.

- T is the time to maturity.

- N is the cumulative distribution function of the standard normal distribution.

- $d_1 = \frac{\ln(S_0 / K) + (r + \sigma^2 / 2) T}{\sigma \sqrt{T}}$

- $d_2 = d_1 - \sigma \sqrt{T}$

Assumption 5: No Dividends

The original Black-Scholes model assumes that the underlying stock pays no dividends during the option's life. Dividends affect the price of the underlying asset, typically causing a drop on the ex-dividend date. By excluding dividends, the model simplifies the pricing process. However, in reality, many stocks do pay dividends, prompting the need for adjustments or alternative models to account for these payments.

An adjusted formula for dividend-paying stocks incorporates the present value of expected dividends:

$$C = S_0 e^{-qT} N(d_1) - K e^{-rT} N(d_2)$$

Where q is the continuous dividend yield.

Assumption 6: Market Liquidity and Efficiency

The Black-Scholes model assumes perfect market liquidity, meaning that the stock and option can be traded freely without impacting their prices. It also presumes market efficiency, where all relevant information is already reflected in the current prices of securities. This assumption ensures that trading can occur without significant transaction costs or delays, and prices respond instantly to new information.

Assumption 7: Constant Volatility

Constant volatility is a cornerstone of the Black-Scholes model. It assumes that the volatility of the underlying asset remains constant over the life of the option. Volatility represents the degree of variation of the stock price, and assuming it to be constant allows for a straightforward mathematical model. In practice, volatility can fluctuate due to market conditions, leading to the development of more sophisticated models like the stochastic volatility models to account for this variability.

Assumption 8: Continuous Trading

The model assumes continuous trading of the underlying asset, meaning that the stock and the option can be bought or sold at any time. This continuous trading assumption ensures the model's differential equations hold true at every moment. In reality, markets operate within specific hours, and this discreteness can introduce additional complexities not captured by the Black-Scholes framework.

Implications of Assumptions

The Black-Scholes model's assumptions provide a simplified

yet powerful framework for option pricing. While each assumption helps in deriving a tractable and elegant formula, they also introduce limitations. Deviations from these assumptions in real markets—such as discrete trading hours, changing volatility, and dividend payments—necessitate modifications or alternative models to address the intricacies of actual market conditions.

Understanding these assumptions is crucial for effectively applying the Black-Scholes model and recognizing its limitations. As you delve deeper into the application of this model using Rust, keeping these foundational assumptions in mind will guide you in developing robust and realistic trading algorithms.

Derivation of the Black-Scholes Formula

The derivation of the Black-Scholes formula is a masterclass in mathematical elegance and financial acumen. The Black-Scholes model, formulated by Fischer Black, Myron Scholes, and Robert Merton, provides a theoretical estimate for the price of European-style options. To derive this formula, we need to weave together concepts from stochastic calculus, partial differential equations, and financial theory.

1. The Stock Price Dynamics

To begin, we model the dynamics of the underlying stock price using a geometric Brownian motion. This is expressed as follows:

$$ dS = \mu S \, dt + \sigma S \, dW $$

where:

- S is the stock price.

- μ is the constant drift rate.

- σ is the constant volatility.

- dW is a Wiener process, representing the random component.

This stochastic differential equation captures the continuous and random nature of stock price movements, with μ representing the expected return and σ the uncertainty or risk.

2. Portfolio Construction and Hedging

Next, imagine a portfolio consisting of a long position in the stock and a short position in the option. Let $V(S,t)$ represent the price of the option as a function of the stock price S and time t. We construct a hedged portfolio Π as follows:

$$\Pi = V - \Delta S$$

where Δ is the number of shares held to hedge against the option position. The goal is to choose Δ such that the portfolio is risk-free over an infinitesimally small time interval dt.

3. Applying Ito's Lemma

To derive the risk-free portfolio, we need to determine how $

(V \) changes with small changes in \(S \) and \(t \). Here, we employ Ito's Lemma, a fundamental result in stochastic calculus, which states:

\[dV = \frac{\partial V}{\partial t} dt + \frac{\partial V}{\partial S} dS + \frac{1}{2} \frac{\partial^2 V}{\partial S^2} (\sigma S)^2 dt \]

Substituting the expression for \(dS \) from the geometric Brownian motion equation, we get:

\[dV = \frac{\partial V}{\partial t} dt + \frac{\partial V}{\partial S} (\mu S dt + \sigma S dW) + \frac{1}{2} \frac{\partial^2 V}{\partial S^2} \sigma^2 S^2 dt \]

4. Making the Portfolio Risk-Free

The change in the value of the portfolio \(\Pi \) over a small time interval \(dt \) is given by:

\[d\Pi = dV - \Delta dS \]

Using Ito's Lemma and substituting for \(dV \):

\[d\Pi = \left(\frac{\partial V}{\partial t} + \frac{\partial V}{\partial S} \mu S + \frac{1}{2} \frac{\partial^2 V}{\partial S^2} \sigma^2 S^2 \right) dt + \frac{\partial V}{\partial S} \sigma S dW - \Delta (\mu S dt + \sigma S dW) \]

For the portfolio to be risk-free, the coefficient of \(dW \) must be zero:

$$\Delta = \frac{\partial V}{\partial S}$$

Thus, the change in the portfolio value $(d\Pi)$ simplifies to:

$$d\Pi = \left(\frac{\partial V}{\partial t} + \frac{1}{2} \frac{\partial^2 V}{\partial S^2} \sigma^2 S^2 \right) dt$$

5. Equating to the Risk-Free Rate

In a risk-free world, the change in the portfolio value must equal the return from a risk-free asset. Let (r) be the risk-free interest rate. Then,

$$d\Pi = r \Pi dt$$

Substituting $(\Pi = V - \Delta S)$ and $(\Delta = \frac{\partial V}{\partial S})$, we get:

$$\left(\frac{\partial V}{\partial t} + \frac{1}{2} \frac{\partial^2 V}{\partial S^2} \sigma^2 S^2 \right) dt = r \left(V - S \frac{\partial V}{\partial S} \right) dt$$

Simplifying, we arrive at the Black-Scholes partial differential equation:

$$\frac{\partial V}{\partial t} + \frac{1}{2} \sigma^2 S^2 \frac{\partial^2 V}{\partial S^2} + r S \frac{\partial V}{\partial S} - r V = 0$$

6. Solving the Black-Scholes PDE

The solution to this partial differential equation gives us the price of the option. For a European call option, the boundary conditions are:

- At maturity $(t = T)$, the option value (V) equals the payoff: $(V(S,T) = \max(S - K, 0))$, where (K) is the strike price.

- As $(S \rightarrow \infty)$, $(V \rightarrow S - K e^{-r(T-t)})$.

Using these boundary conditions, the solution to the Black-Scholes PDE is:

$$ V(S,t) = S N(d_1) - K e^{-r(T-t)} N(d_2) $$

where:

- $(d_1 = \frac{\ln(S / K) + (r + \sigma^2 / 2) (T - t)}{\sigma \sqrt{T - t}})$

- $(d_2 = d_1 - \sigma \sqrt{T - t})$

and $(N(x))$ is the cumulative distribution function of the standard normal distribution.

7. Interpretation and Application

The derived Black-Scholes formula provides a theoretical framework for pricing European call and put options. For a European put option, the pricing formula is:

$$ P(S,t) = K e^{-r(T-t)} N(-d_2) - S N(-d_1) $$

These formulas allow traders to determine the fair value of options based on the current stock price, strike price, time to maturity, risk-free interest rate, and volatility. They underpin much of modern financial practice, from risk management to speculative trading.

8. Real-World Adjustments

While the Black-Scholes model provides an elegant solution for option pricing, real-world conditions often deviate from its assumptions. Practitioners make various adjustments to accommodate dividends, taxes, transaction costs, and non-constant volatility. Nevertheless, the foundational principles of the Black-Scholes model remain central to understanding the dynamics of options pricing.

As you delve into implementing the Black-Scholes formula using Rust, you'll find that translating these mathematical concepts into code requires careful attention to numerical stability and performance optimization. Rust's robust type system and memory safety features make it particularly well-suited for such applications, allowing you to build reliable and efficient financial models.

In the subsequent sections, we'll explore how to implement the Black-Scholes formula in Rust, leveraging its powerful capabilities to create high-performance trading algorithms. With this solid theoretical foundation, you'll be well-equipped to tackle the complexities of real-world financial markets.

Partial Differential Equations in Finance

Partial Differential Equations (PDEs) form the backbone of quantitative finance, underpinning models that describe the evolution of financial variables over time. The Black-Scholes model, which we derive in this book, is a quintessential example of a PDE applied to finance. Understanding PDEs and their applications is crucial for anyone involved in the development of financial models, particularly in the context of options pricing and risk management.

1. Introduction to PDEs

At the heart of many financial models is a PDE, a type of equation that involves multiple independent variables and their partial derivatives. A PDE can describe a variety of phenomena, from heat distribution in a metal rod to the pricing of complex financial derivatives. In finance, PDEs help model the continuous change in asset prices and the evolution of options values over time.

A general form of a second-order linear PDE is:

$$ \frac{\partial^2 u}{\partial x^2} + \frac{\partial^2 u}{\partial y^2} + \cdots = f(u, x, y, \cdots) $$

where u is the dependent variable (e.g., option price), and $x, y, \cdots$ are the independent variables (e.g., stock price, time).

2. The Heat Equation and Its Financial Analogy

The heat equation, a fundamental PDE in physics, serves as an excellent analogy for understanding financial PDEs. It describes the distribution of heat (or temperature) in a given region over time.

$$ \frac{\partial u}{\partial t} = \alpha \frac{\partial^2 u}{\partial x^2} $$

Here, u represents the temperature at position x and time t, and α is the thermal diffusivity.

In finance, a similar equation describes the change in option prices over time, where the diffusion of temperature is analogous to the diffusion of risk. This analogy is a cornerstone of the Black-Scholes model.

3. The Black-Scholes PDE

The Black-Scholes PDE, derived from the principles of no-arbitrage and risk-neutral valuation, is a specific application of PDEs in finance. It describes the price of an option as a function of the underlying asset price and time.

The Black-Scholes PDE is given by:

$$ \frac{\partial V}{\partial t} + \frac{1}{2} \sigma^2 S^2 \frac{\partial^2 V}{\partial S^2} + r S \frac{\partial V}{\partial S} - r V = 0 $$

where:

- V is the option price.

- S is the underlying stock price.

- t is time.

- σ is the volatility of the stock.

- r is the risk-free interest rate.

This equation balances the rate of change of the option price with respect to time and the rate of change with respect to the underlying stock price, along with the risk and return parameters.

4. Solving the Black-Scholes PDE

Solving the Black-Scholes PDE involves finding a function $V(S,t)$ that satisfies the equation with appropriate boundary conditions. For European options, the boundary conditions are specified at maturity when the option payoff is known.

For a European call option, the boundary condition is:

$$V(S,T) = \max(S - K, 0)$$

where T is the maturity date, and K is the strike price.

The Black-Scholes formula we derived earlier is the solution to this PDE, providing a closed-form expression for the price of European call and put options.

$$V(S,t) = S\,N(d_1) - K\,e^{-r(T-t)}\,N(d_2)$$

where d_1 and d_2 are specific transformations of the input parameters, and $N(\cdot)$ is the cumulative distribution function of the standard normal distribution.

5. Numerical Methods for PDEs

While some PDEs, like the Black-Scholes PDE, have closed-form solutions, many real-world problems require numerical methods to find approximate solutions. Common numerical methods for solving PDEs in finance include:

-Finite Difference Methods: These methods discretize the continuous variables and approximate the derivatives using finite differences. The grid points on the discretized domain represent possible values of the underlying asset price and time.

-Monte Carlo Simulation: This method involves simulating a large number of random paths for the underlying asset price and averaging the outcomes to estimate the option price. It is particularly useful for high-dimensional problems and American-style options.

-Finite Element Methods: These methods divide the domain into smaller, simpler pieces (elements) and use variational techniques to approximate the solution. Finite element methods are powerful for solving complex boundary conditions and non-linear PDEs.

Each numerical method has its strengths and weaknesses, and the choice of method depends on the specific problem and the desired level of accuracy and computational efficiency.

6. Practical Applications of PDEs in Finance

The application of PDEs in finance extends beyond option pricing to various other financial problems:

-Interest Rate Models: PDEs are used to model the evolution of interest rates over time, such as the Heath-Jarrow-Morton (HJM) model and the Hull-White model.

-Credit Risk Models: PDEs help model the probability of default and the pricing of credit derivatives, such as credit default swaps (CDS).

-Optimal Control Problems: PDEs are used in portfolio optimization and risk management to determine the optimal allocation of assets and the best strategies for hedging and trading.

7. Implementing PDEs in Rust

Implementing PDEs in Rust involves translating mathematical concepts into efficient and robust code. Rust's performance and safety features make it an excellent choice for this task. Here's a basic outline of how to implement a finite difference method for solving the Black-Scholes PDE in Rust:

1.Set Up the Grid:

Define the grid points for the underlying asset price and time. Allocate arrays to store the option prices at each grid point.

2.Initialize Boundary Conditions:

Apply the boundary conditions at maturity and for extreme values of the underlying asset price.

3.Perform Time Stepping:

Iterate through the grid points and update the option prices using finite difference approximations of the PDE.

4.Optimize for Performance:

Use Rust's concurrency features, such as threads and async programming, to parallelize the computation and improve performance.

Here's a sample Rust code snippet for setting up a simple finite difference grid:

```rust
fn initialize_grid(s_max: f64, t_max: f64, ds: f64, dt: f64) -> (Vec<f64>, Vec<f64>) {

let n_s = (s_max / ds) as usize;

let n_t = (t_max / dt) as usize;


let s_grid: Vec<f64> = (0..=n_s).map(|i| i as f64 * ds).collect();

let t_grid: Vec<f64> = (0..=n_t).map(|j| j as f64 * dt).collect();


(s_grid, t_grid)
```

```
}

fn main() {
let s_max = 100.0;
let t_max = 1.0;
let ds = 1.0;
let dt = 0.01;

let (s_grid, t_grid) = initialize_grid(s_max, t_max, ds, dt);

// Further implementation will include setting up boundary
conditions and time stepping.
}
` ` `
```

This snippet initializes the grid for the finite difference method, which can then be used to solve the Black-Scholes PDE. Further steps would involve implementing the boundary conditions and the time-stepping algorithm.

8. Challenges and Considerations

Implementing PDEs in finance presents several challenges, including ensuring numerical stability and accuracy, handling complex boundary conditions, and optimizing performance. Rust's features, such as memory safety and concurrency, help address these challenges, but careful attention to detail and rigorous testing are essential.

As we progress in this book, we will delve deeper into the

practical aspects of implementing financial models in Rust, providing you with the tools and knowledge to build robust and efficient trading algorithms.

In summary, PDEs are a fundamental tool in quantitative finance, enabling the modeling and solving of complex financial problems. The Black-Scholes model is a prime example of a financial PDE, and its implementation in Rust demonstrates the power of combining advanced mathematical techniques with modern programming languages. As you continue to explore Rust's capabilities, you'll find that it offers unique advantages for developing high-performance financial applications.

Concept of Risk-Free Rate

The risk-free rate is a foundational element in quantitative finance, pivotal to the pricing of derivatives, risk management, and portfolio optimization. It represents the theoretical return on an investment with zero risk, serving as a benchmark against which other investments are measured. Understanding the concept of the risk-free rate is crucial in the context of the Black-Scholes model and other financial models, as it underpins the discounting process and affects the valuation of financial instruments.

1. Definition and Importance

The risk-free rate is the return on an investment that is considered free from risk, typically associated with government bonds of stable countries. In practice, the yield on short-term government securities, such as U.S. Treasury bills, is often used as a proxy for the risk-free rate. This is because these securities are backed by the full faith and credit of the government, making the likelihood of default negligible.

The risk-free rate is vital for several reasons:

-Benchmark for Returns: It serves as a baseline for comparing the performance of other investments. Investors demand a risk premium over the risk-free rate to compensate for taking on additional risk.

-Discounting Cash Flows: In discounted cash flow (DCF) models, the risk-free rate is used to discount future cash flows to their present value, enabling the valuation of various financial assets.

-Arbitrage-Free Pricing: The risk-free rate ensures that derivative prices are consistent with the absence of arbitrage opportunities, maintaining market equilibrium.

2. Role in the Black-Scholes Model

In the Black-Scholes model, the risk-free rate plays a critical role in determining the present value of the expected payoff of an option. The model assumes the ability to continuously trade the underlying asset and a risk-free bond to replicate the option's payoff. The risk-free rate is used to discount the future payoff of the option and calculate its present value.

The Black-Scholes formula for a European call option is:

$$ C = S_0 N(d_1) - K e^{-rT} N(d_2) $$

where:

- C is the call option price.

- S_0 is the current stock price.

- K is the strike price.

- T is the time to maturity.

- r is the risk-free interest rate.

- $N(\cdot)$ is the cumulative distribution function of the standard normal distribution.

- d_1 and d_2 are given by:

$$ d_1 = \frac{\ln(S_0 / K) + (r + \sigma^2 / 2)T}{\sigma \sqrt{T}} $$

$$ d_2 = d_1 - \sigma \sqrt{T} $$

The term e^{-rT} represents the present value factor, discounting the strike price at the risk-free rate over the option's time to maturity.

3. Determining the Risk-Free Rate

Selecting an appropriate risk-free rate is crucial for accurate option pricing and financial modeling. The choice of risk-free rate depends on the time horizon of the investment or derivative being valued. Typically, the following are used:

-Short-Term Risk-Free Rate: For short-term options and investments, the yield on short-term government securities, such as 3-month Treasury bills, is often used.

-Long-Term Risk-Free Rate: For longer-term options and investments, yields on longer-dated government bonds, such as 10-year Treasury bonds, may be more appropriate.

-Interpolated Rate: For options with maturities that do not match the available government bond maturities, an interpolated rate can be calculated using yields from bonds with surrounding maturities.

4. Impact of Risk-Free Rate Changes

Changes in the risk-free rate can significantly impact the pricing of options and other financial derivatives. An increase in the risk-free rate generally leads to higher call option prices and lower put option prices, all else being equal. This is because the present value of the strike price (discounted at the higher rate) decreases, making call options more valuable and put options less valuable.

Conversely, a decrease in the risk-free rate has the opposite effect, lowering call option prices and raising put option prices.

5. Risk-Free Rate in Practice

Despite its theoretical appeal, the risk-free rate in practice may be influenced by various factors, including:

-Market Liquidity: The liquidity of government securities can affect their yields, impacting the observed risk-free rate.

-Central Bank Policies: Actions by central banks, such as setting interest rates and engaging in quantitative easing, can influence the risk-free rate.

-Economic Conditions: The overall economic environment, including inflation expectations and economic growth, can affect the risk-free rate.

To illustrate the practical application of the risk-free rate in financial modeling, let's consider a Rust implementation example for discounting future cash flows.

6. Implementing Discounting in Rust

In Rust, we can implement a function to calculate the present value of a future cash flow using the risk-free rate. Here's a simple example:

```rust
fn present_value(future_cash_flow: f64, risk_free_rate: f64, time: f64) -> f64 {
    future_cash_flow / (1.0 + risk_free_rate).powf(time)
}

fn main() {
    let future_cash_flow = 1000.0;
    let risk_free_rate = 0.03; // 3% annual risk-free rate
    let time = 5.0; // 5 years

    let pv = present_value(future_cash_flow, risk_free_rate, time);
    println!("The present value of the future cash flow is: ${:.2}", pv);
}
```

This Rust code defines a function `present_value` that takes a future cash flow amount, the risk-free rate, and the time to maturity as inputs, and returns the present value. The main function demonstrates how to use this function to discount a future cash flow of $1,000 at a 3% annual risk-free rate over 5 years.

7. Challenges and Considerations

When selecting and using the risk-free rate, there are several challenges and considerations to keep in mind:

-Maturity Matching: Ensure that the maturity of the risk-free rate used matches the maturity of the option or investment being valued.

-Market Conditions: Be aware of current market conditions and economic factors that may affect the risk-free rate.

-Currency: The risk-free rate should be in the same currency as the cash flows being discounted to avoid currency risk.

The risk-free rate is a fundamental concept in finance, essential for pricing derivatives, managing risk, and valuing investments. In the Black-Scholes model, it plays a crucial role in discounting future payoffs to their present value, directly impacting option prices. Understanding how to determine and apply the risk-free rate is vital for accurate financial modeling and decision-making.

Implementing the concept of the risk-free rate in Rust, we can leverage the language's performance and safety features to build robust and efficient financial models. As you continue to explore the intersection of finance and technology, keep in mind the importance of the risk-free rate and its implications for your models and strategies.

Volatility and its Importance

Volatility, a term that frequently echoes in the corridors of financial markets, is a cornerstone concept in the world of options trading and risk management. At its core, volatility measures the degree of variation in the price of a financial instrument over time. It encapsulates the uncertainty and potential fluctuations in the market, serving as a critical input in the valuation of options and other derivatives.

1. Understanding Volatility

Volatility can be categorized into two primary types: historical volatility and implied volatility. Historical volatility, also known as realized volatility, is derived from past price movements of an asset. It provides a statistical measure of the asset's price fluctuation over a specific historical period. Implied volatility, on the other hand, is forward-looking. It is inferred from the market prices of options and reflects the market's expectations of future price movements.

-Historical Volatility: Calculated using historical price data, it quantifies the degree of variation in an asset's price over a specified time frame. It is often computed as the standard deviation of logarithmic returns.

-Implied Volatility: Extracted from the prices of options, it serves as a gauge for the market's expectations of future volatility. It is a crucial parameter in option pricing models and influences the premium of options.

2. Mathematical Representation of Volatility

Volatility is mathematically represented as the standard deviation of the returns of an asset. The formula for historical volatility is as follows:

$$\sigma = \sqrt{\frac{1}{n-1} \sum_{i=1}^{n} (R_i - \bar{R})^2}$$

where:

- σ is the historical volatility.

- n is the number of observations.

- R_i is the logarithmic return of the asset at time i.

- $\bar{R}$ is the average return over the period.

Implied volatility is derived using option pricing models, such as the Black-Scholes model, by finding the volatility value that equates the theoretical option price to the market price.

3. Role of Volatility in Option Pricing

In the Black-Scholes model, volatility plays a pivotal role in determining the price of options. It influences the likelihood that the option will finish in-the-money by the expiration date. Higher volatility increases the probability of significant price movements, thus raising the potential for the option to be profitable.

The Black-Scholes formula for a European call option incorporates volatility as follows:

$$C = S_0 N(d_1) - K e^{-rT} N(d_2)$$

where d_1 and d_2 are given by:

$$d_1 = \frac{\ln(S_0 / K) + (r + \sigma^2 / 2)T}{\sigma \sqrt{T}}$$

$$d_2 = d_1 - \sigma \sqrt{T}$$

Here, σ represents the volatility of the underlying asset. As volatility increases, the values of d_1 and d_2 also change, impacting the overall option price.

4. Practical Implications of Volatility

Understanding and accurately estimating volatility is crucial for traders and risk managers for several reasons:

-Option Pricing: Volatility is a key input in option pricing models. Accurate volatility estimation ensures that options are priced correctly, providing fair value for buyers and sellers.

-Hedging: Volatility forecasts help in designing effective hedging strategies to mitigate risk. By understanding potential price fluctuations, traders can better manage their positions and protect against adverse market movements.

-Portfolio Management: Volatility insights aid in portfolio construction and risk management, enabling investors to balance risk and return. High-volatility assets may offer higher returns but come with increased risk, while low-volatility assets provide stability.

5. Techniques for Estimating Volatility

Several techniques are employed to estimate volatility, each with its own strengths and limitations:

-Historical Volatility Calculation: Based on historical price data, it involves calculating the standard deviation of asset returns over a specified period.

-Implied Volatility Calculation: Derived from the market prices of options, it reflects market expectations of future volatility. Techniques such as the Black-Scholes model are used to back-calculate implied volatility.

-GARCH Models: Generalized Autoregressive Conditional Heteroskedasticity (GARCH) models are statistical models that predict future volatility based on past price data and volatility trends.

-EWMA: Exponentially Weighted Moving Average (EWMA) is a method that gives more weight to recent data, providing a responsive estimate of volatility.

6. Volatility in Practice: Rust Implementation

Let's walk through a simple Rust implementation to calculate historical volatility based on daily closing prices of a stock.

```rust
use std::f64;

fn calculate_daily_returns(prices: &[f64]) -> Vec<f64> {
    let mut returns = Vec::new();
```

```
for i in 1..prices.len() {
let ret = (prices[i] / prices[i - 1]).ln();
returns.push(ret);
}
returns
}

fn calculate_volatility(returns: &[f64]) -> f64 {
let mean: f64 = returns.iter().sum::<f64>() / returns.len() as
f64;
let variance: f64 = returns.iter().map(|&x| (x -
mean).powi(2)).sum::<f64>() / (returns.len() as f64 - 1.0);
variance.sqrt() * f64::consts::SQRT_252 // Annualizing the
daily volatility
}

fn main() {
let prices = vec![100.0, 101.0, 102.0, 101.5, 103.0]; // Example
daily closing prices
let daily_returns = calculate_daily_returns(&prices);
let volatility = calculate_volatility(&daily_returns);
println!("The historical volatility is: {:.2}%", volatility * 100.0);
}
```
```

In this Rust code, we first define a function `calculate_daily_returns` to compute the daily logarithmic returns of a stock based on its closing prices. Then,
```

the `calculate_volatility` function computes the historical volatility by calculating the standard deviation of the daily returns. The `f64::consts::SQRT_252` constant is used to annualize the daily volatility, assuming there are approximately 252 trading days in a year.

7. Challenges in Volatility Estimation

Estimating volatility accurately poses several challenges:

-Market Regimes: Volatility is not constant and can change dramatically across different market regimes. High volatility periods, like during financial crises, can skew historical estimates.

-Non-Stationarity: Financial time series are often non-stationary, meaning their statistical properties change over time. This can complicate the estimation and prediction of volatility.

-Data Quality: Accurate volatility estimation relies on high-quality and granular data. Incomplete or erroneous data can lead to misleading results.

Volatility is indispensable in the domain of options trading and financial risk management. It quantifies the uncertainty and potential price fluctuations of an asset, directly influencing the pricing of options and other derivatives. Understanding both historical and implied volatility, along with their estimation techniques, equips traders and risk managers with the insights needed to navigate the complexities of financial markets.

The Rust implementations provided demonstrate how to

harness the power of this robust programming language to calculate and apply volatility in financial models. As you continue to delve into the intricacies of the Black-Scholes model and beyond, mastering the concept of volatility will be crucial to your success in algorithmic options trading.

Embracing the volatility concept and leveraging Rust's high-performance capabilities, you are well-positioned to build sophisticated and efficient trading algorithms that can thrive in the dynamic landscape of financial markets.

Understanding Option Greeks

In the labyrinthine world of options trading, Option Greeks are invaluable tools that quantify the risk involved in holding an options position. Named after Greek letters, these metrics provide a comprehensive understanding of how different factors like time, volatility, and the price of the underlying asset impact the value of an option. They form the bedrock of sophisticated trading strategies and risk management techniques, making them indispensable for both novice and experienced traders.

1. Delta (Δ): Sensitivity to Underlying Asset Price

Delta measures the sensitivity of an option's price to small changes in the price of the underlying asset. Essentially, it represents the rate of change in the option's value with respect to a one-unit change in the price of the underlying asset.

-Call Options: A delta value between 0 and 1. For example, if the delta of a call option is 0.5, a $1 increase in the price of the underlying asset will result in a $0.50 increase in the option's price.

-Put Options: A delta value between -1 and 0. For instance, a delta of -0.5 means a $1 increase in the price of the underlying asset will cause a $0.50 decrease in the option's price.

Delta also provides insights into the probability of an option finishing in-the-money. A higher delta indicates a higher likelihood that the option will be profitable at expiration.

2. Gamma (Γ): Sensitivity to Delta

Gamma measures the rate of change of delta with respect to changes in the underlying asset's price. While delta tells you the first-order sensitivity, gamma gives you the second-order sensitivity, essentially capturing the curvature of the option's price as the underlying asset's price changes.

-Impact on Hedging: High gamma indicates that delta is highly sensitive to changes in the price of the underlying asset, necessitating frequent rebalancing of hedged positions. Traders often prefer lower gamma for stable positions.

-Volatility Insight: Gamma is higher for options that are at-the-money and near expiration, reflecting the increased sensitivity to price changes during these conditions.

Understanding gamma helps traders manage the risk of dynamic hedging strategies and better anticipate changes in delta.

3. Theta (Θ): Sensitivity to Time Decay

Theta measures the sensitivity of the option's price to the passage of time. It quantifies the rate at which an option's value decreases as it approaches expiration, often referred to as time decay.

-Call and Put Options: Theta is usually negative for both calls and puts, indicating that the option loses value over time. For instance, a theta of -0.05 means the option's price will decrease by $0.05 per day, all else being equal.

-Implications for Traders: Options traders must consider theta when holding positions over time. Options close to expiration will have higher theta, leading to rapid time decay.

Theta is particularly crucial for option sellers, as they benefit from time decay, while option buyers need to overcome the loss in value due to the passage of time.

4. Vega (v): Sensitivity to Volatility

Vega measures the sensitivity of an option's price to changes in the volatility of the underlying asset. It quantifies the amount by which the price of an option will change given a 1% change in implied volatility.

-Volatility Sensitivity: A higher vega indicates that the option's price is more sensitive to changes in volatility. For example, if an option has a vega of 0.10, a 1% increase in implied volatility will increase the option's price by $0.10.

-Strategic Considerations: Traders utilize vega to gauge the impact of volatility changes on their positions. High vega options benefit from increasing volatility, making them attractive during periods of market uncertainty.

Understanding vega is essential for volatility trading strategies, including straddles and strangles, where traders profit from significant moves in volatility.

5. Rho (ρ): Sensitivity to Interest Rates

Rho measures the sensitivity of an option's price to changes in interest rates. It represents the amount by which the price of an option will change given a 1% change in the risk-free interest rate.

-Call Options: Typically, rho is positive for call options, indicating that an increase in interest rates will increase the option's price. For instance, a rho of 0.05 means a 1% increase in interest rates will raise the option's price by $0.05.

-Put Options: Conversely, rho is usually negative for put options, suggesting that an increase in interest rates will decrease the option's price.

Rho is particularly relevant for long-dated options, where changes in interest rates have a more pronounced effect on pricing.

6. Practical Applications of Option Greeks

Understanding and utilizing Option Greeks is fundamental for effective options trading and risk management. Here are some practical applications:

-Hedging: Traders use delta to construct delta-neutral portfolios, where the overall delta of the portfolio is zero, minimizing the impact of small price movements in the underlying asset. Gamma helps in rebalancing these portfolios to maintain delta neutrality.

-Risk Management: Vega is crucial for assessing the impact of volatility changes on options portfolios. By analyzing vegas, traders can construct strategies that benefit from volatility increases or decreases.

-Time Decay: Theta is essential for managing the time decay of options. Option sellers often capitalize on theta decay by writing options with high theta values, while buyers need to be aware of the rapid loss in value as expiration approaches.

-Interest Rate Sensitivity: Rho helps traders understand the impact of interest rate changes on their options positions. This is particularly important in environments where interest rates are volatile or expected to change significantly.

7. Rust Implementation: Calculating Delta

To solidify our understanding, let's implement a simple Rust function to calculate the delta of a European call option using the Black-Scholes model.

```rust
use std::f64::consts::PI;

// Standard normal cumulative distribution function
fn standard_normal_cdf(x: f64) -> f64 {
(1.0 + (x / (2.0f64).sqrt()).erf()) / 2.0
```

```rust
}

// Function to calculate d1
fn calculate_d1(spot: f64, strike: f64, time: f64, rate: f64,
volatility: f64) -> f64 {
(spot.ln() - strike.ln() + (rate + 0.5 * volatility.powi(2)) * time) /
(volatility * time.sqrt())
}

// Function to calculate delta for a European call option
fn calculate_delta(spot: f64, strike: f64, time: f64, rate: f64,
volatility: f64) -> f64 {
let d1 = calculate_d1(spot, strike, time, rate, volatility);
standard_normal_cdf(d1)
}

fn main() {
let spot = 100.0; // Current price of the underlying asset
let strike = 105.0; // Strike price of the option
let time = 1.0; // Time to expiration in years
let rate = 0.05; // Risk-free interest rate
let volatility = 0.2; // Volatility of the underlying asset

let delta = calculate_delta(spot, strike, time, rate, volatility);
println!("The delta of the European call option is: {:.4}", delta);
}
```
` ` `

In this Rust code, we define functions to calculate d_1 and the cumulative distribution function of the standard normal distribution. We then use these functions to calculate the delta for a European call option. The `calculate_delta` function takes the current price of the underlying asset, strike price, time to expiration, risk-free interest rate, and volatility as inputs, returning the delta value.

8. Challenges and Considerations

While Option Greeks are powerful tools, their practical application comes with challenges:

-Dynamic Nature: Option Greeks are not static; they change as market conditions evolve. Traders must continuously monitor and adjust positions to manage risks effectively.

-Complex Interactions: The Greeks often interact in complex ways. For instance, changes in volatility can affect both vega and delta, requiring a holistic approach to risk management.

-Model Assumptions: The accuracy of Option Greeks depends on the assumptions of the underlying pricing models, such as the Black-Scholes model. Deviations from these assumptions can lead to discrepancies in Greek values.

Option Greeks are fundamental to the sophisticated art of options trading and risk management. By quantifying the sensitivities of option prices to various factors, they provide traders with deep insights into potential risks and opportunities. Delta, gamma, theta, vega, and rho each offer unique perspectives, enabling traders to craft well-balanced strategies and dynamically manage their portfolios.

The Rust implementation example illustrates how to calculate one of the key Greeks, delta, integrating theoretical knowledge with practical application. As you advance in mastering Option Greeks, you'll be better equipped to navigate the complexities of options trading, leveraging the precision and efficiency of Rust to enhance your trading algorithms.

Understanding and effectively utilizing Option Greeks will be instrumental in your journey through the intricacies of algorithmic options trading, providing a robust foundation for informed decision-making and strategic execution.

1.18.7 The Normal Distribution and Lognormal Distribution

In the world of financial modeling and options pricing, understanding the distributions of asset prices is paramount. Two distributions stand at the heart of these models—the Normal and Lognormal distributions. These mathematical tools are indispensable for quantifying risk, predicting price movements, and ultimately, formulating robust trading strategies.

Understanding the Normal Distribution

The Normal distribution, often referred to as the Gaussian distribution, is the cornerstone of classical statistics. Characterized by its bell-shaped curve, it is defined by two parameters: the mean (μ) and the standard deviation (σ). The mean represents the central value around which the data points cluster, while the standard deviation measures the dispersion or spread of these points.

Mathematically, the probability density function (PDF) of the Normal distribution is expressed as:

$$ f(x \mid \mu, \sigma) = \frac{1}{\sigma \sqrt{2\pi}} e^{-\frac{(x - \mu)^2}{2\sigma^2}} $$

In the context of finance, the Normal distribution is often used to model the returns of assets, rather than their prices. This is because asset returns tend to exhibit the properties of a Normal distribution, such as symmetry around the mean and a predictable spread.

Consider a stock with a mean return of 5% and a standard deviation of 2%. The distribution of its returns over a period might look something like this:

```rust
extern crate rand;
extern crate rand_distr;

use rand::prelude::*;
use rand_distr::{Normal, Distribution};

fn main() {
let mean = 0.05;
let std_dev = 0.02;
```

```
let normal = Normal::new(mean, std_dev).unwrap();
let mut rng = thread_rng();

let simulated_returns: Vec<f64> = (0..1000).map(|_|
normal.sample(&mut rng)).collect();

for r in &simulated_returns[0..10] {
println!("{:.4}", r);
}
}
```

In this Rust snippet, we use the `rand` and `rand_distr` crates to simulate asset returns based on a Normal distribution. This simulation can be extended to model various scenarios and predict potential outcomes.

The Lognormal Distribution

While the Normal distribution is suitable for modeling returns, the Lognormal distribution is more appropriate for modeling asset prices. This is due to the fact that asset prices cannot be negative and tend to exhibit proportional rather than absolute changes—a behavior aptly captured by the Lognormal distribution.

If a variable X follows a Normal distribution, then e^X follows a Lognormal distribution. Mathematically, if the natural logarithm of a variable follows a Normal distribution, the variable itself follows a Lognormal distribution.

The probability density function (PDF) of the Lognormal distribution is given by:

$$ f(x \mid \mu, \sigma) = \frac{1}{x \sigma \sqrt{2\pi}} e^{-\frac{(\ln x - \mu)^2}{2\sigma^2}} $$

In financial modeling, the Lognormal distribution is used to describe the price of an asset. For instance, if we model the price of a stock as S, we assume that $\ln(S)$ follows a Normal distribution.

To simulate asset prices using the Lognormal distribution in Rust, consider the following:

```rust
extern crate rand;
extern crate rand_distr;

use rand::prelude::*;
use rand_distr::{LogNormal, Distribution};

fn main() {
let mean = 0.05;
let std_dev = 0.02;
let log_normal = LogNormal::new(mean, std_dev).unwrap();
let mut rng = thread_rng();

let simulated_prices: Vec<f64>  =  (0..1000).map(|_|
```

```
log_normal.sample(&mut rng)).collect();

for p in &simulated_prices[0..10] {
println!("{:.2}", p);
}
}
```

This Rust code snippet demonstrates how to generate asset prices assuming they follow a Lognormal distribution. By leveraging the `LogNormal` struct from the `rand_distr` crate, we simulate price movements over time.

Practical Implications in Options Pricing

The Black-Scholes model, a pivotal framework in options pricing, implicitly assumes that the price of the underlying asset follows a Lognormal distribution. This assumption simplifies the mathematical modeling and allows for the derivation of closed-form solutions for option prices.

Consider a European call option on a stock. The Black-Scholes formula for pricing this option is:

$$C = S_0 N(d_1) - K e^{-rT} N(d_2)$$

where

$$d_1 = \frac{\ln(S_0/K) + (r + \sigma^2/2)T}{\sigma \sqrt{T}}$$

$$[d\_2 = d\_1 - \sigma \sqrt{T} \]$$

Here, $N(\cdot)$ represents the cumulative distribution function (CDF) of the standard Normal distribution. The terms S_0 and K are the current stock price and strike price, respectively, r is the risk-free rate, T is the time to expiration, and σ is the volatility of the stock's returns.

This formula highlights the interdependence between the Normal and Lognormal distributions. The $\ln(S_0/K)$ term in d_1 and d_2 stems from the Lognormal assumption, while the $N(\cdot)$ function leverages the properties of the Normal distribution.

In practice, implementing the Black-Scholes formula in Rust requires precise calculation of these terms. Here's a simplified example:

```rust
extern crate statrs;

use statrs::distribution::{Normal, Univariate};

fn black_scholes_call_price(s: f64, k: f64, t: f64, r: f64, sigma: f64) -> f64 {
let d1 = (s.ln() - k.ln() + (r + 0.5 * sigma * sigma) * t) / (sigma * t.sqrt());
let d2 = d1 - sigma * t.sqrt();

let norm = Normal::new(0.0, 1.0).unwrap();
```

```rust
let call_price = s * norm.cdf(d1) - k * (-r * t).exp() * norm.cdf(d2);

    call_price
}

fn main() {
    let s = 100.0;
    let k = 100.0;
    let t = 1.0;
    let r = 0.05;
    let sigma = 0.2;

    let call_price = black_scholes_call_price(s, k, t, r, sigma);
    println!("Call option price: {:.2}", call_price);
}
```
```

In this example, we compute the price of a European call option using the Black-Scholes formula. The `statrs` crate provides the `Normal` distribution functionality necessary to calculate the cumulative distribution functions.

Understanding the Normal and Lognormal distributions is critical for anyone engaged in financial modeling and options pricing. The Normal distribution's role in modeling asset returns and the Lognormal distribution's application to asset prices underpin many of the foundational models in quantitative finance. By leveraging Rust's capabilities, we can efficiently and accurately implement these models, enhancing both our theoretical understanding and practical execution in
```

the ever-evolving world of algorithmic trading.

Time Value of Money

The concept of the Time Value of Money (TVM) is fundamental in finance. It asserts that a dollar today is worth more than a dollar in the future due to its potential earning capacity. This principle underpins the majority of financial decision-making, including investment evaluations, loan amortizations, and options pricing. Understanding TVM is crucial for accurately assessing the present and future value of financial instruments, including derivatives.

The Core Principle of TVM

At its core, TVM is based on the premise that money can earn interest. Therefore, any amount of money is worth more the sooner it is received. This notion is quantified using interest rates, which can be either simple or compound. The calculations of TVM allow us to compare the value of money at different points in time.

Simple and Compound Interest

Simple interest is calculated on the principal amount only. Its formula is straightforward:

$$A = P(1 + rt)$$

where:

- \(A \) is the amount of money accumulated after n years, including interest.

- \(P \) is the principal amount (the initial sum of money).

- \(r \) is the annual interest rate (decimal).

- \(t \) is the time the money is invested for, in years.

However, most financial models utilize compound interest, where interest is calculated on the initial principal and also on the accumulated interest from previous periods. The formula for compound interest is:

\[A = P(1 + \frac{r}{n})^{nt} \]

where:

- \(n \) is the number of times that interest is compounded per unit \(t \).

Let's illustrate these concepts with a Rust code example:

```rust
fn simple_interest(principal: f64, rate: f64, time: f64) -> f64 {
principal * (1.0 + rate * time)
}

fn compound_interest(principal: f64, rate: f64, time: f64, n: u32) -> f64 {
principal * (1.0 + rate / n as f64).powf((n as f64) * time)
}
```

```
fn main() {
let principal = 1000.0;
let rate = 0.05;
let time = 3.0;
let n = 4; // quarterly compounding

let si = simple_interest(principal, rate, time);
let ci = compound_interest(principal, rate, time, n);

println!("Simple Interest: {:.2}", si);
println!("Compound Interest: {:.2}", ci);
}
```

This code snippet demonstrates the calculation of simple and compound interest in Rust. With an initial investment of $1,000 at a 5% annual interest rate over three years, compounded quarterly, the results highlight the significant impact of compound interest.

Present Value (PV) and Future Value (FV)

The TVM principle involves two key concepts: Present Value (PV) and Future Value (FV).

-Future Value (FV): The value of an investment after it has earned interest over a period. The formula for FV using compound interest is:

$$ FV = PV(1 + \frac{r}{n})^{nt} $$

-Present Value (PV): The current value of a future amount of money, discounted at a specific interest rate. The formula for PV is:

$$ PV = \frac{FV}{(1 + \frac{r}{n})^{nt}} $$

Let's extend our Rust example to include PV and FV calculations:

```rust
fn future_value(principal: f64, rate: f64, time: f64, n: u32) ->
f64 {

principal * (1.0 + rate / n as f64).powf((n as f64) * time)

}


fn present_value(future_value: f64, rate: f64, time: f64, n: u32)
-> f64 {

future_value / (1.0 + rate / n as f64).powf((n as f64) * time)

}


fn main() {

let principal = 1000.0;

let rate = 0.05;

let time = 3.0;

let n = 4; // quarterly compounding
```

```
let fv = future_value(principal, rate, time, n);
let pv = present_value(fv, rate, time, n);

println!("Future Value: {:.2}", fv);
println!("Present Value of FV: {:.2}", pv);
}
` ` `
```

This example computes the future value of an investment and then calculates the present value of that future amount. It encapsulates the essence of TVM, demonstrating how an amount grows over time and how future values are discounted back to present terms.

Net Present Value (NPV) and Internal Rate of Return (IRR)

For evaluating investment opportunities, two critical metrics derived from TVM are Net Present Value (NPV) and Internal Rate of Return (IRR).

-Net Present Value (NPV): The difference between the present value of cash inflows and outflows over a period of time. It's calculated as:

$$ NPV = \sum_{t=0}^{n} \frac{C_t}{(1 + r)^t} $$

where C_t is the net cash inflow during the period t and r is the discount rate.

-Internal Rate of Return (IRR): The discount rate that makes the NPV of all cash flows from a particular project equal to zero. It's the rate at which an investment breaks even.

To implement NPV in Rust, consider the following example:

```rust
fn npv(rate: f64, cash_flows: &[f64]) -> f64 {
cash_flows.iter()
.enumerate()
.map(|(t, &cf)| cf / (1.0 + rate).powi(t as i32))
.sum()
}

fn main() {
let rate = 0.1; // discount rate
let cash_flows = [-1000.0, 300.0, 420.0, 680.0];

let npv_value = npv(rate, &cash_flows);

println!("Net Present Value: {:.2}", npv_value);
}
```

This code calculates the NPV of a series of cash flows, with an initial outlay of $1,000 followed by returns of $300, $420, and $680 over the next three years. The discount rate used is 10%.

TVM in Option Pricing

The Time Value of Money is integral to the Black-Scholes model for pricing options. The model discounts future payoffs to their present value, ensuring that the price of an option reflects the time value appropriately.

For a European call option, the Black-Scholes formula includes the term e^{-rT}, which discounts the strike price (K) to its present value. The r represents the risk-free rate, and T is the time to maturity. This ensures the model accounts for the time value of money:

$$C = S_0 N(d\_1) - K e^{-rT} N(d\_2)$$

Here, e^{-rT} is precisely the application of TVM, converting the future payoff into today's terms.

By implementing these principles in Rust, financial professionals can build robust, efficient models that reflect accurate pricing dynamics in the options market. The understanding and application of TVM ensure that all financial decisions, from simple savings plans to complex derivatives pricing, are based on sound financial logic. This consistency and precision are critical in the world of algorithmic trading and financial engineering.

Final Thoughts

The Time Value of Money is an indispensable concept in finance, reflecting the principle that money available now is worth more than the same amount in the future. Understanding and applying TVM allows for more accurate financial modeling and better decision-making. Whether you're calculating simple returns, evaluating investment opportunities, or pricing options, incorporating TVM into your Rust-based financial models ensures precision and reliability.

With this foundation, you're better equipped to navigate the myriad financial instruments and strategies, enhancing your capability to develop sophisticated trading algorithms that stand the test of time.

1.20.9 No-Arbitrage Principle

The no-arbitrage principle is a cornerstone in the world of finance, ensuring market efficiency and the fair pricing of financial instruments. This principle asserts that there are no free lunches in the market—meaning, it is impossible to make a riskless profit without any initial investment. Understanding and applying this principle is vital for financial professionals, particularly in the context of options pricing using models like Black-Scholes and algorithmic trading strategies.

Core Concept of No-Arbitrage

At its essence, the no-arbitrage principle ensures that price discrepancies between equivalent financial instruments are corrected by market forces. If such discrepancies exist, arbitrageurs would exploit them until the prices converge, thereby eliminating the arbitrage opportunity. This principle maintains that the market prices should adjust such that no opportunities for risk-free profit exist.

Arbitrage in Financial Markets

Arbitrage involves the simultaneous purchase and sale of an asset to profit from a difference in the price. It is a fundamental operation that drives the efficiency of financial markets. Consider a simple example of currency arbitrage:

Suppose the exchange rate between USD and EUR in New York is 1 USD = 0.85 EUR, while in London, it's 1 USD = 0.88 EUR. An arbitrageur could buy EUR in New York and sell it in London, locking in a risk-free profit until the exchange rates equalize.

To illustrate this with Rust, let's build a simple arbitrage detection algorithm for currency pairs:

```rust
struct CurrencyPair<'a> {
base: &'a str,
quote: &'a str,
rate: f64,
}

fn find_arbitrage(pairs: Vec<CurrencyPair>) {
for (i, pair1) in pairs.iter().enumerate() {
for (j, pair2) in pairs.iter().enumerate() {
if i != j && pair1.base == pair2.quote && pair1.quote ==
```

```rust
pair2.base {
let profit = pair2.rate - 1.0 / pair1.rate;
if profit > 0.0 {
println!("Arbitrage Opportunity: Buy {} at {} and sell at {} for a profit of {}",
pair1.base, pair1.rate, pair2.rate, profit);
}
}
}
}
}

fn main() {
let pairs = vec![
CurrencyPair { base: "USD", quote: "EUR", rate: 0.85 },
CurrencyPair { base: "EUR", quote: "USD", rate: 1.18 },
CurrencyPair { base: "USD", quote: "GBP", rate: 0.75 },
CurrencyPair { base: "GBP", quote: "USD", rate: 1.32 },
];

find_arbitrage(pairs);
}
```

In this example, the `find_arbitrage` function iterates over currency pairs to identify potential arbitrage opportunities, printing them out when found.

No-Arbitrage Condition in Options Pricing

The no-arbitrage principle is crucial in the context of options pricing. It ensures that the price of an option reflects the fair value based on the underlying asset's price. In the Black-Scholes model, the no-arbitrage condition guarantees that the options pricing formula is consistent with the market dynamics, preventing any arbitrage opportunities.

Consider the European call and put options. According to the put-call parity—a direct consequence of the no-arbitrage principle—the relationship between the prices of European call and put options with the same strike price and expiration date is:

$$C - P = S - K e^{-rT}$$

where:
- C is the price of the call option.
- P is the price of the put option.
- S is the current price of the underlying asset.
- K is the strike price.
- r is the risk-free interest rate.
- T is the time to maturity.

Put-call parity ensures that if any discrepancy exists between these prices, arbitrage opportunities emerge, driving the prices back to equilibrium.

Let's implement this parity check in Rust:

```rust
fn put_call_parity(call_price: f64, put_price: f64, asset_price: f64, strike_price: f64, rate: f64, time: f64) -> bool {
    let lhs = call_price - put_price;
    let rhs = asset_price - strike_price * (-rate * time).exp();
    (lhs - rhs).abs() < 1e-6 // Small tolerance for floating point comparison
}

fn main() {
    let call_price = 10.0;
    let put_price = 7.0;
    let asset_price = 100.0;
    let strike_price = 95.0;
    let rate = 0.05;
    let time = 1.0;

    let parity = put_call_parity(call_price, put_price, asset_price, strike_price, rate, time);
    if parity {
        println!("Put-call parity holds.");
    } else {
        println!("Arbitrage opportunity detected!");
    }
}
```

```
}
```
```
```

This Rust code checks whether the put-call parity condition holds for given option prices. Any deviation signals an arbitrage opportunity.

Practical Implications in Algorithmic Trading

The no-arbitrage principle extends beyond simple pricing checks and into algorithmic trading strategies. Algorithmic traders develop and deploy strategies that exploit small, fleeting arbitrage opportunities across various markets and instruments. These strategies require sophisticated algorithms and high-speed execution to be effective.

For instance, statistical arbitrage involves identifying and exploiting price discrepancies between correlated assets. Another example is index arbitrage, where traders take advantage of mispricings between index futures and individual constituent stocks.

Algorithmic trading systems must ensure compliance with the no-arbitrage principle to avoid incorrect pricing and potential losses. Rust, with its performance and safety features, is well-suited for developing such high-frequency trading systems.

Here's a simplified example of a statistical arbitrage strategy in Rust:

```rust
```

```rust
fn mean_reversion_strategy(asset1_prices: &[f64],
asset2_prices: &[f64], threshold: f64) {

let mean1: f64 = asset1_prices.iter().sum::<f64>() /
asset1_prices.len() as f64;

let mean2: f64 = asset2_prices.iter().sum::<f64>() /
asset2_prices.len() as f64;


let spread: Vec<f64> =
asset1_prices.iter().zip(asset2_prices.iter())

.map(|(&p1, &p2)| p1 - p2).collect();


let mean_spread: f64 = spread.iter().sum::<f64>() /
spread.len() as f64;


if (mean1 - mean2).abs() > threshold {

println!("Arbitrage Opportunity: Mean reversion strategy
signal.");

} else {

println!("No significant arbitrage opportunity.");

}

}


fn main() {

let asset1_prices = vec![100.0, 102.0, 101.0, 103.0, 104.0];

let asset2_prices = vec![98.0, 97.0, 99.0, 100.0, 101.0];

let threshold = 2.0;


mean_reversion_strategy(&asset1_prices, &asset2_prices,
threshold);
```

```
}
` ` `
```

This example implements a mean-reversion strategy by comparing the average prices of two correlated assets. If the price spread exceeds a specified threshold, it signals an arbitrage opportunity.

Ensuring Compliance with No-Arbitrage in Rust

Developing robust financial models and trading algorithms necessitates rigorous testing to ensure compliance with the no-arbitrage principle. Rust offers tools like unit testing and property-based testing to validate that your implementations adhere to this principle.

Here's a simple unit test for the put-call parity function in Rust:

```rust
` ` `rust
#[cfg(test)]
mod tests {
use super::*;

#[test]
fn test_put_call_parity() {
let call_price = 10.0;
let put_price = 7.0;
let asset_price = 100.0;
```

```
let strike_price = 95.0;

let rate = 0.05;

let time = 1.0;


assert!(put_call_parity(call_price,    put_price,    asset_price,
strike_price, rate, time));
}

}
` ` `
```

Running these tests ensures that your financial models and algorithms do not violate the no-arbitrage principle, preserving market efficiency and integrity.

Final Thoughts

The no-arbitrage principle is a fundamental concept in finance, ensuring that markets remain efficient and fair. By eliminating opportunities for risk-free profits, this principle underpins the pricing of financial instruments and the development of trading strategies. Implementing and validating the no-arbitrage condition using Rust provides a robust and efficient foundation for financial modeling and algorithmic trading.

With a deep understanding of the no-arbitrage principle and the ability to implement it in Rust, you are well-equipped to build sophisticated and reliable financial systems that uphold the integrity of the markets while maximizing performance and accuracy.

1.21.10 Introduction to Stochastic Calculus

Stochastic calculus is an essential mathematical framework used to model the randomness inherent in financial markets. It provides the tools to describe and analyze systems influenced by random processes, making it fundamental for pricing derivatives, managing risk, and developing trading algorithms. This subsection introduces the core concepts of stochastic calculus, emphasizing its significance in financial applications, particularly in the Black-Scholes model.

Foundations of Stochastic Processes

At the heart of stochastic calculus lies the concept of stochastic processes—random sequences that evolve over time. These processes are used to model the unpredictable paths of asset prices. A key type of stochastic process in finance is the Wiener process, also known as Brownian motion, which serves as the building block for more complex models.

Wiener Process and Brownian Motion

A Wiener process $W(t)$ is a continuous-time stochastic process with the following properties:

1. $W(0) = 0$ almost surely.

2. $W(t) - W(s) \sim N(0, t-s)$ for $0 \leq s < t$, meaning the increments are normally distributed with mean zero and variance $t-s$.

3. The process has independent increments.

4. \(W(t)\) is continuous with respect to \(t\).

In financial modeling, Brownian motion is used to represent the random fluctuations of asset prices. To illustrate Brownian motion in Rust, consider the following implementation:

```rust
extern crate rand;
use rand::Rng;

fn generate_brownian_motion(n: usize, dt: f64) -> Vec<f64> {
let mut rng = rand::thread_rng();
let mut w: Vec<f64> = Vec::with_capacity(n);
w.push(0.0);

for _ in 1..n {
let dw = rng.sample(rand::distributions::StandardNormal) * dt.sqrt();
w.push(w.last().unwrap() + dw);
}

w
}

fn main() {
let n = 1000; // Number of time steps
let dt = 0.01; // Time increment
let w = generate_brownian_motion(n, dt);
```

```
// Print a few values for illustration
for i in 0..10 {
println!("W({:.2}) = {}", i as f64 * dt, w[i]);
}
}
` ` `
```

This code snippet simulates a Brownian motion by generating increments from a normal distribution and accumulating them over time.

Itô Calculus

A fundamental extension of stochastic calculus is Itô calculus, which allows us to integrate functions with respect to Brownian motion. Unlike standard calculus, Itô calculus accounts for the randomness and non-differentiability of Brownian paths. The Itô integral $\int_0^t \sigma(s) dW(s)$ and Itô's Lemma are central concepts.

Itô's Lemma

Itô's Lemma is the stochastic counterpart of the chain rule in classical calculus. It describes how a function $f(t, W(t))$ of a stochastic process evolves over time. For $f(t, W(t))$, the lemma states:

$$df(t, W(t)) = \left(\frac{\partial f}{\partial t} + \frac{1}{2} \frac{\partial^2 f}{\partial W^2} \right) dt + \frac{\partial f}{\partial W} dW(t)$$

Applying Itô's Lemma is essential in deriving the Black-Scholes partial differential equation. Let's consider a simplified application in Rust:

```rust
fn ito_lemma(x: f64, t: f64, dt: f64, dx: f64) -> f64 {
let df_dt = 0.5 * (1.0 - t).exp(); // Partial derivative w.r.t. time
let df_dx = x; // Partial derivative w.r.t. x
let d2f_dx2 = 1.0; // Second partial derivative w.r.t. x

let df = df_dt * dt + df_dx * dx + 0.5 * d2f_dx2 * dx * dx;
df
}

fn main() {
let x = 1.0; // Initial value of x
let t = 0.0; // Initial time
let dt = 0.01; // Small time increment
let dw = 0.02; // Small increment in Brownian motion

let df = ito_lemma(x, t, dt, dw);
println!("Change in function value according to Itô's Lemma: {}", df);
}
```

This example demonstrates how to compute the change

in a function based on Itô's Lemma, incorporating both deterministic and stochastic components.

Stochastic Differential Equations

Stochastic differential equations (SDEs) are used to model dynamic systems influenced by randomness. In finance, SDEs describe the evolution of asset prices. The Black-Scholes model is a prime example of an SDE, where the price $S(t)$ of an asset follows:

$$ dS(t) = \mu S(t) dt + \sigma S(t) dW(t) $$

where:

- μ is the drift rate.

- σ is the volatility.

- $dW(t)$ is the increment of a Wiener process.

Implementing and solving SDEs in Rust requires numerical methods, such as the Euler-Maruyama method. Below is an implementation for simulating an SDE:

```rust
extern crate rand;
use rand::Rng;

fn simulate_sde(n: usize, dt: f64, mu: f64, sigma: f64, s0: f64) -> Vec<f64> {
let mut rng = rand::thread_rng();
```

```rust
let mut s: Vec<f64> = Vec::with_capacity(n);
s.push(s0);

for _ in 1..n {
let ds = mu * s.last().unwrap() * dt + sigma * s.last().unwrap() *
rng.sample(rand::distributions::StandardNormal) * dt.sqrt();
s.push(s.last().unwrap() + ds);
}

s
}

fn main() {
let n = 1000; // Number of time steps
let dt = 0.01; // Time increment
let mu = 0.05; // Drift rate
let sigma = 0.2; // Volatility
let s0 = 100.0; // Initial asset price

let s = simulate_sde(n, dt, mu, sigma, s0);

// Print a few values for illustration
for i in 0..10 {
println!("S({:.2}) = {}", i as f64 * dt, s[i]);
}
}
```

This code simulates an SDE representing the evolution of an asset price over time, incorporating both drift and volatility.

Applications in Financial Modeling

Stochastic calculus is indispensable for modeling derivative prices and managing financial risks. The Black-Scholes model, for instance, leverages stochastic processes to price European options. By understanding and applying stochastic calculus, financial professionals can develop more accurate pricing models and trading strategies.

In summary, stochastic calculus provides a robust framework for modeling the randomness in financial markets. With tools like Wiener processes, Itô's Lemma, and SDEs, it allows for precise mathematical descriptions of asset price dynamics. Implementing these concepts in Rust enhances the performance and reliability of financial models, equipping you to tackle the complexities of algorithmic trading with confidence and precision.

CHAPTER 3:
IMPLEMENTING
BLACK-SCHOLES
IN RUST

I n Rust, variables are immutable by default, meaning their values cannot be changed once assigned. To declare a variable, you use the `let` keyword, and to make a variable mutable, you add the `mut` keyword.

```rust
fn main() {
let x = 5; // Immutable variable
let mut y = 10; // Mutable variable

println!("Value of x: {}", x);
println!("Initial value of y: {}", y);

y += 5; // Modify y since it is mutable
println!("Modified value of y: {}", y);
```

```
}
```
```
` ` `
```

This snippet demonstrates the declaration and modification of variables. By default, immutability helps prevent unintended side effects, a crucial feature for maintaining the integrity of financial calculations.

Data Types

Rust has a rich type system that ensures type safety and precision. The primary scalar types include integers, floating-point numbers, Booleans, and characters.

```rust
fn main() {
let integer: i32 = 42; // 32-bit signed integer
let floating_point: f64 = 3.14; // 64-bit floating-point number
let boolean: bool = true; // Boolean
let character: char = 'R'; // Character

println!("Integer: {}", integer);
println!("Floating-point: {}", floating_point);
println!("Boolean: {}", boolean);
println!("Character: {}", character);
}
```
```
` ` `
```

Understanding these data types is essential for accurate financial modeling, where the precision and reliability of numerical data are paramount.

Control Flow

Rust provides standard control flow constructs such as `if`, `else`, `loop`, `while`, and `for`. These constructs allow you to implement logic and iteration in your programs.

```rust
fn main() {
let number = 7;

// Conditional statement
if number < 10 {
println!("The number is less than 10");
} else {
println!("The number is greater than or equal to 10");
}

// Loop
let mut count = 0;
loop {
count += 1;
if count == 5 {
break;
```

```
}
}
println!("Loop ran {} times", count);

// While loop
let mut number = 3;
while number != 0 {
println!("{}!", number);
number -= 1;
}

// For loop
for i in 0..5 {
println!("The value of i is: {}", i);
}
}
```
` ` `

These constructs enable you to control the flow of your program, facilitating the execution of complex trading algorithms and decision-making processes.

Functions

Functions in Rust are defined using the `fn` keyword. They can accept parameters and return values, supporting the modularity and reusability of your code.

```rust
fn add(a: i32, b: i32) -> i32 {
a + b
}

fn main() {
let result = add(5, 3);
println!("The sum is: {}", result);
}
```

In the context of algorithmic trading, functions allow you to encapsulate trading strategies and computational models, making your code more organized and maintainable.

Ownership and Borrowing

Ownership is Rust's most distinctive feature, ensuring memory safety without a garbage collector. Each value in Rust has a single owner, and the value is dropped when the owner goes out of scope. Borrowing allows you to reference values without taking ownership.

```rust
fn main() {
let s1 = String::from("Hello");
let s2 = s1; // s1 is moved to s2
```

```
// println!("{}", s1); // This would cause an error

let s3 = String::from("World");
let s4 = &s3; // s3 is borrowed
println!("s3: {}, s4: {}", s3, s4);
}
```

This concept is crucial in preventing data races and ensuring thread safety, which are vital in the development of concurrent, high-frequency trading systems.

Structs

Structs are custom data types that let you package related values together. They are similar to classes in object-oriented languages but with a focus on data rather than behavior.

```rust
struct Trade {
ticker: String,
quantity: u32,
price: f64,
}

fn main() {
let trade = Trade {
```

```
ticker: String::from("AAPL"),

quantity: 100,

price: 150.0,

};


println!("Trade: {} shares of {} at ${}", trade.quantity,
trade.ticker, trade.price);

}
```
` ` `

Structs allow you to represent complex data structures, such as trades or financial instruments, making your code more expressive and easier to manage.

Enums

Enums, short for enumerations, are types that can be any one of several variants. They are powerful for modeling situations where a value can be one of several possible states.

```rust
enum OrderType {
Market,
Limit(f64),
Stop(f64),
}

fn main() {
```

```
let order = OrderType::Limit(200.0);

match order {
OrderType::Market => println!("Market order"),
OrderType::Limit(price) => println!("Limit order at ${}", price),
OrderType::Stop(price) => println!("Stop order at ${}", price),
}
}
```
```

Enums are exceptionally useful in algorithmic trading for handling different order types and states, contributing to more robust and flexible trading systems.

Error Handling

Rust emphasizes safe error handling through the `Result` and `Option` types. The `Result` type is used for operations that can succeed or fail, while the `Option` type is for values that can be present or absent.

```rust
fn divide(dividend: f64, divisor: f64) -> Result<f64, String> {
if divisor == 0.0 {
Err(String::from("Cannot divide by zero"))
} else {
Ok(dividend / divisor)
}
```
```

```rust
}

fn main() {
match divide(10.0, 2.0) {
Ok(result) => println!("Result: {}", result),
Err(e) => println!("Error: {}", e),
}
}
```

Proper error handling is critical in financial applications to ensure the robustness and reliability of your trading algorithms, preventing unexpected crashes and losses.

Ownership and Lifetime Annotations

Understanding ownership and lifetimes is crucial for writing safe and efficient Rust code. Lifetimes ensure that references are valid as long as they are used, preventing dangling references and memory leaks.

```rust
fn main() {
let x = 5; // x is the owner of the value 5
let r = &x; // r borrows the value of x

println!("The value of r: {}", r); // r is valid here
}
```

` ` `

Lifetimes are particularly important in concurrent programs where references are shared across threads, ensuring that your trading algorithms remain performant and safe.

Mastering the basic syntax and structures of Rust provides a strong foundation for implementing sophisticated financial models and algorithms. From variable management and control flow to advanced features like ownership and error handling, each aspect of Rust contributes to creating reliable, high-performance trading systems. As we progress to more complex implementations, these fundamentals will be invaluable in developing robust, efficient, and safe financial applications.

Creating a Rust Project for Option Pricing

In the previous section, we delved into the fundamental syntax and structures of Rust, equipping you with the foundational knowledge necessary for more complex financial applications. Now, we're going to take a practical step forward by creating a Rust project tailored for option pricing. This will be our first foray into building a concrete application, combining theoretical knowledge with Rust's powerful programming capabilities.

Setting Up Your Rust Environment

Before diving into project creation, ensure you have the Rust compiler and Cargo, Rust's package manager, installed on your machine. If you haven't done this yet, follow these steps:

1.Install Rust: Visit [rust-lang.org](https://www.rust-lang.org/) and follow the instructions to install Rust.

2.Verify Installation: Open your terminal and type:

```sh
rustc --version
```

This should display the installed version of Rust.

3.Cargo: Cargo is included with Rust, and it helps manage Rust projects, dependencies, and builds. Verify it by running:

```sh
cargo --version
```

Creating a New Rust Project

With Rust and Cargo set up, let's create a new Rust project. In the terminal, navigate to your desired directory and run:

```sh
cargo new option_pricing
cd option_pricing
```

This will create a new directory named `option_pricing` with the following structure:

```
option_pricing/
├── Cargo.toml
```

└── src

└── main.rs

` ` `

The `Cargo.toml` file is where we define our project's metadata and dependencies, and `src/main.rs` is the main entry point for our application.

Configuring `Cargo.toml`

Open `Cargo.toml` with your preferred text editor. It should look something like this:

```toml
[package]
name = "option_pricing"
version = "0.1.0"
authors = ["Your Name <your.email@example.com>"]
edition = "2018"

[dependencies]
```

To streamline our development process, we'll add dependencies for numerical computations and statistical operations. For this example, let's include the `ndarray` crate for numerical arrays and the `statrs` crate for statistical functions:

```toml
[dependencies]
ndarray = "0.15.3"
```

statrs = "0.15.0"

```
` ` `
```

Save the changes to `Cargo.toml`. These crates will provide the necessary tools for handling complex mathematical operations crucial in option pricing.

Writing the Main Program

Open `src/main.rs` to begin coding our option pricing model. We'll start by importing the required libraries:

```rust
` ` `rust
extern crate ndarray;

extern crate statrs;


use ndarray::Array1;

use statrs::distribution::{Normal, Continuous};
` ` `
```

Next, define a function to calculate the Black-Scholes option price. We'll create a function for the European call option as an example:

```rust
` ` `rust
fn black_scholes_call(

stock_price: f64,

strike_price: f64,

time_to_maturity: f64,

risk_free_rate: f64,

volatility: f64

) -> f64 {
```

```rust
let d1 = (stock_price / strike_price).ln() + (risk_free_rate + 0.5 *
volatility.powi(2)) * time_to_maturity;

let d1 = d1 / (volatility * time_to_maturity.sqrt());

let d2 = d1 - volatility * time_to_maturity.sqrt();


let norm_dist = Normal::new(0.0, 1.0).unwrap();

let call_price = stock_price * norm_dist.cdf(d1) - strike_price * (-
risk_free_rate * time_to_maturity).exp() * norm_dist.cdf(d2);

call_price

}
```

This function takes the stock price, strike price, time to maturity, risk-free rate, and volatility as inputs, and returns the calculated call option price using the Black-Scholes formula.

Incorporating User Inputs

To make our program more interactive, we'll add functionality to read user inputs from the command line. Modify `main.rs` to include this:

```rust
use std::io;

fn main() {
println!("Enter the stock price:");

let mut stock_price = String::new();

io::stdin().read_line(&mut stock_price).expect("Failed to read line");
```

```rust
let stock_price: f64 = stock_price.trim().parse().expect("Please
type a number!");

println!("Enter the strike price:");

let mut strike_price = String::new();

io::stdin().read_line(&mut strike_price).expect("Failed to read
line");

let strike_price: f64 = strike_price.trim().parse().expect("Please
type a number!");

println!("Enter the time to maturity (in years):");

let mut time_to_maturity = String::new();

io::stdin().read_line(&mut    time_to_maturity).expect("Failed
to read line");

let            time_to_maturity:           f64          =
time_to_maturity.trim().parse().expect("Please      type     a
number!");

println!("Enter the risk-free rate (as a decimal):");

let mut risk_free_rate = String::new();

io::stdin().read_line(&mut    risk_free_rate).expect("Failed    to
read line");

let            risk_free_rate:            f64              =
risk_free_rate.trim().parse().expect("Please type a number!");

println!("Enter the volatility (as a decimal):");

let mut volatility = String::new();

io::stdin().read_line(&mut    volatility).expect("Failed    to read
line");
```

```rust
let volatility: f64 = volatility.trim().parse().expect("Please type a number!");

let call_price = black_scholes_call(stock_price, strike_price, time_to_maturity, risk_free_rate, volatility);
println!("The calculated call option price is: ${:.2}", call_price);

}
```

This code snippet captures user inputs for the required parameters and calls the `black_scholes_call` function to compute the option price, subsequently displaying the result.

Testing the Implementation

Before running the program, it's prudent to add some basic tests to ensure our function works correctly. Create a new file named `tests.rs` in the `src` directory and add the following content:

```rust
#[cfg(test)]
mod tests {
use super::*;

#[test]
fn test_black_scholes_call() {
let stock_price = 100.0;
let strike_price = 100.0;
let time_to_maturity = 1.0;
```

```
let risk_free_rate = 0.05;
```

```
let volatility = 0.2;
```

```
let expected_price = 10.45; // Example expected price, you may
need to adjust based on precise calculations
```

```
let calculated_price = black_scholes_call(stock_price,
strike_price, time_to_maturity, risk_free_rate, volatility);
```

```
assert!((calculated_price - expected_price).abs() < 0.01); //
Allowing small margin for floating-point errors
```

```
}
```

```
}
```

` ` `

Run the test using Cargo:

` ` `sh

```
cargo test
```

` ` `

This command will compile and execute your tests, verifying the correctness of the Black-Scholes call option pricing function.

Running the Program

With everything set up, you can now run your Rust program:

` ` `sh

```
cargo run
```

` ` `

Follow the prompts to input the necessary parameters, and the program will output the calculated call option price.

Implementing the Black-Scholes Formula in Rust

The Black-Scholes model provides a theoretical estimate for the price of European-style options. The formula for the price of a call option C is given by:

$$C = S_0 N(d_1) - X e^{-rt} N(d_2)$$

Where:

- S_0 is the current stock price
- X is the strike price
- t is the time to maturity (in years)
- r is the risk-free interest rate
- σ is the volatility of the stock
- $N(\cdot)$ is the cumulative distribution function (CDF) of the standard normal distribution
- d_1 and d_2 are calculated as:

$$d_1 = \frac{\ln\left(\frac{S_0}{X}\right) + \left(r + \frac{\sigma^2}{2}\right)t}{\sigma \sqrt{t}}$$

$$d_2 = d_1 - \sigma \sqrt{t}$$

Implementing the Formula in Rust

Let's break down the implementation into manageable steps. We will use the `ndarray` and `statrs` crates, which provide the necessary tools for numerical and statistical operations.

Step 1: Setting Up the Project

If you haven't already, ensure your `Cargo.toml` includes the following dependencies:

```toml
[dependencies]
ndarray = "0.15.3"
statrs = "0.15.0"
```

Ensure your project structure is as follows:

```
option_pricing/
├── Cargo.toml
└── src
└── main.rs
```

Step 2: Importing Necessary Libraries

Open `src/main.rs` and import the necessary libraries:

```rust
extern crate ndarray;
extern crate statrs;

use ndarray::Array1;
use statrs::distribution::{Normal, Continuous};
```

```
` ` `
```

Step 3: Defining the Black-Scholes Function

We will define a function `black_scholes_call` that calculates the price of a European call option using the Black-Scholes formula:

```rust
fn black_scholes_call(
stock_price: f64,
strike_price: f64,
time_to_maturity: f64,
risk_free_rate: f64,
volatility: f64
) -> f64 {
let d1 = (stock_price / strike_price).ln() + (risk_free_rate + 0.5 * volatility.powi(2)) * time_to_maturity;
let d1 = d1 / (volatility * time_to_maturity.sqrt());
let d2 = d1 - volatility * time_to_maturity.sqrt();

let norm_dist = Normal::new(0.0, 1.0).unwrap();
let call_price = stock_price * norm_dist.cdf(d1) - strike_price * (-risk_free_rate * time_to_maturity).exp() * norm_dist.cdf(d2);
call_price
}
` ` `
```

Step 4: Adding User Interaction

To make our implementation user-friendly, let's add functionality to read inputs from the command line. Modify `main.rs` to include:

```rust
use std::io;

fn main() {
println!("Enter the stock price:");
let mut stock_price = String::new();
io::stdin().read_line(&mut stock_price).expect("Failed to read line");
let stock_price: f64 = stock_price.trim().parse().expect("Please type a number!");

println!("Enter the strike price:");
let mut strike_price = String::new();
io::stdin().read_line(&mut strike_price).expect("Failed to read line");
let strike_price: f64 = strike_price.trim().parse().expect("Please type a number!");

println!("Enter the time to maturity (in years):");
let mut time_to_maturity = String::new();
io::stdin().read_line(&mut time_to_maturity).expect("Failed to read line");
let time_to_maturity: f64 = time_to_maturity.trim().parse().expect("Please type a number!");
```

```rust
println!("Enter the risk-free rate (as a decimal):");

let mut risk_free_rate = String::new();

io::stdin().read_line(&mut   risk_free_rate).expect("Failed   to
read line");

let              risk_free_rate:              f64              =
risk_free_rate.trim().parse().expect("Please type a number!");


println!("Enter the volatility (as a decimal):");

let mut volatility = String::new();

io::stdin().read_line(&mut  volatility).expect("Failed  to  read
line");

let volatility: f64 = volatility.trim().parse().expect("Please type
a number!");


let  call_price  =  black_scholes_call(stock_price,  strike_price,
time_to_maturity, risk_free_rate, volatility);

println!("The calculated call option price is: ${:.2}", call_price);

}
```
` ` `

Step 5: Incorporating Error Handling

Rust's powerful error handling capabilities ensure stable and
reliable applications. We'll add error handling to our input
parsing:
` ` `rust

```rust
fn read_input(prompt: &str) -> f64 {

println!("{}", prompt);
```

```rust
let mut input = String::new();
io::stdin().read_line(&mut input).expect("Failed to read line");
input.trim().parse().expect("Please type a valid number!")
}

fn main() {
let stock_price = read_input("Enter the stock price:");
let strike_price = read_input("Enter the strike price:");
let time_to_maturity = read_input("Enter the time to maturity (in years):");
let risk_free_rate = read_input("Enter the risk-free rate (as a decimal):");
let volatility = read_input("Enter the volatility (as a decimal):");

let call_price = black_scholes_call(stock_price, strike_price, time_to_maturity, risk_free_rate, volatility);
println!("The calculated call option price is: ${:.2}", call_price);
}
```

Step 6: Testing the Implementation

Testing is crucial to verify correctness. Add a `tests.rs` file with the following content:

```rust
#[cfg(test)]
mod tests {
use super::*;
```

```rust
#[test]
fn test_black_scholes_call() {
let stock_price = 100.0;
let strike_price = 100.0;
let time_to_maturity = 1.0;
let risk_free_rate = 0.05;
let volatility = 0.2;
let expected_price = 10.45; // Adjust based on precise calculations
let calculated_price = black_scholes_call(stock_price, strike_price, time_to_maturity, risk_free_rate, volatility);

assert!((calculated_price - expected_price).abs() < 0.01); // Allowing small margin for floating-point errors
}
}
```

Run the tests using:
```sh
cargo test
```

Step 7: Running the Program

Finally, execute your program:
```sh
```

cargo run

```
` ` `
```

Follow the prompts to input the necessary parameters, and the program will output the calculated call option price.

Implementing the Black-Scholes formula in Rust bridges the gap between theoretical financial models and practical applications. By following the steps outlined above, you have created a robust, interactive Rust application capable of calculating European call option prices. This implementation not only solidifies your understanding of the Black-Scholes model but also enhances your skills in Rust programming, setting the stage for more sophisticated financial applications in subsequent sections.

Handling Inputs: Reading and Validating Data

In the context of our Black-Scholes implementation, inputs typically include the current stock price, the strike price, time to maturity, the risk-free interest rate, and volatility. Each of these inputs must be correctly read, parsed, and validated to ensure the integrity of the calculations. Incorrect or malformed data can lead to erroneous results, compromising the model's accuracy.

Step-by-Step Guide to Input Handling

Let's break down the process into well-defined steps:

Step 1: Setting Up the Project

Ensure that your project directory is properly set up with the following structure:

```
option_pricing/
├── Cargo.toml
└── src
└── main.rs
```

Your `Cargo.toml` should include necessary dependencies:

```toml
[dependencies]
ndarray = "0.15.3"
statrs = "0.15.0"
```

Step 2: Reading User Input

Reading user input in Rust is straightforward using the `std::io` library. Open `src/main.rs` and add the following code to read inputs from the command line:

```rust
use std::io;

fn read_input(prompt: &str) -> String {
println!("{}", prompt);
let mut input = String::new();
```

```rust
io::stdin().read_line(&mut input).expect("Failed to read line");
input.trim().to_string()
}
```

Step 3: Parsing and Validating Inputs

Parsing and validating inputs is essential to ensure that the data conforms to expected formats and ranges. A well-constructed function will not only parse the input but also handle potential errors gracefully:

```rust
fn parse_input(input: &str) -> Result<f64, &'static str> {
match input.trim().parse::<f64>() {
Ok(value) => {
if value.is_sign_positive() {
Ok(value)
} else {
Err("Value must be positive")
}
},
Err(_) => Err("Invalid input; please enter a valid number"),
}
}
```

Step 4: Integrating Input Handling in Main Function

Now, we integrate our reading and validating functions into the main Rust function:

```rust
fn main() {
let stock_price = loop {
let input = read_input("Enter the stock price:");
match parse_input(&input) {
Ok(value) => break value,
Err(e) => println!("{}", e),
}
};

let strike_price = loop {
let input = read_input("Enter the strike price:");
match parse_input(&input) {
Ok(value) => break value,
Err(e) => println!("{}", e),
}
};

let time_to_maturity = loop {
let input = read_input("Enter the time to maturity (in years):");
match parse_input(&input) {
Ok(value) => break value,
Err(e) => println!("{}", e),
}
```

```rust
};

let risk_free_rate = loop {
let input = read_input("Enter the risk-free rate (as a decimal):");
match parse_input(&input) {
Ok(value) => break value,
Err(e) => println!("{}", e),
}
};

let volatility = loop {
let input = read_input("Enter the volatility (as a decimal):");
match parse_input(&input) {
Ok(value) => break value,
Err(e) => println!("{}", e),
}
};

let call_price = black_scholes_call(stock_price, strike_price, time_to_maturity, risk_free_rate, volatility);
println!("The calculated call option price is: ${:.2}", call_price);
}

fn black_scholes_call(
stock_price: f64,
strike_price: f64,
time_to_maturity: f64,
```

```
risk_free_rate: f64,

volatility: f64

) -> f64 {

let d1 = (stock_price / strike_price).ln() + (risk_free_rate + 0.5 *
volatility.powi(2)) * time_to_maturity;

let d1 = d1 / (volatility * time_to_maturity.sqrt());

let d2 = d1 - volatility * time_to_maturity.sqrt();


let norm_dist = statrs::distribution::Normal::new(0.0,
1.0).unwrap();

let call_price = stock_price * norm_dist.cdf(d1) - strike_price * (-
risk_free_rate * time_to_maturity).exp() * norm_dist.cdf(d2);

call_price

}
```
` ` `

Step 5: Defining Edge Cases and Error Messages

Effective validation should account for edge cases and provide clear, helpful error messages. For instance, all numerical inputs should be positive, and rates should be within a realistic range:

` ` `rust

```
fn parse_input(input: &str) -> Result<f64, &'static str> {

match input.trim().parse::<f64>() {

Ok(value) => {

if value.is_sign_positive() {

Ok(value)
```

```rust
} else {
Err("Value must be positive")
}
},
Err(_) => Err("Invalid input; please enter a valid number"),
}
}

fn read_input(prompt: &str) -> String {
println!("{}", prompt);
let mut input = String::new();
io::stdin().read_line(&mut input).expect("Failed to read line");
input.trim().to_string()
}

fn main() {
let stock_price = loop {
let input = read_input("Enter the stock price:");
match parse_input(&input) {
Ok(value) => break value,
Err(e) => println!("{}", e),
}
};

let strike_price = loop {
let input = read_input("Enter the strike price:");
```

```
match parse_input(&input) {
Ok(value) => break value,
Err(e) => println!("{}", e),
}
};

let time_to_maturity = loop {
let input = read_input("Enter the time to maturity (in years):");
match parse_input(&input) {
Ok(value) => break value,
Err(e) => println!("{}", e),
}
};

let risk_free_rate = loop {
let input = read_input("Enter the risk-free rate (as a decimal):");
match parse_input(&input) {
Ok(value) => break value,
Err(e) => println!("{}", e),
}
};

let volatility = loop {
let input = read_input("Enter the volatility (as a decimal):");
match parse_input(&input) {
Ok(value) => break value,
```

```rust
        Err(e) => println!("{}", e),
    }
};

let call_price = black_scholes_call(stock_price, strike_price,
time_to_maturity, risk_free_rate, volatility);
println!("The calculated call option price is: ${:.2}", call_price);
}
```

Step 6: Enhancing User Experience

To enhance the user experience, consider providing default values or ranges for input. This not only aids users unfamiliar with typical values but also ensures smoother operation:

```rust
fn read_input_with_default(prompt: &str, default: f64) -> f64 {
println!("{} (default: {}):", prompt, default);
let mut input = String::new();
io::stdin().read_line(&mut input).expect("Failed to read line");
if input.trim().is_empty() {
return default;
}
input.trim().parse().expect("Please type a valid number!")
}

fn main() {
```

```
let stock_price = read_input_with_default("Enter the stock
price", 100.0);

let strike_price = read_input_with_default("Enter the strike
price", 100.0);

let time_to_maturity = read_input_with_default("Enter the
time to maturity (in years)", 1.0);

let risk_free_rate = read_input_with_default("Enter the risk-
free rate (as a decimal)", 0.05);

let volatility = read_input_with_default("Enter the volatility
(as a decimal)", 0.2);


let call_price = black_scholes_call(stock_price, strike_price,
time_to_maturity, risk_free_rate, volatility);

println!("The calculated call option price is: ${:.2}", call_price);

}
```
```

Handling inputs in Rust involves more than just reading data from the user or other sources. It requires a meticulous approach to parsing and validating that data to ensure the accuracy and robustness of your financial models. By implementing the steps outlined above, you have fortified your Black-Scholes application against erroneous inputs, thus enhancing its reliability and user experience.

Mastering these input handling techniques, you are well-prepared to tackle more complex financial computations and integrations in the subsequent sections of this book. The next steps will build on this strong foundation, guiding you through advanced Rust programming strategies tailored for high-performance financial applications.
```

Calculating d1 and d2 Terms

Before diving into the Rust implementation, let's revisit the mathematical definitions of $d1$ and $d2$:

$$
d1 = \frac{\ln(\frac{S}{K}) + \left(r + \frac{\sigma^2}{2} \right) T}{\sigma \sqrt{T}}
$$

$$
d2 = d1 - \sigma \sqrt{T}
$$

Where:

- S is the current price of the underlying asset

- K is the strike price of the option

- r is the risk-free interest rate

- σ is the volatility of the underlying asset

- T is the time to maturity (in years)

- $\ln$ represents the natural logarithm

The $d1$ term incorporates all the relevant market parameters, including the logarithmic ratio of the asset price to the strike price, adjusted for the risk-free rate and volatility over the time to maturity. The $d2$ term is derived from $d1$ by subtracting the volatility term scaled by the square root of the time to maturity.

Implementing d1 and d2 in Rust

To bring these equations to life, we need a robust and precise implementation in Rust. We'll start by setting up a function to calculate $d1$ and $d2$. First, let's define a struct to hold the necessary parameters:

```rust
// Define a struct to encapsulate option parameters
struct OptionParameters {
spot_price: f64,
strike_price: f64,
risk_free_rate: f64,
volatility: f64,
time_to_maturity: f64,
}

// Implement the calculation of d1 and d2 within the OptionParameters struct
impl OptionParameters {
fn calculate_d1(&self) -> f64 {
let numerator = (self.spot_price / self.strike_price).ln()
+ (self.risk_free_rate + 0.5 * self.volatility.powi(2)) * self.time_to_maturity;
let denominator = self.volatility * self.time_to_maturity.sqrt();
numerator / denominator
}
```

```
fn calculate_d2(&self) -> f64 {
self.calculate_d1()          -              self.volatility          *
self.time_to_maturity.sqrt()
}
}
` ` `
```

In the above code, we define an `OptionParameters` struct to encapsulate the necessary parameters for our calculations. The `calculate_d1` and `calculate_d2` functions are implemented as methods of this struct.

Detailed Explanation

1.Struct Definition:

- We define the `OptionParameters` struct to encapsulate the parameters $\(S \)$, $\(K \)$, $\(r \)$, $\(\sigma \)$, and $\(T \)$. Each field is assigned the `f64` type to ensure precision in floating-point arithmetic.

2.d1 Calculation:

- We compute the numerator of the $\(d1 \)$ formula by first taking the natural logarithm of the spot price divided by the strike price. This is achieved using Rust's `ln` method on `f64`.

- Next, we add the product of the risk-free rate and time to maturity plus half the square of the volatility multiplied by the time to maturity.

- The denominator is simply the product of the volatility and the square root of the time to maturity.

- Finally, the value of \(d1 \) is obtained by dividing the numerator by the denominator.

3.d2 Calculation:

- The calculation of \(d2 \) leverages the result of the `calculate_d1` method. We subtract the product of the volatility and the square root of the time to maturity from \(d1 \).

Example Usage

To ensure our implementation is both accurate and efficient, let's walk through an example of using this struct and its methods:

```rust
fn main() {
// Define the parameters for our option
let option_params = OptionParameters {
spot_price: 100.0,    // Current price of the underlying asset
strike_price: 95.0,    // Strike price of the option
risk_free_rate: 0.05,  // Risk-free interest rate (5%)
volatility: 0.2,     // Volatility (20%)
time_to_maturity: 1.0, // Time to maturity (1 year)
};

// Calculate d1 and d2
```

```
let d1 = option_params.calculate_d1();
let d2 = option_params.calculate_d2();

// Print the results
println!("d1: {:.4}", d1);
println!("d2: {:.4}", d2);
}
```

Explanation of Example Usage

1.Main Function:

- We define the parameters for an example option with specific values for the spot price, strike price, risk-free rate, volatility, and time to maturity.

- We then create an instance of `OptionParameters` using these values.

2.Calculating d1 and d2:

- We call the `calculate_d1` and `calculate_d2` methods on our `option_params` instance to compute the values of $d1$ and $d2$.

3.Printing Results:

- Finally, we use the `println!` macro to format and print the results to the console with four decimal places for clarity.

The calculation of $d1$ and $d2$ is a critical step in the Black-Scholes model, underpinning the accurate pricing of options. By implementing these calculations in Rust, we leverage the language's strengths in precision, performance, and safety. The code provided is not only a practical tool for your trading algorithms but also a foundation for deeper exploration into more complex financial models. As you integrate these calculations into your broader trading strategies, you'll find that Rust's capabilities enhance both the reliability and efficiency of your implementations, ultimately contributing to more robust and profitable trading decisions.

Integrating Standard Library Functions

Rust's standard library is a trove of powerful functions and utilities designed to handle a wide range of programming tasks. For financial computations, certain modules stand out, particularly those related to numerical operations, input/ output handling, and error management. The `std::f64` module, for example, offers extensive functionality for floating-point arithmetic, which is crucial for our purposes.

Using Mathematical Functions

To implement the Black-Scholes formula, we frequently perform operations like exponentiation, natural logarithms, and cumulative distribution functions. Rust's standard library provides built-in methods for these operations, ensuring high performance and accuracy.

Natural Logarithm and Exponents

The calculation of $d1$ and $d2$ involves the natural logarithm (`ln`) and exponentiation. Here's how to use these functions in Rust:

```rust
use std::f64::consts::E;

// Example of using natural logarithm and exponentiation
fn main() {
let value = 2.71828; // Approximation of Euler's number
let log_value = value.ln();
let exp_value = E.powf(log_value);
println!("Natural Logarithm: {}", log_value);
println!("Exponentiation: {}", exp_value);
}
```

In this example, we use the `ln` method provided by the `f64` type to compute the natural logarithm and the `powf` method for exponentiation. The constant `E` from `std::f64::consts` represents Euler's number, which is foundational in these calculations.

Implementing Cumulative Distribution Function

The Black-Scholes model relies on the cumulative distribution function (CDF) of the standard normal distribution. Unfortunately, Rust's standard library does not provide a direct function for this. However, we can use the `statrs` crate, a third-party library, which offers a comprehensive suite of statistical functions.

First, add the `statrs` crate to your `Cargo.toml`:

```toml
[dependencies]
statrs = "0.15.0"
```

Then, implement the CDF for the standard normal distribution:

```rust
extern crate statrs;

use statrs::distribution::{Normal, Univariate};

fn main() {
let normal = Normal::new(0.0, 1.0).unwrap();  // Standard normal distribution
let x = 1.96;
let cdf = normal.cdf(x);
println!("CDF at {}: {}", x, cdf);
}
```

Here, we create an instance of the `Normal` distribution with a mean of 0 and a standard deviation of 1. The `cdf` method calculates the cumulative distribution function at the given value, providing the probability that a standard normal variable is less than or equal to that value.

Integrating I/O Functions

Efficiently reading and writing data is vital for real-time trading algorithms. Rust's standard library offers several modules to handle input/output operations, such as `std::fs` for file handling and `std::io` for more general I/O tasks.

Reading Data from Files

Let's assume we need to read historical price data from a CSV file. Rust's `std::fs` and `csv` crates are perfect tools for this task.

First, add the `csv` crate to your `Cargo.toml`:

```toml
[dependencies]
csv = "1.1.6"
```

Then, implement the function to read data:

```rust
extern crate csv;

use std::error::Error;
use std::fs::File;
```

```
fn read_csv(file_path: &str) -> Result<(), Box<dyn Error>> {
let file = File::open(file_path)?;
let mut rdr = csv::Reader::from_reader(file);

for result in rdr.records() {
let record = result?;
println!("{:?}", record);
}
Ok(())
}

fn main() {
if let Err(err) = read_csv("data/historical_prices.csv") {
println!("Error reading CSV: {}", err);
}
}
```

In this snippet, we define the `read_csv` function, which opens the specified file and reads its contents into a CSV reader. The `records` method iterates over each row, and we print each record to the console.

Error Handling

Robust error handling is crucial for maintaining the stability and reliability of your trading algorithms. Rust's standard library provides powerful constructs for error management, notably the `Result` and `Option` types.

Using the Result Type

In the previous example, we returned a `Result` from the `read_csv` function to handle potential errors in file operations. Here's a brief explanation of how to use the `Result` type for error handling:

```rust
fn calculate_d1(spot_price: f64, strike_price: f64, risk_free_rate: f64, volatility: f64, time_to_maturity: f64) -> Result<f64, &'static str> {

if spot_price <= 0.0 || strike_price <= 0.0 || volatility < 0.0 || time_to_maturity <= 0.0 {

return Err("Invalid input values");

}


let numerator = (spot_price / strike_price).ln()

+ (risk_free_rate + 0.5 * volatility.powi(2)) * time_to_maturity;

let denominator = volatility * time_to_maturity.sqrt();

Ok(numerator / denominator)

}


fn main() {

match calculate_d1(100.0, 95.0, 0.05, 0.2, 1.0) {

Ok(d1) => println!("d1: {:.4}", d1),

Err(e) => println!("Error: {}", e),
```

```
}

}

` ` `
```

In this code, `calculate_d1` returns a `Result<f64, &'static str>`, indicating either a successful calculation (`Ok`) or an error message (`Err`). The `match` statement in the `main` function handles both cases, ensuring any errors are gracefully managed.

Integrating Rust's standard library functions into your Black-Scholes implementation is essential for building efficient and accurate trading models. By leveraging mathematical functions, input/output handling, and robust error management, you ensure that your algorithms are not only precise but also resilient and performant. As you incorporate these tools into your broader trading strategies, you'll find that Rust's standard library provides a solid foundation for tackling even the most complex financial computations. The integration of these functions underscores the versatility and power of Rust, empowering you to craft sophisticated, high-performance trading solutions.

Memory Safety and Performance Considerations

Memory safety is a cornerstone of Rust's design, achieved through its ownership system, borrowing, and lifetimes. These features eliminate the common pitfalls of other languages, such as null pointer dereferencing, buffer overflows, and data races.

Ownership System

Rust's ownership system enforces strict rules about how memory is accessed, ensuring that each piece of data has a single owner at any given time. This eliminates the need for garbage collection and prevents dangling pointers.

Here's a simple example to illustrate ownership:

```rust
fn main() {
let data = String::from("Hello, Rust!"); // `data` owns the memory
let length = calculate_length(&data); // Borrow `data` immutably
println!("The length of '{}' is {}.", data, length);
}

fn calculate_length(s: &String) -> usize {
s.len()
}
```

In this example, the `data` variable owns the memory for the string. When `calculate_length` borrows `data` immutably, Rust enforces that no other mutable borrow can occur simultaneously, thereby preventing potential data races and ensuring safe access.

Borrowing and Lifetimes

Rust's borrowing system allows you to reference data without taking ownership. Lifetimes further ensure that references do not outlive the data they point to, preventing dangling references. Here's an example demonstrating lifetimes:

```rust
fn main() {
let string1 = String::from("abcd");
let string2 = "xyz";

let result = longest(string1.as_str(), string2);
println!("The longest string is {}", result);
}

fn longest<'a>(x: &'a str, y: &'a str) -> &'a str {
if x.len() > y.len() {
x
} else {
y
}
}
```

In this case, the `longest` function takes two string slices with the same lifetime `'a`, ensuring that the returned reference is valid as long as both input references are.

Performance Optimization

Apart from ensuring safety, Rust excels in performance. It offers low-level control akin to C or C++, allowing you to write highly optimized code while ensuring safety through compile-time checks.

Zero-Cost Abstractions

Rust's abstractions have zero runtime overhead, meaning that high-level constructs are compiled down to efficient machine code. This is critical for algorithmic trading, where performance can significantly impact profitability.

Consider a scenario where you must compute multiple options prices concurrently. Rust's iterator and parallelism features can be leveraged for this purpose:

```rust
use rayon::prelude::*;

fn main() {
let prices: Vec<f64> = vec![100.0, 105.0, 110.0, 115.0];
let strike_price = 100.0;
let risk_free_rate = 0.05;
let volatility = 0.2;
let time_to_maturity = 1.0;

let option_prices: Vec<f64> = prices.par_iter()
```

```
.map(|&price| black_scholes(price, strike_price, risk_free_rate,
volatility, time_to_maturity))
.collect();

    println!("Option prices: {:?}", option_prices);
}

fn    black_scholes(spot_price:    f64,    strike_price:    f64,
risk_free_rate: f64, volatility: f64, time_to_maturity: f64) ->
f64 {
// Black-Scholes formula implementation
// Calculate d1 and d2 terms, call price, etc.
0.0 // Placeholder for actual option price
}
` ` `
```

In this example, the `par_iter` method from the `rayon` crate enables parallel iteration, significantly reducing computation time for large datasets by leveraging multiple cores.

Memory Allocation and Deallocation

Rust's strict control over memory allocation and deallocation avoids the overhead of garbage collection. When you need to allocate memory dynamically, Rust provides safe abstractions without compromising performance.

For instance, using `Vec` for dynamic arrays ensures that memory is managed efficiently:

```rust
fn main() {
let mut data = Vec::new();
for i in 0..1000 {
data.push(i);
}
println!("Data length: {}", data.len());
}
```

The `Vec` type automatically handles memory allocation and deallocation, ensuring efficient use of resources.

Profiling and Benchmarking

To achieve optimal performance, profiling and benchmarking your code are essential. Rust provides tools like `cargo bench` and the `criterion` crate to measure and analyze performance.

Using Criterion for Benchmarking

First, add `criterion` to your `Cargo.toml`:

```toml
[dependencies]
criterion = "0.3"
```

```
```
```

Then, create a benchmark for your Black-Scholes implementation:

```rust
extern crate criterion;
extern crate black_scholes; // Assuming your Black-Scholes code is in this crate

use criterion::{criterion_group, criterion_main, Criterion};
use black_scholes::black_scholes;

fn benchmark_black_scholes(c: &mut Criterion) {
c.bench_function("black_scholes", |b| {
b.iter(|| black_scholes(100.0, 95.0, 0.05, 0.2, 1.0))
});
}

criterion_group!(benches, benchmark_black_scholes);
criterion_main!(benches);
```

Running `cargo bench` will execute the benchmark, providing detailed performance metrics that can guide further optimizations.

Rust's emphasis on memory safety and performance makes it a powerful tool for algorithmic trading and financial
```

computations. By leveraging its ownership system, borrowing rules, and zero-cost abstractions, you can write code that is both safe and performant. The ability to profile and benchmark ensures that your algorithms remain optimized, giving you a competitive edge in the fast-paced world of trading. Embracing these principles will not only enhance the robustness of your implementations but also pave the way for more sophisticated and efficient trading strategies.

Error Handling in Rust

Rust employs a combination of compile-time and runtime checks to ensure that errors are handled gracefully. It primarily uses two types of errors: panics and results.

-Panic: This is Rust's way of dealing with unrecoverable errors. When a panic occurs, the program terminates, providing a detailed stack trace for debugging. It's useful for situations where continuing execution would be unsafe or meaningless.

-Result: This is the preferred method for handling recoverable errors. The `Result` type is an enum with `Ok` and `Err` variants, allowing functions to return either a success value or an error.

The `Result` Type

The `Result` type is central to Rust's error handling. It enables functions to signal errors without using exceptions, facilitating explicit error management.

```rust
enum Result<T, E> {
```

```rust
Ok(T),

Err(E),

}
```

In financial computations, where precision is critical, the `Result` type ensures that errors are propagated and handled appropriately. Consider a function that calculates the price of an option. If the input parameters are invalid, the function should return an error.

```rust
fn calculate_option_price(spot_price: f64, strike_price: f64) -> Result<f64, String> {

if spot_price <= 0.0 || strike_price <= 0.0 {

return Err("Invalid input parameters".to_string());

}

// Implement the option pricing logic

Ok(0.0) // Placeholder for the actual option price

}
```

In this example, the `calculate_option_price` function returns a `Result<f64, String>`, indicating that it can either succeed with a `f64` value or fail with a `String` error message.

Handling Errors with `match`

One way to handle `Result` values is by using the `match` expression. This allows you to define specific actions for both success and error cases.

```rust
fn main() {
let spot_price = 100.0;
let strike_price = 0.0; // Invalid input

match calculate_option_price(spot_price, strike_price) {
Ok(price) => println!("Option price: {}", price),
Err(e) => println!("Error calculating option price: {}", e),
}
}
```

The `match` expression provides a clear, exhaustive way to handle all possible outcomes of a function that returns a `Result`.

The `?` Operator

For more concise error handling, Rust offers the `?` operator, which can be used to propagate errors upward. If a function returns an `Err`, the `?` operator will cause the current function to return the error immediately.

```rust
```

```rust
fn get_option_price(spot_price: f64, strike_price: f64) ->
Result<f64, String> {

let price = calculate_option_price(spot_price, strike_price)?;

Ok(price)

}


fn main() {

match get_option_price(100.0, 0.0) {

Ok(price) => println!("Option price: {}", price),

Err(e) => println!("Error: {}", e),

}

}
```

In this example, if `calculate_option_price` returns an error, the `?` operator ensures that `get_option_price` also returns the error, simplifying error propagation.

Custom Error Types

For complex financial systems, custom error types can provide more detailed and specific error information. Rust's enums are particularly well-suited for this purpose.

```rust
#[derive(Debug)]

enum OptionError {

InvalidInput(String),
```

```
CalculationError(String),
}


fn calculate_option_price(spot_price: f64, strike_price: f64) ->
Result<f64, OptionError> {
if spot_price <= 0.0 || strike_price <= 0.0 {
return        Err(OptionError::InvalidInput("Invalid        input
parameters".to_string()));
}
// Implement the option pricing logic
Ok(0.0) // Placeholder for the actual option price
}


fn main() {
match calculate_option_price(100.0, 0.0) {
Ok(price) => println!("Option price: {}", price),
Err(e) => println!("Error: {:?}", e),
}
}
` ` `
```

Here, the `OptionError` enum provides more granular error information, distinguishing between different types of errors.

Error Handling in Real-World Applications

In real-world financial applications, error handling becomes even more critical. Consider a Rust-based algorithmic trading system that interfaces with multiple external data sources and services. Each interaction point is a potential source of failure, from network issues to data inconsistencies. Robust error handling ensures that such failures are managed gracefully, maintaining system stability and reliability.

Example: Fetching Market Data

Let's illustrate error handling in the context of fetching market data from an external API. This involves network requests, which are inherently unreliable.

```rust
extern crate reqwest;

#[derive(Debug)]
enum MarketDataError {
NetworkError(reqwest::Error),
ParseError,
}

async fn fetch_market_data(api_url: &str) -> Result<String, MarketDataError> {
let response = reqwest::get(api_url).await.map_err(MarketDataError::NetworkError)?;
let data = response.text().await.map_err(|_| MarketDataError::ParseError)?;
Ok(data)
}
```

```
#[tokio::main]
async fn main() {
let api_url = "http://example.com/marketdata";
match fetch_market_data(api_url).await {
Ok(data) => println!("Market data: {}", data),
Err(e) => println!("Failed to fetch market data: {:?}", e),
}
}
```
` ` `

In this example, potential errors from the network request and response parsing are handled using the `Result` type. The custom `MarketDataError` enum provides detailed error information, aiding in debugging and recovery.

Best Practices for Error Handling in Financial Algorithms

1.Explicit Error Propagation: Use the `Result` type to make error handling explicit, ensuring that errors are not silently ignored.

2.Granular Error Types: Define custom error types to provide detailed and specific error information.

3.Early Error Detection: Validate inputs early to catch errors as soon as possible, reducing the risk of cascading failures.

4.Graceful Degradation: Design your system to handle errors gracefully, maintaining partial functionality where possible.

5.Logging and Monitoring: Implement comprehensive logging and monitoring to track errors and system health in real-time.

Robust error handling is essential for developing reliable and efficient algorithmic trading systems. Rust's approach to error management, through the `Result` type and custom error handling mechanisms, provides a solid foundation for building resilient financial algorithms. By adopting best practices and leveraging Rust's powerful error handling features, you can ensure that your trading systems are both fault-tolerant and performant, capable of thriving in the dynamic and unpredictable world of financial markets.

Running and Testing the Implementation

Before diving into running and testing, ensure your development environment is properly configured. This includes having Rust and necessary dependencies installed.

1.Install Rust: Ensure you have the latest version of Rust installed. You can install Rust using the following command:
```sh
curl --proto '=https' --tlsv1.2 -sSf https://sh.rustup.rs | sh
```

2.Create a New Project: Set up a new Rust project for your Black-Scholes implementation:
```sh
cargo new black_scholes
cd black_scholes
```

3.Add Dependencies: Modify your `Cargo.toml` file to include any necessary dependencies, such as for numerical calculations and testing:

```toml
[dependencies]
rand = "0.8.3"
```

Writing Unit Tests

Unit tests are essential for verifying the correctness of individual components in your implementation. In Rust, unit tests are typically included in the same file as the code they test, within a `mod tests` module.

Consider a function that calculates the price of a European call option. We'll write a test to ensure this function produces the expected results.

```rust
pub fn calculate_call_price(spot_price: f64, strike_price: f64, time_to_expiry: f64, risk_free_rate: f64, volatility: f64) -> f64 {
// Implement the Black-Scholes formula
0.0 // Placeholder return value
}

#[cfg(test)]
mod tests {
```

```
use super::*;

#[test]
fn test_calculate_call_price() {
let spot_price = 100.0;
let strike_price = 100.0;
let time_to_expiry = 1.0;
let risk_free_rate = 0.05;
let volatility = 0.2;

let price = calculate_call_price(spot_price, strike_price,
time_to_expiry, risk_free_rate, volatility);
assert!((price - 10.45).abs() < 0.01);
}
}
```

In this example, the `test_calculate_call_price` function checks if the call option price calculation is within a small tolerance of the expected value.

Running Tests

To run your tests, use the `cargo test` command. This will compile your project and execute all the tests defined in your code.

```sh
```

```
cargo test
```
` ` `

Ensure your tests cover a wide range of scenarios, including edge cases such as zero volatility or extremely high risk-free rates. This thorough testing will help identify potential issues before deploying your algorithm in a live trading environment.

Integration Testing

Integration tests verify that different parts of your system work together correctly. In Rust, integration tests are placed in the `tests` directory at the root of your project.

Here's an example of an integration test that verifies the overall functionality of the Black-Scholes model:

```rust
extern crate black_scholes;

use black_scholes::calculate_call_price;

#[test]
fn test_integration() {
let spot_price = 100.0;
let strike_price = 100.0;
let time_to_expiry = 1.0;
let risk_free_rate = 0.05;
```

```
let volatility = 0.2;

let price = calculate_call_price(spot_price, strike_price,
time_to_expiry, risk_free_rate, volatility);
assert!((price - 10.45).abs() < 0.01);
}
```

Run integration tests using the same `cargo test` command. Integration tests help ensure that individual components work together as expected, providing a higher level of confidence in your system's overall functionality.

Performance Testing

Performance is critical in algorithmic trading, where even slight delays can impact profitability. Rust's `criterion` crate provides a powerful framework for benchmarking and performance testing.

Add `criterion` to your `Cargo.toml`:

```toml
[dev-dependencies]
criterion = "0.3"
```

Create a new benchmark file in the `benches` directory:

```rust
extern crate criterion;
extern crate black_scholes;

use criterion::{criterion_group, criterion_main, Criterion};
use black_scholes::calculate_call_price;

fn benchmark_call_price(c: &mut Criterion) {
    c.bench_function("calculate_call_price", |b| {
        b.iter(|| {
            let spot_price = 100.0;
            let strike_price = 100.0;
            let time_to_expiry = 1.0;
            let risk_free_rate = 0.05;
            let volatility = 0.2;
            calculate_call_price(spot_price, strike_price, time_to_expiry,
            risk_free_rate, volatility);
        })
    });
}

criterion_group!(benches, benchmark_call_price);
criterion_main!(benches);
```

Run the benchmarks using:

```sh
cargo bench
```

Performance tests will help you identify bottlenecks and optimize your implementation for maximum efficiency.

Debugging and Logging

Effective debugging and logging are essential for identifying and resolving issues in your implementation. Rust's standard library provides robust support for both.

Use the `println!` macro for simple debugging:

```rust
fn calculate_call_price(spot_price: f64, strike_price: f64, time_to_expiry: f64, risk_free_rate: f64, volatility: f64) -> f64 {
println!("Calculating call price for spot price: {}", spot_price);
// Implement the Black-Scholes formula
0.0 // Placeholder return value
}
```

For more sophisticated logging, consider using the `log` and `env_logger` crates:

```toml
```

```
[dependencies]
log = "0.4"
env_logger = "0.9"
```

Initialize the logger in your main function:

```rust
extern crate env_logger;
#[macro_use]
extern crate log;

fn main() {
env_logger::init();
info!("Starting the application");
// Your code here
}
```

With logging in place, you can provide detailed runtime information, which is invaluable for debugging and monitoring your trading system.

Continuous Integration

Incorporating continuous integration (CI) into your development process ensures that your codebase remains stable and reliable. Tools like GitHub Actions or GitLab CI/CD can automate the testing and deployment of your Rust project.

Here's an example GitHub Actions workflow for a Rust project:

```yaml
name: Rust

on:
push:
branches: [ main ]
pull_request:
branches: [ main ]

jobs:
build:

runs-on: ubuntu-latest

steps:
- uses: actions/checkout@v2
- name: Set up Rust
uses: actions-rs/toolchain@v1
with:
toolchain: stable
- name: Build
run: cargo build --verbose
- name: Run tests
```

run: cargo test --verbose

` ` `

This workflow automatically builds and tests your project on every push or pull request, helping maintain code quality and catching issues early.

Running and testing your Rust implementation of the Black-Scholes model is a critical step in developing reliable and efficient algorithmic trading systems. By setting up a robust testing framework, performing thorough unit and integration tests, benchmarking performance, and implementing effective debugging and logging practices, you ensure that your code is both correct and performant.

In the dynamic and competitive world of financial markets, these practices provide the foundation for building resilient trading algorithms capable of thriving in real-world conditions. As you continue to refine and optimize your implementation, you'll be well-equipped to tackle the challenges and opportunities that lie ahead.

Optimizing Computational Efficiency

Before embarking on optimization, it's essential to identify the parts of your code that need improvement. Profiling tools help pinpoint performance bottlenecks, guiding your optimization efforts.

Install the `cargo-flamegraph` tool for profiling:

` ` `sh

cargo install flamegraph

```
` ` `
```

Run your application with `cargo flamegraph` to generate a visual representation of your code's performance, highlighting areas that require optimization.

Leveraging Rust's Ownership and Borrowing System

Rust's ownership and borrowing system ensures memory safety without a garbage collector but can also be leveraged for optimization. Efficient memory management reduces unnecessary allocations and deallocations, improving performance.

Consider using references (`&`) instead of owned values where possible to minimize copying:

```rust
fn calculate_call_price(spot_price: &f64, strike_price: &f64, time_to_expiry: &f64, risk_free_rate: &f64, volatility: &f64) -> f64 {
// Implement the Black-Scholes formula
0.0 // Placeholder return value
}
```

Using references reduces the overhead of passing around large data structures and ensures that data is only copied when necessary.

Inlining Functions

Inlining small, frequently called functions can reduce function call overhead and improve performance. The `#[inline(always)]` attribute suggests to the compiler to inline a function:

```rust
#[inline(always)]
pub fn calculate_d1(...) -> f64 {
// Calculation logic
}
```

Inlining should be used judiciously, as excessive inlining can increase binary size and potentially degrade performance.

Utilizing Multithreading and Concurrency

Rust's concurrency model, based on ownership and borrowing, makes it safe and efficient to use multithreading to parallelize computations. The `rayon` crate provides an easy-to-use interface for parallelism:

```toml
[dependencies]
rayon = "1.5"
```

Use Rayon to parallelize a computation-intensive task:

```rust
extern crate rayon;
```

```rust
use rayon::prelude::*;

fn calculate_multiple_prices(params: Vec<Params>) -> Vec<f64> {
params.par_iter()
.map(|p| calculate_call_price(&p.spot_price, &p.strike_price, &p.time_to_expiry, &p.risk_free_rate, &p.volatility))
.collect()
}
```

Parallelizing computations can significantly speed up your application, particularly for tasks that are embarrassingly parallel, like pricing multiple options.

Minimizing Floating-Point Operations

Floating-point operations are often more expensive than integer operations. Where possible, minimize their usage or consolidate multiple operations into fewer steps.

For instance, instead of:
```rust
let result = a * b * c * d;
```

Consider:
```rust
let intermediate = a * b;
```

```rust
let result = intermediate * c * d;
```

This change reduces the number of floating-point multiplications from three to two, slightly improving performance.

Efficient Use of Data Structures

Choosing the right data structures can have a significant impact on performance. For instance, using a `Vec` for dynamic arrays is common, but adding elements individually can be slow due to potential reallocations.

Preallocate memory if the size is known:

```rust
let mut prices: Vec<f64> = Vec::with_capacity(1000);
```

This avoids multiple memory allocations, improving performance when populating the vector.

Avoiding Unnecessary Computations

Ensure that computations are only performed when necessary. Memoization can be used to store the results of expensive functions and reuse them instead of recalculating.

For example, if `calculate_d1` is called multiple times with the same parameters, consider caching the result:

```rust
use std::collections::HashMap;

fn calculate_call_price_with_cache(params: &Params, cache: &mut HashMap<Params, f64>) -> f64 {
if let Some(&price) = cache.get(params) {
return price;
}
let price = calculate_call_price(&params.spot_price, &params.strike_price, &params.time_to_expiry, &params.risk_free_rate, &params.volatility);
cache.insert(params.clone(), price);
price
}
```

Optimizing Mathematical Computations

Utilize specialized libraries that are optimized for various mathematical computations. Libraries like `nalgebra` for linear algebra or `statrs` for statistical functions can significantly speed up your computations.

Add `nalgebra` to your `Cargo.toml`:
```toml
[dependencies]
nalgebra = "0.29"
```

Use `nalgebra` for matrix operations:

```rust
extern crate nalgebra as na;
use na::{DMatrix, DVector};

fn solve_linear_system(a: DMatrix<f64>, b: DVector<f64>) ->
DVector<f64> {
a.lu().solve(&.unwrap()
}
```

These libraries are highly optimized and can provide better performance than hand-rolled implementations.

Compiler Optimizations

Rust's compiler provides various optimization levels, which can be set in the `Cargo.toml` file:

```toml
[profile.release]
opt-level = "z" # Optimize for size
```

For computationally intensive applications, optimizing for speed (`opt-level = "3"`) can yield significant improvements:

```toml
[profile.release]
```

```
opt-level = "3"
` ` `
```

Building your project with `cargo build --release` enables these optimizations, ensuring that your application runs as efficiently as possible.

Optimizing computational efficiency in your Rust implementation of the Black-Scholes model involves a combination of profiling, leveraging Rust's unique features, and applying advanced techniques for memory management, concurrency, and mathematical computations. By following these best practices, you can significantly enhance the performance of your algorithmic trading systems, ensuring they are capable of operating in the demanding environment of real-time financial markets.

CHAPTER 4:
ALGORITHMIC
OPTIONS TRADING

Algorithmic trading leverages mathematical models and complex algorithms to make trading decisions. These algorithms can analyze vast amounts of data, identify trading opportunities, and execute trades within milliseconds. The primary objective is to achieve optimal trading outcomes by minimizing costs, maximizing profits, and managing risks.

A typical algorithmic trading system comprises several key components:

1.Market Data Feed: This component provides real-time data on stock prices, volumes, and other relevant market information.

2.Trading Algorithms: These are the mathematical models that analyze market data to identify potential trades.

3.Execution Systems: These systems execute the trades identified by the algorithms.

4.Order Management Systems: These systems manage the placement, routing, and execution of trade orders.

5.Risk Management Systems: These systems monitor and mitigate potential risks associated with trading activities.

Advantages of Algorithmic Trading

Algorithmic trading offers numerous benefits compared to traditional manual trading. Some of the key advantages include:

1.Speed and Efficiency: Algorithms can process and analyze data at lightning speeds, executing trades in milliseconds. This speed is crucial in markets where prices can change within seconds.

2.Precision and Accuracy: Algorithms follow predefined rules and strategies, ensuring precision and accuracy in trade execution. This reduces the likelihood of human errors and emotional biases affecting trading decisions.

3.Cost Reduction: Automated trading reduces transaction costs by optimizing trade execution and minimizing the impact of market spreads.

4.Consistency: Algorithms operate based on consistent and repeatable rules, providing a level of discipline that is difficult to achieve with human traders.

5.Market Monitoring: Algorithms can continuously monitor multiple markets and instruments simultaneously, identifying opportunities that might be missed by human traders.

Types of Algorithmic Trading Strategies

Algorithmic trading encompasses a wide range of strategies, each with its own set of objectives and methodologies. Some of the most common types include:

1.Market Making: Market making algorithms provide liquidity to the market by simultaneously placing buy and sell orders. They profit from the bid-ask spread and aim to execute a high volume of trades with minimal risk.

2.Trend Following: These algorithms identify and exploit trends in price movements. They buy assets that are trending upwards and sell those that are trending downwards, aiming to profit from sustained market trends.

3.Arbitrage: Arbitrage algorithms exploit price discrepancies between different markets or instruments. For instance, they might buy an asset in one market where it's undervalued and sell it in another market where it's overvalued.

4.Statistical Arbitrage: These algorithms use statistical models to identify and exploit temporary price deviations between correlated assets. They typically involve pairs trading, where two correlated assets are traded simultaneously.

5.Mean Reversion: Mean reversion algorithms assume that asset prices will revert to their historical mean over time. They buy assets that are below their historical average price and sell those that are above it.

6.Execution-Based Strategies: These algorithms focus on executing large trades in a manner that minimizes market impact and transaction costs. Examples include VWAP (Volume Weighted Average Price) and TWAP (Time Weighted Average Price) strategies.

Key Considerations in Algorithmic Trading

While algorithmic trading offers numerous advantages, it also presents several challenges and considerations that traders must address:

1.Data Quality and Accuracy: The accuracy of trading algorithms depends heavily on the quality of the market data they analyze. Inaccurate or delayed data can lead to incorrect trading decisions.

2.Latency: Latency, or the delay between data capture and trade execution, can significantly impact trading performance. Low-latency systems are essential for high-frequency trading strategies.

3.Regulatory Compliance: Algorithmic traders must adhere to regulatory requirements and ensure their trading practices are compliant with market regulations.

4.Risk Management: Effective risk management is crucial in algorithmic trading. Traders must implement robust risk management systems to monitor and mitigate potential risks, such as market volatility and system failures.

5.System Reliability: Algorithmic trading systems must be reliable and resilient to avoid failures that could result in significant financial losses. This includes implementing redundancy and backup systems.

6.Algorithm Testing and Validation: Thorough testing and validation of trading algorithms are essential to ensure their effectiveness and reliability. This involves backtesting algorithms using historical data and stress testing them under various market conditions.

Implementing Algorithmic Trading with Rust

Rust, with its emphasis on performance, safety, and concurrency, is an ideal language for developing algorithmic trading systems. Its memory safety guarantees and lack of a garbage collector make it suitable for high-frequency trading applications.

To implement an algorithmic trading system in Rust, consider the following steps:

1.Setting Up the Environment: Install Rust and set up your development environment. This includes installing necessary crates and configuring your project.

2.Fetching Market Data: Use Rust libraries and APIs to fetch real-time market data. Ensure the data is accurate and up-to-date.

3.Developing Trading Algorithms: Implement your trading

algorithms in Rust, leveraging the language's features for performance and safety.

4.Executing Trades: Integrate your system with trading platforms to execute trades based on the algorithms' decisions.

5.Risk Management: Implement robust risk management systems to monitor and mitigate potential risks.

6.Testing and Optimization: Thoroughly test your algorithmic trading system using historical data and optimize it for performance and reliability.

Algorithmic trading represents a significant advancement in financial markets, offering speed, efficiency, and precision that manual trading cannot match. By leveraging Rust's powerful features, you can develop robust and efficient algorithmic trading systems that capitalize on market opportunities and manage risks effectively. In the subsequent sections, we will explore specific trading algorithms and their implementation in Rust, providing you with the tools and knowledge to excel in the world of algorithmic trading.

Different Types of Trading Algorithms

1.Market Making Algorithms

Market making algorithms play a pivotal role in providing liquidity to financial markets. These algorithms simultaneously place buy and sell orders for a specific security, profiting from the bid-ask spread. The primary goal is to make a market in a security by ensuring that there is always a price at which it can be bought or sold.

*Principle: Market makers benefit from the difference between the bid price (the price at which they buy) and the ask price (the price at which they sell).

*Advantages: By continuously offering to buy and sell, these algorithms help to stabilize the market and reduce volatility.

*Considerations: Effective market making requires rapid execution and low latency to respond to market changes and maintain profitability.

2.Trend Following Algorithms

Trend following algorithms capitalize on the momentum of market trends. These algorithms identify assets that are trending—either upward or downward—and place trades accordingly. The underlying assumption is that trends tend to persist, enabling these algorithms to ride the trend for profit.

*Principle: Trend following strategies typically involve moving averages, breakout systems, and other technical indicators to detect trends.

*Advantages: These strategies can generate significant returns during prolonged market trends.

*Considerations: Trend following can be less effective in choppy or sideways markets, where trends are not clearly defined.

3.Arbitrage Algorithms

Arbitrage algorithms exploit price discrepancies between different markets or related financial instruments. The essence of arbitrage lies in buying a lower-priced asset in one market and simultaneously selling it at a higher price in another, thus locking in a risk-free profit.

*Principle: Examples include cross-exchange arbitrage, where the same asset is traded at different prices on different exchanges, and statistical arbitrage, which leverages statistical models to identify temporary price deviations.

*Advantages: Arbitrage opportunities offer low-risk profits and can help to correct market inefficiencies.

*Considerations: The window for arbitrage can be fleeting, requiring high-speed execution and low latency.

4.Statistical Arbitrage Algorithms

Statistical arbitrage goes beyond simple price discrepancies and involves complex quantitative models to identify and exploit relative mispricings between securities. This strategy often involves pairs trading, where two correlated assets are simultaneously traded based on their historical correlation.

*Principle: Pairs trading strategies identify mispriced pairs of assets, typically buying the undervalued and shorting the overvalued.

*Advantages: This strategy can be market-neutral, reducing exposure to broader market movements.

*Considerations: Accurate statistical models and high-frequency data analysis are essential for success.

5.Mean Reversion Algorithms

Mean reversion algorithms operate on the premise that asset prices tend to revert to their historical mean over time. These algorithms identify assets that have deviated significantly from their average price and place trades to profit from the anticipated reversion.

*Principle: Mean reversion strategies often use indicators such as Bollinger Bands and moving averages to identify overbought or oversold conditions.

*Advantages: These strategies can perform well in markets characterized by frequent price reversals.

*Considerations: Mean reversion can be challenging in trending markets, where prices may stray further from their historical mean.

6.Execution-Based Algorithms

Execution-based algorithms focus on optimizing the execution of large trades to minimize market impact and transaction costs. These strategies are used by institutional investors to execute large orders without significantly affecting the market price.

*Principle: Common execution algorithms include VWAP (Volume Weighted Average Price), which spreads an order over time based on historical volume patterns, and TWAP (Time Weighted Average Price), which executes trades evenly over a specified period.

*Advantages: These algorithms help to achieve better

execution prices and reduce slippage.

*Considerations: Execution algorithms require sophisticated market data and real-time adjustments to trade execution strategies.

7.High-Frequency Trading (HFT) Algorithms

High-frequency trading algorithms are characterized by their high speed and volume of trading. HFT algorithms use advanced technology to execute a large number of orders in fractions of a second, capitalizing on small price discrepancies.

*Principle: HFT strategies can include market making, arbitrage, and liquidity provision, all executed at ultra-high speeds.

*Advantages: HFT can be highly profitable due to the volume and speed of trades.

*Considerations: HFT requires significant investment in technology and infrastructure to maintain competitive latency and execution speed.

Implementing Trading Algorithms with Rust

Rust's performance and safety features make it a compelling choice for developing trading algorithms, especially those requiring high-speed execution and low latency. Here's a step-by-step guide to implementing trading algorithms in Rust:

1.Setting Up Rust Environment: Install Rust and set up your development environment. Utilize crates such as `tokio` for asynchronous programming and `serde` for data serialization.

2.Fetching Market Data: Use APIs and libraries to fetch real-time and historical market data. Libraries such as `reqwest` can facilitate HTTP requests, while `serde` can help in parsing JSON data.

3.Developing Algorithms: Implement the core logic of your chosen trading algorithm. Leverage Rust's powerful type system and memory safety features to ensure robust code.

4.Backtesting and Optimization: Test your algorithms against historical data to evaluate their performance. Use crates like `backtrader` to simulate trading scenarios and refine your strategies.

5.Executing Trades: Integrate your system with trading platforms using APIs. Ensure seamless and secure connections for executing trades in real-time.

6.Risk Management: Implement risk management protocols to monitor and mitigate potential risks. This includes stop-loss mechanisms, position sizing, and real-time risk assessments.

Understanding the different types of trading algorithms is crucial for developing effective trading strategies. Each algorithm has unique strengths and considerations, and selecting the right one depends on your trading objectives and market conditions. By leveraging Rust's capabilities, you can develop robust and efficient trading systems that capitalize on these diverse strategies. In the next sections, we will explore specific examples and implementations, providing you with practical insights and tools to excel in algorithmic trading.

Market Inefficiencies and Arbitrage

To begin, we must understand the concept of market inefficiencies. These are scenarios where the price of an asset deviates from its fair value, creating opportunities for profit.

One common type of inefficiency is arbitrage—where a trader can exploit price differences of the same asset across different markets or forms. For example, if a stock is priced lower on one exchange compared to another, a trader can buy the stock low and sell it high, pocketing the difference. Rust's speed and concurrency capabilities make it an ideal tool for capturing these fleeting opportunities.

Rust Code Example – Detecting Arbitrage Opportunities:

```rust
use reqwest;
use serde_json::Value;
use std::collections::HashMap;

async fn fetch_prices() -> Result<HashMap<String, f64>, reqwest::Error> {
let mut prices = HashMap::new();
let exchanges = vec!["exchange1", "exchange2", "exchange3"];

for exchange in exchanges {
let url = format!("https://api.{}.com/prices", exchange);
let response = reqwest::get(&url).await?.text().await?;
let json: Value = serde_json::from_str(&response)?;
prices.insert(exchange.to_string(),
json["price"].as_f64().unwrap());
}

Ok(prices)
}
```

```
fn detect_arbitrage(prices: HashMap<String, f64>) {

let min_price = prices.values().cloned().min_by(|a, b|
a.partial_cmp(.unwrap()).unwrap();

let max_price = prices.values().cloned().max_by(|a, b|
a.partial_cmp(.unwrap()).unwrap();


if max_price > min_price {

println!("Arbitrage opportunity detected: Buy at ${} and sell at
${}", min_price, max_price);

} else {

println!("No arbitrage opportunity detected.");

}

}


#[tokio::main]

async fn main() {

match fetch_prices().await {

Ok(prices) => detect_arbitrage(prices),

Err(e) => eprintln!("Error fetching prices: {}", e),

}

}
```

\ \ \

This example illustrates how Rust's asynchronous capabilities can be harnessed to fetch real-time prices from multiple exchanges and identify potential arbitrage opportunities.

Statistical Analysis and Machine Learning

Beyond simple arbitrage, statistical analysis and machine learning models can be employed to identify more complex trading opportunities. Techniques such as regression analysis, time-series forecasting, and pattern recognition are instrumental in predicting price movements and market trends.

For instance, a machine learning model trained on historical options data can be used to predict future volatility or price movements. Rust's powerful data processing libraries and integration with machine learning frameworks such as TensorFlow or PyTorch allow for efficient implementation of these models.

Rust Code Example – Linear Regression for Price Prediction:

```rust
use ndarray::Array2;
use linregress::RegressionDataBuilder;
use linregress::FormulaRegression;

fn main() {
let data: Array2<f64> = Array2::from_shape_vec((5, 2), vec![
1.0, 2.0,
2.0, 2.8,
3.0, 3.6,
4.0, 4.5,
5.0, 5.1
]).unwrap();
```

```rust
let                    regression_data              =
RegressionDataBuilder::new().build_from(data).unwrap();

let formula = "y ~ x";

let                    model                        =
FormulaRegression::new(formula).fit(&regression_data).unw
rap();

println!("Intercept: {}", model.intercept());

println!("Slope: {}", model.parameters().get("x").unwrap());
}
```
```
` ` `
```

This example demonstrates a simple linear regression model using Rust, which can be extended to more complex predictive models for analyzing trading opportunities.

Sentiment Analysis and Market Sentiment

Market sentiment, often gleaned from news articles, social media feeds, and expert opinions, plays a significant role in influencing asset prices. Sentiment analysis involves extracting subjective information from text data to gauge the overall mood or sentiment of the market.

Rust's natural language processing (NLP) crates, such as `rust-nlp`, facilitate the implementation of sentiment analysis. By analyzing large volumes of text from various sources, traders can identify bullish or bearish trends and adjust their strategies accordingly.

Rust Code Example – Sentiment Analysis with NLP:

```rust
use rust_nlp::{SentimentAnalyzer, Sentiment};

fn main() {
let analyzer = SentimentAnalyzer::new();
let text = "The market is expected to rise due to positive earnings reports.";
let sentiment = analyzer.analyze(text);

match sentiment {
Sentiment::Positive => println!("Positive sentiment detected."),
Sentiment::Negative => println!("Negative sentiment detected."),
Sentiment::Neutral => println!("Neutral sentiment detected."),
}
}
```

In this example, a sentiment analyzer is used to determine the sentiment of a given piece of text, aiding in the identification of market sentiment-driven trading opportunities.

Technical Indicators and Quantitative Signals

Technical indicators, such as moving averages, Bollinger Bands, and the Relative Strength Index (RSI), are crucial tools for analyzing price trends and identifying trading signals. These indicators are derived from historical price data and are used to forecast future price movements.

Rust's efficient handling of numerical computations allows for the real-time calculation and analysis of these technical indicators. Combining multiple indicators can provide a robust framework for identifying high-probability trading opportunities.

Rust Code Example – Calculating Moving Averages:

```rust
fn moving_average(prices: &[f64], period: usize) -> Vec<f64> {
prices.windows(period)
.map(|window| window.iter().sum::<f64>() / period as f64)
.collect()
}

fn main() {
let prices = vec![1.0, 2.0, 3.0, 4.0, 5.0, 6.0, 7.0, 8.0, 9.0, 10.0];
let period = 3;
let averages = moving_average(&prices, period);

println!("Moving Averages: {:?}", averages);
}
```

This example showcases the calculation of simple moving averages, a foundational technical indicator, used to identify trends and potential trading opportunities.

Risk Management and Position Sizing

Finally, effective risk management and position sizing are critical components of a successful trading strategy. Identifying trading opportunities is only half the battle; ensuring that trades are executed with appropriate risk controls is equally important. Techniques such as Value at Risk (VaR), stop-loss orders, and position sizing algorithms help in mitigating risk and enhancing the overall performance of the trading strategy.

Rust Code Example – Simple Position Sizing Algorithm:

```rust
fn position_size(account_balance: f64, risk_per_trade: f64, trade_risk: f64) -> f64 {
(account_balance * risk_per_trade) / trade_risk
}

fn main() {
let account_balance = 10000.0;
let risk_per_trade = 0.01; // 1% of account balance
let trade_risk = 100.0; // risk per trade

let size = position_size(account_balance, risk_per_trade, trade_risk);
println!("Position Size: {}", size);
}
```

In this example, a simple position sizing algorithm is implemented to determine the appropriate trade size based on the account balance and risk parameters.

Identifying and analyzing trading opportunities is a multi-faceted process involving market inefficiencies, statistical analysis, sentiment analysis, technical indicators, and robust risk management. Rust, with its speed, safety, and concurrency, offers a powerful toolkit for implementing these techniques effectively. By leveraging Rust's capabilities, traders can gain a significant edge in the competitive world of algorithmic options trading, transforming theoretical models into practical success.

Covered Call Strategy

The covered call strategy is one of the simplest and most conservative options trading techniques, making it a popular choice for investors seeking to generate additional income from their existing stock holdings. In this strategy, an investor holds a long position in a stock while simultaneously selling call options on the same stock. The premium received from selling the call options serves as an additional income stream.

Implementation in Rust

To implement a covered call strategy in Rust, we need to simulate the process of holding a stock position and selling call options against it. Here is a basic example:

```rust
struct StockPosition {
symbol: String,
shares: u32,
purchase_price: f64,
```

```
}

struct CallOption {
strike_price: f64,
premium: f64,
expiration: String,
}

fn main() {
let stock = StockPosition {
symbol: "AAPL".to_string(),
shares: 100,
purchase_price: 150.0,
};

let call_option = CallOption {
strike_price: 160.0,
premium: 5.0,
expiration: "2023-12-31".to_string(),
};

let income = call_option.premium * stock.shares as f64;
println!("Covered Call Income: ${}", income);
}
```

This example demonstrates the basic principle of calculating the income generated from selling call options. In a real-world scenario, you would need to consider additional factors such as transaction costs, tax implications, and the potential for the stock to be called away if its price exceeds the strike price.

Protective Put Strategy

A protective put strategy involves holding a long position in a stock while purchasing put options for the same stock. This approach acts as an insurance policy against a decline in the stock's price. If the stock price falls, the put option increases in value, offsetting the loss from the stock position.

Implementation in Rust

Below is an example of how to implement a protective put strategy in Rust:

```rust
struct StockPosition {
symbol: String,
shares: u32,
purchase_price: f64,
}

struct PutOption {
strike_price: f64,
premium: f64,
expiration: String,
```

```
}

fn main() {
let stock = StockPosition {
symbol: "AAPL".to_string(),
shares: 100,
purchase_price: 150.0,
};

let put_option = PutOption {
strike_price: 140.0,
premium: 3.0,
expiration: "2023-12-31".to_string(),
};

let protection_cost = put_option.premium * stock.shares as
f64;
println!("Protective Put Cost: ${}", protection_cost);
}
```
` ` `

This example calculates the cost of buying put options to protect the stock position. It's essential to weigh the cost of protection against the potential loss to determine if this strategy is suitable for your investment goals.

Straddle Strategy

The straddle strategy involves buying a call option and a put option at the same strike price and expiration date. This strategy benefits from significant price movements in either direction, making it ideal for volatile markets.

Implementation in Rust

Here is an example of implementing a straddle strategy in Rust:

```rust
struct OptionPosition {
strike_price: f64,
premium: f64,
expiration: String,
option_type: String, // "call" or "put"
}

fn main() {
let call_option = OptionPosition {
strike_price: 150.0,
premium: 5.0,
expiration: "2023-12-31".to_string(),
option_type: "call".to_string(),
};

let put_option = OptionPosition {
```

```
strike_price: 150.0,

premium: 5.0,

expiration: "2023-12-31".to_string(),

option_type: "put".to_string(),

};


let total_cost = call_option.premium + put_option.premium;

println!("Straddle Total Cost: ${}", total_cost);

}
```
` ` `

This example calculates the total cost of entering a straddle position. The profitability of this strategy hinges on the stock price moving significantly away from the strike price, either upwards or downwards.

Iron Condor Strategy

An iron condor strategy involves selling a lower strike put, buying an even lower strike put, selling a higher strike call, and buying an even higher strike call. This strategy is designed to profit from low volatility and aims to capture premium income from the options sold.

Implementation in Rust

Below is an example of implementing an iron condor strategy in Rust:

```rust
struct OptionPosition {
strike_price: f64,
premium: f64,
expiration: String,
option_type: String, // "call" or "put"
}

fn main() {
let lower_strike_put = OptionPosition {
strike_price: 140.0,
premium: 2.0,
expiration: "2023-12-31".to_string(),
option_type: "put".to_string(),
};

let higher_strike_put = OptionPosition {
strike_price: 130.0,
premium: 1.0,
expiration: "2023-12-31".to_string(),
option_type: "put".to_string(),
};

let lower_strike_call = OptionPosition {
strike_price: 160.0,
```

```
premium: 3.0,
expiration: "2023-12-31".to_string(),
option_type: "call".to_string(),
};

let higher_strike_call = OptionPosition {
strike_price: 170.0,
premium: 1.5,
expiration: "2023-12-31".to_string(),
option_type: "call".to_string(),
};

let total_premium_received = lower_strike_call.premium + lower_strike_put.premium;
let total_premium_paid = higher_strike_call.premium + higher_strike_put.premium;
let net_premium = total_premium_received - total_premium_paid;

println!("Iron Condor Net Premium: ${}", net_premium);
}
```
` ` `

This example calculates the net premium received from entering an iron condor position. The key to this strategy is to ensure that the stock price remains within the range defined by the strike prices, allowing the trader to capture the net premium as profit.

Butterfly Spread Strategy

The butterfly spread strategy combines a bull spread and a bear spread by using three different strike prices. The trader buys one option at the lowest strike price, sells two options at the middle strike price, and buys one option at the highest strike price. This strategy is effective when the trader anticipates minimal movement in the stock price.

Implementation in Rust

Here is an example of implementing a butterfly spread strategy in Rust:

```rust
struct OptionPosition {
strike_price: f64,
premium: f64,
expiration: String,
option_type: String, // "call" or "put"
}

fn main() {
let lower_strike_call = OptionPosition {
strike_price: 140.0,
premium: 2.0,
expiration: "2023-12-31".to_string(),
option_type: "call".to_string(),
```

```
};

let middle_strike_call1 = OptionPosition {
strike_price: 150.0,
premium: 4.0,
expiration: "2023-12-31".to_string(),
option_type: "call".to_string(),
};

let middle_strike_call2 = OptionPosition {
strike_price: 150.0,
premium: 4.0,
expiration: "2023-12-31".to_string(),
option_type: "call".to_string(),
};

let upper_strike_call = OptionPosition {
strike_price: 160.0,
premium: 1.0,
expiration: "2023-12-31".to_string(),
option_type: "call".to_string(),
};

let total_premium_paid = lower_strike_call.premium + upper_strike_call.premium;
let total_premium_received = middle_strike_call1.premium + middle_strike_call2.premium;
```

```
let net_cost = total_premium_paid - total_premium_received;

println!("Butterfly Spread Net Cost: ${}", net_cost);
}
```
```

This example calculates the net cost of entering a butterfly spread position. The strategy aims to profit if the stock price remains near the middle strike price at expiration.

Implementing various options trading strategies requires a blend of theoretical knowledge and practical application. Rust, with its high performance and safety features, provides a robust framework for developing, testing, and executing these strategies. By leveraging Rust's capabilities, traders can enhance their strategies' efficiency, accuracy, and profitability, gaining a significant edge in the competitive world of options trading.

Setting Up Your Rust Environment

Before diving into specific algorithms, ensure your Rust environment is correctly set up. Install Rust and Cargo (Rust's package manager) following these steps:

1.Install Rust:
``` sh
curl --proto '=https' --tlsv1.2 -sSf https://sh.rustup.rs | sh
```
```

2.Verify Installation:

```sh
rustc --version
```

3.Create a New Project:

```sh
cargo new trading_algorithms
cd trading_algorithms
```

This setup forms the foundation for our algorithmic trading examples.

Moving Average Crossover Strategy

The Moving Average Crossover Strategy is a simple yet effective algorithm used to identify trends in financial markets. It involves two moving averages of different lengths —a short-term and a long-term one. The strategy generates buy or sell signals based on the crossover of these moving averages.

Code Implementation

1.Adding Dependencies:

Open `Cargo.toml` and add the necessary dependencies:

```toml
[dependencies]
csv = "1.1"
serde = { version = "1.0", features = ["derive"] }
```

2.Reading Historical Data:

First, we need to read historical price data. Here's a function to accomplish this:

```rust
use serde::Deserialize;
use std::error::Error;
use std::fs::File;
use std::io::Read;

#[derive(Debug, Deserialize)]
struct Record {
date: String,
close: f64,
}

fn read_csv(file_path: &str) -> Result<Vec<Record>, Box<dyn Error>> {
let mut rdr = csv::Reader::from_path(file_path)?;
let mut records = Vec::new();
```

```rust
for result in rdr.deserialize() {
let record: Record = result?;
records.push(record);
}
Ok(records)
}
```
```

3.Calculating Moving Averages:

Implement functions to calculate the short-term and long-term moving averages:

```rust
fn moving_average(data: &[f64], period: usize) -> Vec<f64> {
let mut ma = Vec::new();
for i in 0..data.len() {
if i >= period - 1 {
let sum: f64 = data[i + 1 - period..=i].iter().sum();
ma.push(sum / period as f64);
}
}
ma
}
```
```

4.Generating Buy/Sell Signals:

Next, generate buy or sell signals based on the crossover of moving averages:

```rust
fn generate_signals(short_ma: &[f64], long_ma: &[f64]) -> Vec<String> {

let mut signals = Vec::new();

for i in 1..short_ma.len() {

if short_ma[i] > long_ma[i] && short_ma[i - 1] <= long_ma[i - 1] {

signals.push("BUY".to_string());

} else if short_ma[i] < long_ma[i] && short_ma[i - 1] >= long_ma[i - 1] {

signals.push("SELL".to_string());

} else {

signals.push("HOLD".to_string());

}

}

signals

}
```

5.Integrating the Components:

Finally, integrate all components in the `main` function:

```rust
```

```
fn main() -> Result<(), Box<dyn Error>> {
let records = read_csv("historical_data.csv")?;
let close_prices: Vec<f64> = records.iter().map(|r| r.close).collect();
let short_ma = moving_average(&close_prices, 20);
let long_ma = moving_average(&close_prices, 50);

let signals = generate_signals(&short_ma, &long_ma);

for (i, signal) in signals.iter().enumerate() {
println!("{}: {}", records[i + 50].date, signal);
}

Ok(())
}
```
` ` `

This code reads historical data, calculates moving averages, and generates buy/sell signals based on the crossover strategy.

Momentum Trading Strategy

Momentum trading involves buying securities that have shown an upward price movement or short-selling those that have shown a downward movement. The idea is that securities that have been rising will continue to rise and vice versa.

Code Implementation

BLACK SCHOLES: ALGORITHMIC OPTIONS TRADING WITH RUST

1.Adding Required Dependencies:

Ensure you have the `chrono` library for date manipulation:

```toml
[dependencies]
chrono = "0.4"
```

2.Calculating Momentum:

Implement a function to calculate momentum:

```rust
fn calculate_momentum(prices: &[f64], period: usize) ->
Vec<f64> {
let mut momentum = Vec::new();
for i in period..prices.len() {
momentum.push(prices[i] - prices[i - period]);
}
momentum
}
```

3.Generating Signals:

Generate buy/sell signals based on momentum:

```rust

fn generate_momentum_signals(momentum: &[f64],
threshold: f64) -> Vec<String> {

momentum.iter().map(|&m| {

if m > threshold {

"BUY".to_string()

} else if m < -threshold {

"SELL".to_string()

} else {

"HOLD".to_string()

}

}).collect()

}

```

4.Integrating the Strategy:

Integrate the momentum strategy into the `main` function:

```rust
fn main() -> Result<(), Box<dyn Error>> {

let records = read_csv("historical_data.csv")?;

let close_prices: Vec<f64> = records.iter().map(|r|
r.close).collect();


let momentum = calculate_momentum(&close_prices, 10);
```

```rust
let signals = generate_momentum_signals(&momentum, 1.0);

for (i, signal) in signals.iter().enumerate() {
println!("{}: {}", records[i + 10].date, signal);
}

Ok(())
}
```

This implementation calculates the momentum of stock prices over a period and generates trading signals based on the calculated momentum values.

Mean Reversion Strategy

The mean reversion strategy is based on the principle that asset prices tend to revert to their historical averages. It involves identifying overbought or oversold conditions and trading accordingly.

Code Implementation

1.Calculating the Mean:

Implement a function to calculate the mean of a series:

```rust
fn calculate_mean(data: &[f64]) -> f64 {
```

```rust
let sum: f64 = data.iter().sum();
sum / data.len() as f64
}
```

2.Generating Mean Reversion Signals:

Generate buy/sell signals based on deviation from the mean:

```rust
fn generate_mean_reversion_signals(prices: &[f64], period: usize, threshold: f64) -> Vec<String> {
let mut signals = Vec::new();
for i in period..prices.len() {
let mean = calculate_mean(&prices[i - period..i]);
if prices[i] > mean + threshold {
signals.push("SELL".to_string());
} else if prices[i] < mean - threshold {
signals.push("BUY".to_string());
} else {
signals.push("HOLD".to_string());
}
}
signals
}
```

3.Integrating the Strategy:

Integrate the mean reversion strategy into the `main` function:

```rust
fn main() -> Result<(), Box<dyn Error>> {
let records = read_csv("historical_data.csv")?;
let close_prices: Vec<f64> = records.iter().map(|r| r.close).collect();

let signals = generate_mean_reversion_signals(&close_prices, 20, 2.0);

for (i, signal) in signals.iter().enumerate() {
println!("{}: {}", records[i + 20].date, signal);
}

Ok(())
}
```

This code calculates the mean price over a period and generates trading signals based on the deviation from this mean.

Implementing basic trading algorithms in Rust showcases the language's efficiency and safety features. By leveraging Rust, traders can develop robust and high-performance trading strategies. From moving average crossovers to momentum and mean reversion strategies, Rust provides a solid foundation for building and executing sophisticated trading algorithms. As you continue to explore and refine these strategies, remember that the key to successful algorithmic trading lies in continuous learning and adaptation to market conditions.

Backtesting Trading Strategies

Backtesting is an essential component in the development and validation of trading strategies. It involves running a trading algorithm on historical data to evaluate its performance and reliability. By backtesting, traders can gain insights into how a strategy might perform in real market conditions, identify potential flaws, and make necessary adjustments before deploying it live.

Setting Up the Backtesting Environment

To begin backtesting, you need an environment that simulates historical market conditions. Rust, with its robust performance and safety features, is well-suited for this task. Ensure you have your Rust environment set up and the necessary libraries installed.

1.Install Rust and Cargo (if not already installed):

```sh
curl --proto '=https' --tlsv1.2 -sSf https://sh.rustup.rs | sh
```

2.Verify Installation:

``` sh
rustc --version
```

3.Create a New Project for Backtesting:

``` sh
cargo new backtesting
cd backtesting
```

4.Add Dependencies:

Open `Cargo.toml` and add dependencies for handling CSV data and date-time operations:

``` toml
[dependencies]
csv = "1.1"
serde = { version = "1.0", features = ["derive"] }
chrono = "0.4"
```

Loading Historical Data

To perform backtesting, we first need to load historical market data. This data will serve as the foundation for simulating trades and evaluating strategy performance.

1.Define a Data Structure for Historical Records:

```rust
use serde::Deserialize;

#[derive(Debug, Deserialize)]
struct Record {
date: String,
close: f64,
}
```

2.Implement a Function to Read CSV Data:

```rust
use std::error::Error;
use std::fs::File;
use std::io::Read;

fn read_csv(file_path: &str) -> Result<Vec<Record>, Box<dyn Error>> {
let mut rdr = csv::Reader::from_path(file_path)?;
let mut records = Vec::new();
for result in rdr.deserialize() {
let record: Record = result?;
records.push(record);
}
Ok(records)
```

```
}
```
` ` `

Implementing a Simple Trading Strategy

For demonstration, we will implement a simple Moving Average Crossover Strategy. This strategy generates buy and sell signals based on the crossover of short-term and long-term moving averages.

1.Calculate Moving Averages:

` ` `rust

```rust
fn moving_average(data: &[f64], period: usize) -> Vec<f64> {
let mut ma = Vec::new();
for i in 0..data.len() {
if i >= period - 1 {
let sum: f64 = data[i + 1 - period..=i].iter().sum();
ma.push(sum / period as f64);
}
}
ma
}
```
` ` `

2.Generate Buy/Sell Signals:

` ` `rust

```rust
fn generate_signals(short_ma: &[f64], long_ma: &[f64]) ->
Vec<String> {
```

```rust
let mut signals = Vec::new();

for i in 1..short_ma.len() {

if short_ma[i] > long_ma[i] && short_ma[i - 1] <= long_ma[i - 1]
{

signals.push("BUY".to_string());

} else if short_ma[i] < long_ma[i] && short_ma[i - 1] >=
long_ma[i - 1] {

signals.push("SELL".to_string());

} else {

signals.push("HOLD".to_string());

}

}

signals

}
```

Simulating Trades and Performance Metrics

Backtesting involves simulating trades based on generated signals and calculating performance metrics such as profit, loss, and drawdown.

1.Simulate Trades:

```rust
fn simulate_trades(mut cash: f64, initial_shares: f64, prices:
&[f64], signals: &[String]) -> (f64, f64) {

let mut shares = initial_shares;

for (i, signal) in signals.iter().enumerate() {
```

```rust
match &signal[..] {
"BUY" => {
if cash >= prices[i] {
shares += 1.0;
cash -= prices[i];
}
}
"SELL" => {
if shares > 0.0 {
shares -= 1.0;
cash += prices[i];
}
}
_ => (),
}
}
(cash, shares)
}
```

2.Calculate Performance Metrics:

```rust
fn calculate_performance(cash: f64, shares: f64, final_price: f64) -> f64 {
cash + shares * final_price
}
```

```
` ` `
```

Running the Backtest

Integrate all components and run the backtest to evaluate the strategy.

1.Main Function:

```rust
fn main() -> Result<(), Box<dyn Error>> {
let records = read_csv("historical_data.csv")?;
let close_prices: Vec<f64> = records.iter().map(|r| r.close).collect();

let short_ma = moving_average(&close_prices, 20);
let long_ma = moving_average(&close_prices, 50);

let signals = generate_signals(&short_ma, &long_ma);

let (final_cash, final_shares) = simulate_trades(10000.0, 0.0, &close_prices, &signals);

let final_value = calculate_performance(final_cash, final_shares, close_prices.last().unwrap().to_owned());
println!("Final Portfolio Value: ${:.2}", final_value);

Ok(())
}
```

This code reads historical data, calculates moving averages, generates trading signals, simulates trades, and calculates the final portfolio value, providing an insight into the strategy's performance.

Optimizing and Iterating

Backtesting is an iterative process. It's crucial to evaluate the strategy's performance, identify areas for improvement, and refine the algorithm. Consider the following steps for optimization:

1. Parameter Tuning:

Adjust parameters such as the periods for moving averages or thresholds for momentum strategies to optimize performance.

2. Adding Transaction Costs:

Incorporate transaction costs to simulate real-world trading conditions more accurately.

3. Risk Management:

Implement risk management techniques such as stop-loss orders or position sizing to enhance the strategy's robustness.

4. Performance Metrics:

Evaluate additional performance metrics such as Sharpe ratio, maximum drawdown, and win/loss ratio to gain a comprehensive understanding of the strategy's effectiveness.

5.Visualizing Results:

Use data visualization tools to plot trading signals, price movements, and performance metrics over time, aiding in the analysis and refinement of the strategy.

Incorporating these steps into your backtesting process will help you develop more reliable and effective trading algorithms.

Backtesting is a critical step in the development of trading algorithms, providing valuable insights into a strategy's performance and reliability before live deployment. By leveraging Rust's performance and safety features, you can efficiently implement and evaluate trading strategies. As you continue to refine your algorithms, remember that backtesting is an ongoing process of iteration and optimization, essential for achieving long-term success in algorithmic trading.

Data Sourcing: The Backbone of Algorithmic Trading

The initial step in any trading strategy is collecting historical market data. This data serves as the cornerstone for backtesting and, consequently, the development of profitable trading strategies. Several avenues are available for sourcing this data:

1.Public Data Sources:

-Yahoo Finance API: This is a popular source for obtaining historical stock prices, offering ease of access and a comprehensive dataset.

-Alpha Vantage: This API provides historical and real-time data on stocks, forex, and cryptocurrencies. It requires an API key for access.

2.Subscription-Based Services:

-Bloomberg Terminal: Known for its extensive range of financial data, the Bloomberg Terminal is a premium service offering real-time and historical data.

-Reuters Eikon: Similar to Bloomberg, Reuters Eikon provides a wealth of financial data, albeit at a subscription cost.

3.Brokerage APIs:

-Interactive Brokers: For those already trading with Interactive Brokers, their API provides a seamless way to access historical and real-time data.

-TD Ameritrade: Another brokerage offering API access to a vast dataset.

To demonstrate, let's start by sourcing data from Alpha Vantage using Rust.

1.Set Up the Project:

``` sh
cargo new data_sourcing
cd data_sourcing
```

2.Add Dependencies:

Open `Cargo.toml` and include the necessary crates:

````toml
[dependencies]
reqwest = { version = "0.11", features = ["blocking", "json"] }
serde = { version = "1.0", features = ["derive"] }
serde_json = "1.0"
````

3.Fetch Data from Alpha Vantage:
````rust
use reqwest;
use serde::Deserialize;
use std::collections::HashMap;
use std::error::Error;

#[derive(Debug, Deserialize)]
struct TimeSeries {
#[serde(rename = "Time Series (Daily)")]
daily: HashMap<String, DayInfo>,
}

#[derive(Debug, Deserialize)]
struct DayInfo {
#[serde(rename = "4. close")]
close: String,
}
````

```rust
fn fetch_data(symbol: &str, api_key: &str) -> Result<(),
Box<dyn Error>> {

let url = format!("https://www.alphavantage.co/query?
function=TIME_SERIES_DAILY&symbol={}&apikey={}",
symbol, api_key);

let                       response                       =
reqwest::blocking::get(&url)?.json::<TimeSeries>()?;

for (date, info) in response.daily {
println!("{}: ${}", date, info.close);
}

Ok(())
}

fn main() {
let symbol = "AAPL";
let api_key = "your_api_key_here"; // Replace with your actual
API key

if let Err(e) = fetch_data(symbol, api_key) {
println!("Error fetching data: {}", e);
}
}
```

This code snippet fetches daily closing prices for a given stock symbol from Alpha Vantage and prints them. Replace `"your_api_key_here"` with your actual Alpha Vantage API key.

Data Preprocessing: Cleaning and Structuring

Once the data is sourced, preprocessing is essential to ensure it's usable for algorithmic trading. This involves cleaning, normalizing, and transforming the data into a suitable format.

1.Handling Missing Data:

Missing data points are common in financial datasets and can skew your algorithm's performance. Rust's powerful standard library and ecosystem offer tools for handling such anomalies.

```rust
fn handle_missing_data(data: Vec<Option<f64>>) -> Vec<f64> {
    data.into_iter().map(|x| x.unwrap_or(0.0)).collect()
}

fn main() {
    let raw_data = vec![Some(100.0), None, Some(102.5), Some(101.0), None];
    let clean_data = handle_missing_data(raw_data);
    println!("{:?}", clean_data);
}
```

This example replaces missing data points (`None`) with

zeros, a simple yet effective method for maintaining dataset continuity.

2.Normalization:

To ensure different datasets are comparable, normalization scales the data between a specific range, typically 0 to 1.

```rust
fn normalize(data: &[f64]) -> Vec<f64> {
let min = data.iter().cloned().fold(f64::INFINITY, f64::min);
let max = data.iter().cloned().fold(f64::NEG_INFINITY, f64::max);

data.iter().map(|x| (x - min) / (max - min)).collect()
}

fn main() {
let prices = vec![100.0, 102.5, 101.0, 105.0, 110.0];
let normalized_prices = normalize(&prices);
println!("{:?}", normalized_prices);
}
```

Normalization helps in comparing price movements on a standardized scale, crucial for many trading strategies.

3.Feature Engineering:

Beyond basic preprocessing, feature engineering transforms

raw data into informative features that better capture the patterns and trends in the market.

Example: Calculating Moving Averages as Features

```rust
fn calculate_moving_average(data: &[f64], period: usize) -> Vec<f64> {
    data.windows(period).map(|window|
    window.iter().sum::<f64>() / period as f64).collect()
}

fn main() {
    let prices = vec![100.0, 102.5, 101.0, 105.0, 110.0];
    let moving_average_3 = calculate_moving_average(&prices, 3);
    println!("{:?}", moving_average_3);
}
```

Moving averages smooth out price data, making trends more observable and aiding in the generation of trading signals.

Data Storage: Efficient and Accessible

Efficient storage of preprocessed data ensures quick access and retrieval during backtesting and live trading. Rust's performance capabilities make it an excellent choice for handling large datasets.

1.Using CSV Files:

CSV files are a common format for storing financial data due to their simplicity and widespread support.

```rust
use std::fs::File;
use std::io::Write;

fn save_to_csv(data: &[f64], file_path: &str) -> Result<(), Box<dyn Error>> {
let mut wtr = csv::Writer::from_path(file_path)?;
for value in data {
wtr.write_record(&[value.to_string()])?;
}
wtr.flush()?;
Ok(())
}

fn main() {
let prices = vec![100.0, 102.5, 101.0, 105.0, 110.0];
if let Err(e) = save_to_csv(&prices, "cleaned_data.csv") {
println!("Error saving to CSV: {}", e);
}
}
```

This example saves a vector of prices to a CSV file, ensuring data persistence for future use.

2.Using Databases:

For more complex applications, especially those dealing with large volumes of data, databases are preferable. Rust integrates well with various databases like PostgreSQL and SQLite.

```toml
[dependencies]
postgres = "0.19"
tokio = { version = "1", features = ["full"] }
```

```rust
use tokio_postgres::{NoTls, Error};

async fn save_to_db(data: &[f64]) -> Result<(), Error> {
let (client, connection) = tokio_postgres::connect("host=localhost    user=postgres", NoTls).await?;

tokio::spawn(async move {
if let Err(e) = connection.await {
eprintln!("connection error: {}", e);
}
});
```

```
for value in data {
client.execute("INSERT INTO prices (value) VALUES ($1)",
&[value]).await?;
}

Ok(())
}

#[tokio::main]
async fn main() {
let prices = vec![100.0, 102.5, 101.0, 105.0, 110.0];
if let Err(e) = save_to_db(&prices).await {
println!("Error saving to database: {}", e);
}
}
```

This asynchronous Rust code snippet demonstrates how to insert price data into a PostgreSQL database, providing a scalable solution for data storage.

Data sourcing and preprocessing are critical steps in the life cycle of an algorithmic trading strategy. Quality data, meticulously cleaned and prepared, forms the bedrock upon which robust and profitable algorithms are built. Leveraging Rust's powerful capabilities, you can create efficient, performant, and reliable data pipelines, setting the stage for sophisticated and effective trading strategies. As you continue to refine your approach, remember that the quality of your data can significantly influence the success of your trading endeavours.

Risk Management Techniques

Risk in trading is the probability of losing capital. It stems from various sources such as market volatility, liquidity issues, and operational failures. Effective risk management identifies these risks and implements measures to mitigate them. Here, we categorize the main types of risks:

1.Market Risk:

-Volatility Risk: The risk that the price of securities will fluctuate.

-Trend Risk: The risk of losses due to unfavorable market trends.

2.Liquidity Risk:

- The risk that a security cannot be traded quickly enough in the market without impacting its price.

3.Operational Risk:

- The risk of loss due to failures in systems, processes, or controls.

4.Credit Risk:

- The risk of a counterparty failing to fulfill its financial obligations.

Implementing Risk Management Techniques in Rust

To manage these risks, we employ various techniques, such as setting stop-loss orders, using position sizing algorithms, and performing scenario analysis. Let's delve into each of these techniques with practical Rust implementations.

1.Stop-Loss Orders:

- A stop-loss order automatically sells a security when its price falls to a certain level, limiting potential losses.

```rust
fn execute_stop_loss(current_price: f64, stop_loss_price: f64) -> bool {
if current_price <= stop_loss_price {
println!("Stop-loss triggered. Selling the security.");
return true;
}
println!("Stop-loss not triggered.");
false
}

fn main() {
let current_price = 98.0;
let stop_loss_price = 100.0;
execute_stop_loss(current_price, stop_loss_price);
}
```

```
` ` `
```

In this example, if the current price of the security drops to or below the stop-loss price, the function triggers a sell action.

2.Position Sizing Algorithms:

- Determining the appropriate amount of capital to allocate to a specific trade is crucial. Popular methods include the Kelly Criterion and Fixed Fractional Position Sizing.

Kelly Criterion:

```rust
fn kelly_criterion(win_probability: f64, win_loss_ratio: f64) -> f64 {

(win_probability - (1.0 - win_probability) / win_loss_ratio).max(0.0)

}


fn main() {

let win_probability = 0.6;

let win_loss_ratio = 1.5;

let kelly_fraction = kelly_criterion(win_probability, win_loss_ratio);

println!("Kelly Criterion suggests investing {:.2}% of capital.", kelly_fraction * 100.0);

}
```
```
` ` `
```

This implementation calculates the optimal fraction of capital to invest based on the probability of winning and the win/loss ratio.

3.Scenario Analysis:

- Scenario analysis involves evaluating the potential impact of different market conditions on your portfolio. Rust's computational efficiency makes it suitable for running numerous simulations quickly.

```rust
fn simulate_scenarios(initial_price: f64, scenarios: &[f64]) -> Vec<f64> {

scenarios.iter().map(|&change|    initial_price   *   (1.0   + change)).collect()
}


fn main() {
let initial_price = 100.0;
let scenarios = vec![-0.1, 0.0, 0.1, 0.2]; // -10%, 0%, +10%, +20%
let simulated_prices  =  simulate_scenarios(initial_price, &scenarios);
println!("Simulated prices: {:?}", simulated_prices);
}
```

This example simulates potential future prices of a security based on different percentage changes, helping to assess risk under various market conditions.

4.Diversification:

- Diversifying your portfolio can reduce risk by spreading investments across different assets, thereby minimizing the impact of a single asset's poor performance.

```rust
struct Portfolio {
assets: Vec<(String, f64)>, // (Asset name, allocation percentage)
}

impl Portfolio {
fn new(assets: Vec<(String, f64)>) -> Self {
Portfolio { assets }
}

fn evaluate_diversification(&self) -> f64 {
let total_allocation: f64 = self.assets.iter().map(|(_, alloc)| alloc).sum();
total_allocation
}
}

fn main() {
let assets = vec![
("Stock A".to_string(), 0.4),
("Stock B".to_string(), 0.3),
```

```rust
("Bond C".to_string(), 0.2),

("Commodity D".to_string(), 0.1),

];

let portfolio = Portfolio::new(assets);

let diversification_score = portfolio.evaluate_diversification();

println!("Total Allocation: {:.2}", diversification_score);

}
```

This code helps manage diversification by evaluating the total allocation across different assets, ensuring it aligns with your risk management strategy.

5.Risk-Adjusted Return Metrics:

- Metrics such as the Sharpe Ratio and Sortino Ratio help evaluate the performance of your trading strategy adjusted for risk.

Sharpe Ratio Calculation:

```rust
fn calculate_sharpe_ratio(returns: &[f64], risk_free_rate: f64) -> f64 {

let mean_return = returns.iter().sum::<f64>() / returns.len() as f64;

let excess_return = mean_return - risk_free_rate;

let standard_deviation = (returns.iter().map(|r| (r - mean_return).powi(2)).sum::<f64>() / returns.len() as f64).sqrt();
```

```rust
    excess_return / standard_deviation
}

fn main() {
    let returns = vec![0.01, 0.02, 0.015, 0.03, 0.025];
    let risk_free_rate = 0.005;
    let sharpe_ratio = calculate_sharpe_ratio(&returns, risk_free_rate);
    println!("Sharpe Ratio: {:.2}", sharpe_ratio);
}
```

The Sharpe Ratio measures the performance of an investment compared to a risk-free asset, adjusted for its risk. Higher values indicate better risk-adjusted returns.

6.Volatility Control:

- Controlling volatility within your portfolio is crucial. Techniques like Volatility Targeting adjust the proportion of risk taken based on the current level of market volatility.

```rust
fn volatility_targeting(returns: &[f64], target_volatility: f64) -> f64 {
    let std_deviation = (returns.iter().map(|r| r.powi(2)).sum::<f64>() / returns.len() as f64).sqrt();
    target_volatility / std_deviation
}
```

```rust
fn main() {
let returns = vec![0.01, 0.02, 0.015, 0.03, 0.025];
let target_volatility = 0.02;
let allocation_factor = volatility_targeting(&returns, target_volatility);
println!("Allocation Factor: {:.2}", allocation_factor);
}
```

This example demonstrates how to calculate an allocation factor based on the desired volatility target, helping to maintain consistent risk levels.

Integrating Risk Management into Trading Algorithms

Risk management is not a standalone process but an integral part of your trading algorithms. By embedding these techniques into your Rust-based trading systems, you can create robust, resilient, and adaptive strategies.

1.Combining Techniques:
```rust
fn manage_risk(current_price: f64, stop_loss_price: f64, returns: &[f64], target_volatility: f64) -> bool {
let stop_loss_triggered = execute_stop_loss(current_price, stop_loss_price);
if stop_loss_triggered {
return false;
```

```
}

let allocation_factor = volatility_targeting(returns, target_volatility);
println!("Allocated {:.2}% of capital based on volatility targeting.", allocation_factor * 100.0);

true
}

fn main() {
let current_price = 98.0;
let stop_loss_price = 100.0;
let returns = vec![0.01, 0.02, 0.015, 0.03, 0.025];
let target_volatility = 0.02;

let risk_managed = manage_risk(current_price, stop_loss_price, &returns, target_volatility);
println!("Risk management result: {}", risk_managed);
}
```
```

This example combines a stop-loss order with volatility targeting, enhancing the overall risk management capabilities of the trading algorithm.
```

Integration with Trading Platforms

Trading platforms are software systems that facilitate the buying and selling of financial instruments. These platforms offer critical functionalities such as order execution, market data feeds, portfolio management, and risk management. Some of the most popular trading platforms include Interactive Brokers, MetaTrader, and TradeStation, each offering its own unique set of APIs and integration methods.

APIs and Protocols

To integrate your Rust-based trading algorithms with these platforms, you need to understand and leverage their Application Programming Interfaces (APIs) and communication protocols. APIs provide a set of rules and tools for building software applications, allowing your algorithm to interact with the trading platform.

1.REST APIs:

- Representational State Transfer (REST) APIs use HTTP requests to GET, PUT, POST, and DELETE data. Many trading platforms offer REST APIs for ease of integration.

```rust
extern crate reqwest;
```

```rust
use std::collections::HashMap;

async fn place_order(api_url: &str, api_key: &str,
order_data: HashMap<&str, &str>) -> Result<(), Box<dyn
std::error::Error>> {
let client = reqwest::Client::new();
let res = client.post(api_url)
.header("API-KEY", api_key)
.json(&order_data)
.send()
.await?;

println!("Order Response: {:?}", res);
Ok(())
}

#[tokio::main]
async fn main() {
let api_url = "https://api.tradingplatform.com/v1/orders";
let api_key = "your_api_key_here";

let mut order_data = HashMap::new();
order_data.insert("symbol", "AAPL");
order_data.insert("quantity", "10");
order_data.insert("type", "buy");

match place_order(api_url, api_key, order_data).await {
```

```rust
        Ok(_) => println!("Order placed successfully."),
        Err(e) => println!("Failed to place order: {:?}", e),
    }
}
```

In this example, we use an asynchronous HTTP client to place an order through a REST API. The API key and order data are included in the HTTP request header and body, respectively.

2.WebSockets:

- WebSockets provide a full-duplex communication channel over a single, long-lasting connection. This is particularly useful for real-time market data streaming.

```rust
use tokio_tungstenite::connect_async;
use url::Url;

#[tokio::main]
async fn main() {
    let url = Url::parse("wss://api.tradingplatform.com/stream").unwrap();

    let (mut socket, response) = connect_async(url).await.expect("Failed to connect");

    println!("Connected to the server: {:?}", response);

    while let Some(message) = socket.next().await {
```

```
match message {

Ok(msg) => println!("Received: {:?}", msg),

Err(e) => println!("Error: {:?}", e),

}

}

}
```

` ` `

This example demonstrates how to connect to a WebSocket server and listen for real-time updates. This continuous stream of data is essential for time-sensitive trading strategies.

Authentication and Security

When integrating trading algorithms with platforms, security is paramount. Most trading platforms require some form of authentication, such as API keys, OAuth tokens, or even multi-factor authentication (MFA). Ensuring secure communication and data handling is crucial to protect your trading operations.

1.API Key Management:

- Store API keys securely using environment variables or secure vault services. Avoid hardcoding sensitive information directly into your code.

` ` `rust

```
use std::env;

fn main() {
```

```rust
let api_key = env::var("API_KEY").expect("API_KEY not set");
println!("API Key: {}", api_key);
}
```

By using environment variables, you can keep your API keys secure and manage them more easily across different deployment environments.

2.Encrypted Communication:

- Use HTTPS for REST APIs and secure WebSocket connections (wss://) to ensure data encryption in transit.

Order Execution and Management

Efficient order execution and management are the backbones of successful algorithmic trading. Integrating with trading platforms involves not only placing orders but also managing them post-execution.

1.Placing Orders:

- Your algorithm needs to place various types of orders, such as market orders, limit orders, and stop-loss orders. Ensure your integration supports different order types and their respective parameters.

```rust
extern crate reqwest;

use std::collections::HashMap;
```

```rust
async fn place_limit_order(api_url: &str, api_key: &str,
symbol: &str, quantity: u32, limit_price: f64) -> Result<(),
Box<dyn std::error::Error>> {

let client = reqwest::Client::new();

let mut order_data = HashMap::new();

order_data.insert("symbol", symbol);

order_data.insert("quantity", &quantity.to_string());

order_data.insert("type", "limit");

order_data.insert("limit_price", &limit_price.to_string());


let res = client.post(api_url)

.header("API-KEY", api_key)

.json(&order_data)

.send()

.await?;


println!("Limit Order Response: {:?}", res);

Ok(())

}


#[tokio::main]

async fn main() {

let api_url = "https://api.tradingplatform.com/v1/orders";

let api_key = "your_api_key_here";


match place_limit_order(api_url, api_key, "AAPL", 10,
150.0).await {
```

```rust
    Ok(_) => println!("Limit order placed successfully."),
    Err(e) => println!("Failed to place limit order: {:?}", e),
    }
}
```
` ` `

2.Order Status and Management:

- Continuously monitor the status of placed orders to handle partial fills, cancellations, and executions. Implementing a robust order management system ensures your algorithm can adapt to changes in order status dynamically.

` ` `rust

```rust
extern crate reqwest;

async fn check_order_status(api_url: &str, api_key: &str, order_id: &str) -> Result<(), Box<dyn std::error::Error>> {
let client = reqwest::Client::new();
let res = client.get(format!("{}/{}", api_url, order_id))
.header("API-KEY", api_key)
.send()
.await?;

let order_status: serde_json::Value = res.json().await?;
println!("Order Status: {:?}", order_status);
Ok(())
}
```

```
#[tokio::main]
async fn main() {
let api_url = "https://api.tradingplatform.com/v1/orders";
let api_key = "your_api_key_here";
let order_id = "your_order_id_here";

match check_order_status(api_url, api_key, order_id).await {
Ok(_) => println!("Order status checked successfully."),
Err(e) => println!("Failed to check order status: {:?}", e),
}
}
```

This code snippet checks the status of an order by querying the trading platform's API. By continuously monitoring order status, your algorithm can manage trades more effectively.

Data Integration

Access to real-time and historical market data is essential for developing and backtesting algorithms. Trading platforms provide data through various channels, including REST APIs, WebSockets, and proprietary data feeds.

1.Real-time Market Data:

- Subscribe to market data streams to receive live updates on prices, volumes, and other relevant metrics.

```rust
use tokio_tungstenite::connect_async;
use url::Url;

#[tokio::main]
async fn main() {
let url = Url::parse("wss://api.tradingplatform.com/marketdata").unwrap();
let (mut socket, response) = connect_async(url).await.expect("Failed to connect");

println!("Connected to the market data stream: {:?}", response);

while let Some(message) = socket.next().await {
match message {
Ok(msg) => println!("Market Data: {:?}", msg),
Err(e) => println!("Error: {:?}", e),
}
}
}
```

2.Historical Data:

- Fetch historical data for backtesting your algorithms. Use REST APIs to download data in various formats (e.g., JSON, CSV).

```rust
extern crate reqwest;

async fn fetch_historical_data(api_url: &str, api_key: &str, symbol: &str) -> Result<(), Box<dyn std::error::Error>> {
let client = reqwest::Client::new();
let res = client.get(format!("{}/historical/{}", api_url, symbol))
.header("API-KEY", api_key)
.send()
.await?;

let historical_data: serde_json::Value = res.json().await?;
println!("Historical Data: {:?}", historical_data);
Ok(())
}

#[tokio::main]
async fn main() {
let api_url = "https://api.tradingplatform.com/v1/data";
let api_key = "your_api_key_here";
let symbol = "AAPL";

match fetch_historical_data(api_url, api_key, symbol).await {
Ok(_) => println!("Historical data fetched successfully."),
Err(e) => println!("Failed to fetch historical data: {:?}", e),
}
}
```

```
}
` ` `
```

Performance and Latency Considerations

In algorithmic trading, performance and low latency are crucial. Rust's high performance and concurrency capabilities make it an ideal choice for developing low-latency trading systems. When integrating with trading platforms, consider the following:

1.Network Latency:

- Minimize network latency by co-locating your trading servers close to the trading platform's data centers. Use low-latency network protocols and optimize your network stack.

2.Efficient Data Processing:

- Process market data and orders efficiently using Rust's concurrency features, such as async/await, and leveraging multi-threading where appropriate.

```rust
use tokio::task;
use tokio::time::{sleep, Duration};

async fn process_market_data(data: Vec<u8>) {
// Simulate data processing
sleep(Duration::from_millis(10)).await;
println!("Processed market data: {:?}", data);
```

```
}

#[tokio::main]
async fn main() {
let market_data = vec![1, 2, 3, 4, 5];

let handles: Vec<_> = (0..5)
.map(|_| {
let data = market_data.clone();
task::spawn(async move {
process_market_data(data).await;
})
})
.collect();

for handle in handles {
handle.await.unwrap();
}
}
```
` ` `

This example demonstrates how to process market data concurrently, reducing the time taken for data processing and decision-making.

Best Practices for Integration

1.Robust Error Handling:

- Implement robust error handling to manage API rate limits, connection timeouts, and other potential issues.

```rust
extern crate reqwest;

async fn fetch_api_data(api_url: &str, api_key: &str) -> Result<serde_json::Value, reqwest::Error> {
let client = reqwest::Client::new();
let res = client.get(api_url)
.header("API-KEY", api_key)
.send()
.await?;

if res.status().is_success() {
let data = res.json::<serde_json::Value>().await?;
Ok(data)
} else {
Err(reqwest::Error::new(reqwest::StatusCode::from(res.status()), res.text().await?))
}
}

#[tokio::main]
async fn main() {
let api_url = "https://api.tradingplatform.com/v1/data";
let api_key = "your_api_key_here";
```

```
match fetch_api_data(api_url, api_key).await {
Ok(data) => println!("Fetched data: {:?}", data),
Err(e) => println!("Failed to fetch data: {:?}", e),
}
}
` ` `
```

2.Scalability:

- Design your integration to be scalable, enabling your system to handle increased trading volumes and data feeds without compromising performance.

3.Documentation and Testing:

- Thoroughly document your integration processes and perform extensive testing to ensure reliability and robustness in real-world scenarios.

Performance Monitoring and Optimization

Performance monitoring involves continuously tracking the execution and performance metrics of your trading algorithms. This process is essential for identifying bottlenecks, understanding system behavior under different market conditions, and ensuring that your algorithms are functioning as intended.

Key Performance Metrics

1.Latency: The time delay between the occurrence of a market event and the execution of a corresponding trading action. Low latency is critical for high-frequency trading strategies.

2.Throughput: The number of transactions processed per unit of time. High throughput indicates that your system can handle large volumes of trading activity efficiently.

3.Resource Utilization: The consumption of system resources such as CPU, memory, and network bandwidth. Monitoring resource utilization helps in identifying overuse and preventing system crashes.

4.Error Rates: The frequency of errors or failures in the system. High error rates can indicate issues with data handling, external API interactions, or internal logic.

Tools for Performance Monitoring

Several tools and libraries can aid in monitoring the performance of Rust-based trading systems:

1.Metrics Collection:

- Libraries such as `prometheus` and `metrics` provide easy integration for collecting and exposing performance metrics.

```rust
use metrics::{histogram, increment_counter};

pub fn monitor_order_processing_time(duration: f64) {
histogram!("order_processing_time", duration);
}

pub fn increment_order_count() {
```

```rust
increment_counter!("order_count");
}
```

Here, we use the `metrics` library to monitor the processing time of orders and increment the order count. These metrics can be exposed to a monitoring system like Prometheus for visualization and analysis.

2.Logging:

- Comprehensive logging is essential for debugging and performance monitoring. The `log` and `env_logger` crates are commonly used for logging in Rust applications.

```rust
#[macro_use]
extern crate log;
extern crate env_logger;

fn main() {
env_logger::init();
info!("Application started");
warn!("This is a warning message");
error!("This is an error message");
}
```

Logging critical events and performance data helps in

understanding the system's behavior and diagnosing issues.

3.Profiling:

- Profiling tools such as `perf` and `criterion` can be used to analyze the performance of your Rust code in detail.

```rust
#[macro_use]
extern crate criterion;
use criterion::{Criterion, black_box};

fn fibonacci(n: u64) -> u64 {
match n {
0 => 0,
1 => 1,
n => fibonacci(n-1) + fibonacci(n-2),
}
}

fn criterion_benchmark(c: &mut Criterion) {
c.bench_function("fibonacci 20", |b| b.iter(|| fibonacci(black_box(20))));
}

criterion_group!(benches, criterion_benchmark);
criterion_main!(benches);
```

This example shows how to use `criterion` to benchmark a Fibonacci function. Profiling helps identify slow code paths and optimize performance-critical sections.

Techniques for Performance Optimization

Once you have identified performance bottlenecks through monitoring, the next step is to optimize your trading algorithms. Various techniques can be applied to enhance the performance of Rust-based trading systems:

1.Algorithmic Optimization:

- Review and optimize the core algorithms to reduce complexity and improve efficiency. For example, replacing $O(n^2)$ algorithms with $O(n \log n)$ algorithms can yield significant performance gains.

2.Memory Management:

- Efficient memory management is crucial for performance. Rust's ownership and borrowing system helps in preventing memory leaks, but additional techniques such as pooling and reusing objects can further optimize memory usage.

```rust
struct Order {
id: u64,
symbol: String,
quantity: u32,
}
```

```rust
struct OrderPool {
pool: Vec<Order>,
}

impl OrderPool {
fn new() -> Self {
OrderPool { pool: Vec::new() }
}

fn get_order(&mut self) -> Order {
self.pool.pop().unwrap_or(Order {
id: 0,
symbol: String::new(),
quantity: 0,
})
}

fn return_order(&mut self, order: Order) {
self.pool.push(order);
}
}
```

This example demonstrates a simple object pool for reusing `Order` objects, reducing the overhead of frequent allocations and deallocations.

3.Concurrency and Parallelism:

- Leveraging Rust's concurrency features, such as threads and async/await, can improve the throughput and responsiveness of your trading system.

```rust
use tokio::task;

async fn process_order(order: Order) {
// Simulate order processing
}

#[tokio::main]
async fn main() {
let orders = vec![/* orders to process */];

let handles: Vec<_> = orders.into_iter()
.map(|order| task::spawn(process_order(order)))
.collect();

for handle in handles {
handle.await.unwrap();
}
}
```

Processing orders concurrently can significantly enhance the system's ability to handle large volumes of trading activity.

4.Network Optimization:

- Optimize network communication by reducing latency and minimizing data transfer overhead. This can be achieved by using efficient network protocols, compressing data, and reducing the frequency of network requests.

5.Caching:

- Implementing caching strategies for frequently accessed data can reduce the need for repetitive computations and external data fetches.

```rust
use std::collections::HashMap;

struct Cache {
store: HashMap<String, f64>,
}

impl Cache {
fn new() -> Self {
Cache { store: HashMap::new() }
}

fn get(&self, key: &str) -> Option<&f64> {
self.store.get(key)
}
```

```
fn set(&mut self, key: String, value: f64) {
self.store.insert(key, value);
}
}
```
` ` `

A simple in-memory cache can store the results of expensive computations or frequently accessed data, reducing the need for redundant processing.

Continuous Improvement and Adaptation

Performance optimization is an ongoing process. As market conditions and trading volumes change, continuous monitoring and adaptation are necessary to maintain optimal performance. Regularly review and update your performance monitoring and optimization strategies to keep your trading algorithms competitive.

1.Regular Audits:

- Conduct regular performance audits to identify new bottlenecks and areas for improvement. Use the insights gained from monitoring to inform your optimization efforts.

2.Adaptive Algorithms:

- Develop adaptive algorithms that can adjust their behavior based on real-time performance metrics. For example, dynamically adjusting the frequency of data polling based on network latency can improve overall system performance.

3.Feedback Loops:

- Implement feedback loops that use performance data to automatically tune system parameters. This can help in maintaining optimal performance without manual intervention.

Performance monitoring and optimization are critical for the success of Rust-based algorithmic trading systems. By continuously tracking key performance metrics, leveraging the right tools for monitoring and profiling, and applying effective optimization techniques, you can ensure that your trading algorithms are both efficient and reliable. As you navigate the dynamic landscape of financial markets, maintaining a robust performance monitoring and optimization framework will enable you to capitalize on market opportunities with precision and confidence.

CHAPTER 5: ADVANCED RUST PROGRAMMING FOR FINANCE

T he Rust ecosystem is rich with crates that cater to a multitude of needs. From mathematical computations to data manipulation, crates offer reusable code that simplifies complex tasks. Crates are hosted on crates.io, the official Rust package registry, where you can browse and integrate them into your projects effortlessly.

For instance, the `nalgebra` crate is indispensable for numerical linear algebra computations, a cornerstone in financial modeling and quantitative analysis. Similarly, the `serde` crate provides powerful serialization and deserialization capabilities, essential for handling financial data formats.

Setting Up Your Project with Crates

To begin utilizing crates, you need to configure your

project's `Cargo.toml` file. This file manages your project's dependencies and other metadata. Here's a step-by-step guide to incorporating crates into your Rust project.

1.Initialize a New Project:

` ` `bash

cargo new options_trading

cd options_trading

` ` `

2.Edit `Cargo.toml`:

Open the `Cargo.toml` file and add the desired crate dependencies. For our purposes, let's add `nalgebra` and `serde`.

` ` `toml

[dependencies]

nalgebra = "0.29"

serde = { version = "1.0", features = ["derive"] }

` ` `

3.Run `cargo build`:

This command fetches the crates from crates.io and compiles them along with your project.

` ` `bash

cargo build

` ` `

Implementing Financial Models with Crates

Now that we have integrated our dependencies, let's explore how these crates enhance functionality. Consider implementing a simple Black-Scholes option pricing model using the `nalgebra` crate for matrix operations and the `serde` crate for handling input/output.

1. Matrix Operations with `nalgebra`:

```rust
extern crate nalgebra as na;

use na::{DMatrix};

fn calculate_option_price() {
// Example matrix for financial computations
let matrix = DMatrix::from_row_slice(3, 3, &[
1.0, 2.0, 3.0,
4.0, 5.0, 6.0,
7.0, 8.0, 9.0,
]);

println!("Matrix:\n{}", matrix);
}

fn main() {
calculate_option_price();
```

```
}
` ` `
```

This simple example demonstrates how to create and manipulate matrices, which can be extended to complex financial models involving covariance matrices or portfolio optimization.

2.Data Serialization with `serde`:

```rust
extern crate serde;
#[macro_use]
extern crate serde_derive;
extern crate serde_json;

#[derive(Serialize, Deserialize)]
struct OptionData {
symbol: String,
strike: f64,
expiration: String,
}

fn main() {
// Serialize data
let option = OptionData {
symbol: String::from("AAPL"),
strike: 150.0,
```

```
expiration: String::from("2022-12-31"),
};

let serialized = serde_json::to_string(&option).unwrap();
println!("Serialized: {}", serialized);

// Deserialize data
let             deserialized:          OptionData          =
serde_json::from_str(&serialized).unwrap();
println!("Deserialized: {:?}", deserialized);
}
```
` ` `

In financial applications, managing data input/output efficiently is crucial. The `serde` crate allows you to serialize data structures to JSON, facilitating easy data exchange between systems and storage formats.

Advanced Usage and Best Practices

While the basic usage of crates is relatively straightforward, mastering advanced functionalities and best practices can elevate your projects. Here are some tips:

1.Dependency Management:

Regularly update your crates to benefit from the latest features and security patches. Use `cargo update` to upgrade dependencies.

2.Feature Flags:

Some crates offer feature flags to enable only the parts of the crate you need, reducing the binary size and improving performance. For example, `serde` uses feature flags for derive macros.

3.Documentation and Community Support:

Leverage the extensive documentation and active community support available for most crates. The Rust community is known for its collaborative spirit, and you can often find solutions to common issues on forums like the Rust Users Forum or Stack Overflow.

4.Modular Design:

Structure your code to be modular, allowing easy integration of different crates. This approach enhances code readability and maintainability, making it easier to manage large projects.

Crates are an indispensable part of Rust programming, especially in the context of developing sophisticated financial applications. By harnessing the power of crates like `nalgebra` and `serde`, you can streamline your development process, enhance functionality, and ensure that your applications are both robust and performant. As you continue to explore the Rust ecosystem, you'll find that the versatility and power of crates will significantly amplify your capabilities as a developer in the financial domain.

Leveraging Concurrency and Parallelism

Before diving into Rust's specific tools, it's crucial

to understand the difference between concurrency and parallelism. Concurrency involves managing multiple tasks at the same time, allowing them to make progress without necessarily running simultaneously. Parallelism, on the other hand, refers to executing multiple tasks simultaneously to leverage multi-core processors.

In financial applications, concurrency is essential for tasks such as handling multiple data streams or executing trades concurrently. Parallelism can be used to distribute computationally intensive tasks like option pricing models or backtesting strategies across multiple cores, significantly speeding up execution.

Concurrency in Rust: The Basics

Rust's concurrency model is built on the principles of safety and performance. The language's ownership system ensures that data races are impossible, making concurrent programming safer and more predictable. Rust provides several tools for concurrency, including threads, async programming, and channels for communication between threads.

Using Threads

Threads are the basic unit of concurrent execution in Rust. The `std::thread` module provides the tools to create and manage threads. Here's a simple example demonstrating how to spawn threads in Rust:

```rust
```

```rust
use std::thread;
use std::time::Duration;

fn main() {
let handle = thread::spawn(|| {
for i in 1..5 {
println!("Thread: {}", i);
thread::sleep(Duration::from_millis(100));
}
});

for i in 1..5 {
println!("Main: {}", i);
thread::sleep(Duration::from_millis(50));
}

handle.join().unwrap();
}
```
` ` `

In this example, a new thread is spawned to execute a series of print statements. The main thread continues its execution independently, demonstrating how tasks can progress concurrently.

Asynchronous Programming

For IO-bound tasks, asynchronous programming can be more

efficient than threads. Rust's `async` and `await` keywords, along with the `tokio` and `async-std` crates, provide powerful abstractions for writing asynchronous code.

Here's an example of asynchronous programming using the `tokio` crate:

```rust
use tokio::time::{sleep, Duration};

#[tokio::main]
async fn main() {
let handle = tokio::spawn(async {
for i in 1..5 {
println!("Async Task: {}", i);
sleep(Duration::from_millis(100)).await;
}
});

for i in 1..5 {
println!("Main Task: {}", i);
sleep(Duration::from_millis(50)).await;
}

handle.await.unwrap();
}
```

In this example, an asynchronous task is spawned using `tokio::spawn`. The `sleep` function from the `tokio::time` module is used to simulate asynchronous delays, allowing other tasks to run during the wait period.

Parallelism with the Rayon Crate

For computationally intensive tasks, parallelism can drastically reduce execution time. The `rayon` crate is a powerful tool for data parallelism in Rust, allowing you to parallelize collections and iterators easily.

Parallel Iterators

The `rayon` crate provides parallel iterators that can process elements in parallel. Here's an example demonstrating how to use parallel iterators to speed up computations:

```rust
use rayon::prelude::*;

fn main() {
let data = vec![1, 2, 3, 4, 5, 6, 7, 8, 9, 10];

let result: i32 = data.par_iter()
.map(|&x| x * x)
.sum();

println!("Sum of squares: {}", result);
```

```
}
` ` `
```

In this example, the `par_iter` method is used to create a parallel iterator over the data vector. The `map` function applies a computation to each element, and `sum` aggregates the results. This code leverages multiple cores to perform the computations concurrently.

Applying Concurrency and Parallelism to Financial Models

Now, let's apply these concepts to a practical financial application. Consider a scenario where we need to price a large number of options using the Black-Scholes model. The computation for each option is independent, making it an ideal candidate for parallel execution.

Parallel Option Pricing

Here's an example of how to parallelize the Black-Scholes option pricing using the `rayon` crate:

```rust
use rayon::prelude::*;
use std::f64::consts::E;

fn black_scholes(price: f64, strike: f64, time: f64, rate: f64, volatility: f64) -> f64 {
let d1 = (price / strike).ln() + (rate + 0.5 * volatility.powi(2)) * time;
```

```rust
let d2 = d1 - volatility * time.sqrt();
price * norm_cdf(d1) - strike * (E.powf(-rate * time)) * norm_cdf(d2)
}

fn norm_cdf(x: f64) -> f64 {
(1.0 + (x / (2.0_f64).sqrt()).erf()) / 2.0
}

fn main() {
let options = vec![
(50.0, 55.0, 1.0, 0.05, 0.2),
(60.0, 65.0, 0.5, 0.03, 0.25),
// More options
];

let prices: Vec<f64> = options.par_iter()
.map(|&(price, strike, time, rate, volatility)| {
black_scholes(price, strike, time, rate, volatility)
})
.collect();

for price in prices {
println!("Option price: {}", price);
}
}
```
```
```

In this example, the `par_iter` method is used to create a parallel iterator over the list of options. The `map` function applies the Black-Scholes pricing model to each option, and `collect` gathers the results into a vector. This approach leverages multiple cores to price options concurrently, significantly speeding up the computation.

Best Practices for Concurrency and Parallelism

To maximize the benefits of concurrency and parallelism in your Rust applications, consider the following best practices:

1.Avoid Data Races:

Rust's ownership system and borrow checker make it difficult to introduce data races, but you should still be cautious when sharing data between threads. Use synchronization primitives like `Mutex` and `RwLock` when necessary.

2.Minimize Lock Contention:

Use fine-grained locking to minimize contention and improve performance. Where possible, prefer lock-free data structures and algorithms.

3.Leverage Async for IO-bound Tasks:

For tasks that involve waiting on IO, such as network requests or file operations, use asynchronous programming to keep your application responsive and efficient.

4.Profile and Optimize:

Use profiling tools to identify bottlenecks in your code.

Optimize critical sections to ensure that your application takes full advantage of concurrent and parallel execution.

5.Test Thoroughly:

Concurrent and parallel code can be challenging to test. Use tools like `cargo test` and `loom` to write comprehensive tests that cover edge cases and potential race conditions.

Leveraging concurrency and parallelism in Rust can significantly enhance the performance and responsiveness of your financial applications. By understanding and applying Rust's concurrency tools, such as threads, async programming, and the `rayon` crate, you can build sophisticated, high-performance systems that excel in the demanding world of algorithmic trading. As you continue to explore and refine these techniques, you'll discover new ways to optimize and innovate, driving forward the capabilities of Rust in the financial domain.

Rust for High-Frequency Trading

The Need for Speed: Latency Optimization

In HFT, latency—the time delay between receiving market data and executing a trade—is critical. Lower latency means faster reaction times to market events, offering a competitive edge. Rust's system-level control and performance characteristics make it an excellent choice for minimizing latency.

Low-Level Control

Rust provides fine-grained control over system resources, enabling developers to optimize for speed. Features like zero-cost abstractions ensure that high-level constructs incur no runtime cost, maintaining performance at the system level.

To illustrate, consider the need for precise time measurements. Rust's `std::time` module provides tools for high-resolution timing:

```rust
use std::time::Instant;

fn main() {
let now = Instant::now();

// Perform some high-frequency trading tasks here
do_hft_task();

let elapsed = now.elapsed();
println!("Elapsed time: {:.2?}", elapsed);
}

fn do_hft_task() {
// Simulate a high-frequency trading task
for _ in 0..1000 {
// trading logic
```

```
}
}
` ` `
```

Using `Instant::now` and `elapsed`, you can measure and optimize the execution time of critical sections in your HFT system.

Real-Time Data Handling

Handling real-time data efficiently is paramount in HFT. Rust's concurrency features, such as async programming and channels, enable responsive, non-blocking data processing. Consider using the `tokio` crate for handling asynchronous tasks:

```rust
use tokio::net::TcpStream;
use tokio::io::{self, AsyncReadExt, AsyncWriteExt};

#[tokio::main]
async fn main() -> io::Result<()> {
let mut stream = TcpStream::connect("127.0.0.1:8080").await?;

let (mut reader, mut writer) = stream.split();

tokio::spawn(async move {
let mut buf = vec![0; 1024];
```

```
loop {
let n = reader.read(&mut buf).await.unwrap();
if n == 0 {
break;
}
println!("Received: {:?}", &buf[..n]);
}
});

writer.write_all(b"Hello world!").await?;
Ok(())
}
` ` `
```

This example demonstrates how to handle real-time data streams asynchronously, ensuring that your HFT system remains responsive and efficient.

Ensuring Reliability and Safety

In the high-stakes world of HFT, reliability is as crucial as speed. Rust's strong type system and ownership model provide guarantees that help prevent common bugs and runtime errors, such as data races and memory leaks.

Data Races and Ownership

Rust's ownership model ensures memory safety without a garbage collector, preventing data races at compile time. When developing HFT systems, where multiple threads may access shared data, Rust's ownership and borrowing rules provide a solid foundation for safe concurrency.

Consider the following example using `Mutex` for shared state:

```rust
use std::sync::{Arc, Mutex};
use std::thread;

fn main() {
let data = Arc::new(Mutex::new(0));
let mut handles = vec![];

for _ in 0..10 {
let data = Arc::clone(&data);
handles.push(thread::spawn(move || {
let mut num = data.lock().unwrap();
*num += 1;
}));
}

for handle in handles {
handle.join().unwrap();
}

println!("Result: {}", *data.lock().unwrap());
```

```
}
```
` ` `

Using `Arc` and `Mutex`, this code safely shares and modifies state across multiple threads, ensuring data consistency without risking data races.

Leveraging Concurrency and Parallelism

As discussed previously, Rust's concurrency and parallelism capabilities are a key advantage in HFT. Utilizing threads and parallel iterators can significantly speed up computations and data processing.

Example: Parallel Order Matching

Consider a scenario where you need to match buy and sell orders concurrently. Using the `rayon` crate, you can process these orders in parallel:

` ` `rust

```rust
use rayon::prelude::*;
use std::sync::mpsc::{channel, Receiver};

fn main() {
let (tx, rx) = channel();

let buy_orders = vec![Order::new(50.0, 100), Order::new(51.0, 200)];
let sell_orders = vec![Order::new(49.0, 100), Order::new(48.0,
```

```
200)];

let orders = vec![buy_orders, sell_orders];

orders.into_par_iter().for_each_with(tx, |s, order_list| {
for order in order_list {
s.send(process_order(order)).unwrap();
}
});

process_results(rx);
}

fn process_order(order: Order) -> Result {
// Simulate processing an order
Result::new(order.price, order.quantity)
}

fn process_results(rx: Receiver<Result>) {
for result in rx {
println!("Processed result: {:?}", result);
}
}

#[derive(Debug)]
struct Order {
price: f64,
```

```
quantity: u32,
}

impl Order {
fn new(price: f64, quantity: u32) -> Self {
Order { price, quantity }
}
}

#[derive(Debug)]
struct Result {
price: f64,
quantity: u32,
}

impl Result {
fn new(price: f64, quantity: u32) -> Self {
Result { price, quantity }
}
}
```
```

In this example, `par_iter` is used to process buy and sell orders in parallel, leveraging multi-core processors to enhance performance. The results are sent through a channel and processed sequentially.

Profiling and Performance Optimization
```

Profiling tools are essential for identifying and eliminating performance bottlenecks in your HFT system. Rust provides various tools for profiling and benchmarking.

Using `cargo bench`

You can use the `cargo bench` command to run benchmarks and analyze performance:

```rust
#[macro_use]
extern crate criterion;
use criterion::Criterion;

fn fibonacci(n: u64) -> u64 {
match n {
0 => 0,
1 => 1,
n => fibonacci(n - 1) + fibonacci(n - 2),
}
}

fn criterion_benchmark(c: &mut Criterion) {
c.bench_function("fib 20", |b| b.iter(|| fibonacci(20)));
}

criterion_group!(benches, criterion_benchmark);
```

```
criterion_main!(benches);
```
` ` `

This example benchmarks the ` fibonacci ` function, providing insights into its performance characteristics and potential optimization opportunities.

Real-World Application: HFT System Architecture

Building a complete HFT system involves integrating various components—data acquisition, order management, risk management, and execution. Rust's ecosystem offers the tools and libraries needed to develop these components efficiently.

Data Acquisition

Real-time market data is the lifeblood of HFT. Using Rust's networking capabilities, you can build efficient data acquisition systems that handle high volumes of market data with minimal latency.

Order Management

Managing orders involves tracking their status, matching them against market conditions, and executing trades. Rust's concurrency model ensures that these operations can be performed safely and efficiently.

Risk Management

Risk management is crucial in HFT to prevent significant

losses due to market volatility. Rust's strong type system and compile-time checks help ensure that risk management algorithms are robust and error-free.

Execution

Finally, executing trades with minimal latency is essential for HFT success. Rust's performance characteristics make it an ideal choice for developing low-latency execution systems.

Rust's powerful concurrency and parallelism features, combined with its system-level control and safety guarantees, make it a formidable tool for high-frequency trading. By leveraging Rust's capabilities, you can build HFT systems that are not only fast and efficient but also reliable and safe. As you continue to explore and refine your HFT strategies, Rust will be a valuable ally in your quest for trading excellence.

Efficient Data Storage: HashMaps and BTreeMaps

Two fundamental data structures for storing and querying associative data are HashMaps and BTreeMaps. In financial applications, these structures are often used for storing key-value pairs such as ticker symbols and their corresponding prices, or dates and their associated market data.

Using HashMaps

HashMaps provide average O(1) time complexity for insertions, deletions, and lookups, making them ideal for scenarios where fast access is required. Here's how you can use HashMaps in Rust:

```rust
use std::collections::HashMap;

fn main() {
let mut stock_prices = HashMap::new();
stock_prices.insert("AAPL", 150.0);
stock_prices.insert("MSFT", 250.0);
stock_prices.insert("GOOG", 2800.0);

match stock_prices.get("AAPL") {
Some(price) => println!("The price of AAPL is ${}", price),
None => println!("Stock not found"),
}
}
```

In this example, `HashMap::new` creates a new HashMap, and `insert` adds key-value pairs. The `get` method retrieves the value associated with a key, allowing for fast data access.

Using BTreeMaps

BTreeMaps, on the other hand, offer ordered storage with O(log n) time complexity for insertions, deletions, and lookups. They are beneficial when maintaining a sorted order of elements is necessary, such as in time-series data.

```rust
```

```rust
use std::collections::BTreeMap;

fn main() {
let mut market_data = BTreeMap::new();
market_data.insert("2023-01-01", 150.0);
market_data.insert("2023-01-02", 153.0);
market_data.insert("2023-01-03", 148.0);

for (date, price) in &market_data {
println!("On {}, the price was ${}", date, price);
}
}
```

Here, `BTreeMap::new` initializes a BTreeMap, and `insert` ensures that the data remains ordered by date. Iterating over the BTreeMap maintains the sorted order, which is useful for time-series analysis.

Handling Large Data Sets: Vectors and Deques

Vectors and Deques are dynamic arrays that allow for efficient access and manipulation of data. In financial applications, these data structures are often used to store large datasets such as historical price data or trade logs.

Vectors

Vectors provide O(1) time complexity for accessing elements

and O(n) for insertions and deletions. They are suitable for scenarios where data access is more frequent than modifications.

```rust
fn main() {
let mut prices: Vec<f64> = vec![150.0, 152.0, 148.0, 155.0];
prices.push(153.0);

for price in &prices {
println!("Price: ${}", price);
}

let average_price: f64 = prices.iter().sum::<f64>() / prices.len() as f64;
println!("Average Price: ${}", average_price);
}
```

In this example, `vec!` initializes a Vector, and `push` adds a new element. Iterating over the Vector and calculating the average price demonstrates the efficient access and manipulation of data.

Deques

Deques (double-ended queues) provide O(1) time complexity for both insertions and deletions at both ends. They are useful for applications that require frequent additions and removals from both ends, such as maintaining a sliding window of recent prices.

```rust
use std::collections::VecDeque;

fn main() {
let mut recent_trades: VecDeque<f64> = VecDeque::new();
recent_trades.push_back(150.0);
recent_trades.push_back(152.0);
recent_trades.push_back(148.0);

recent_trades.push_front(153.0);
recent_trades.pop_back();

for trade in &recent_trades {
println!("Recent Trade: ${}", trade);
}
}
```

Here, `VecDeque::new` creates a new deque, and `push_back`, `push_front`, and `pop_back` demonstrate the efficient addition and removal of elements from both ends.

Advanced Data Structures: Trees and Graphs

For more complex financial applications, advanced data structures such as trees and graphs are often required. These structures enable sophisticated data modeling and efficient algorithm implementation.

Binary Trees

Binary trees are used for hierarchical data storage and fast searching. In financial applications, they can be used for building decision trees for trading strategies or storing hierarchical market data.

```rust
#[derive(Debug)]
struct Node {
value: f64,
left: Option<Box<Node>>,
right: Option<Box<Node>>,
}

impl Node {
fn new(value: f64) -> Self {
Node { value, left: None, right: None }
}

fn insert(&mut self, value: f64) {
if value < self.value {
match self.left {
Some(ref mut left) => left.insert(value),
None => self.left = Some(Box::new(Node::new(value))),
```

```
}
} else {
match self.right {
Some(ref mut right) => right.insert(value),
None => self.right = Some(Box::new(Node::new(value))),
}
}
}
}

fn main() {
let mut root = Node::new(150.0);
root.insert(148.0);
root.insert(152.0);
root.insert(145.0);

println!("{:#?}", root);
}
` ` `
```

This code defines a binary tree with insertion logic, allowing hierarchical storage and fast searching of values.

Graphs

Graphs are essential for representing relationships between entities in financial networks, such as influence networks or transaction graphs. Rust's `petgraph` crate provides comprehensive support for graph operations.

```rust
use petgraph::graph::{Graph, NodeIndex};
use petgraph::algo::dijkstra;

fn main() {
let mut graph = Graph::new();
let a = graph.add_node("A");
let b = graph.add_node("B");
let c = graph.add_node("C");
let d = graph.add_node("D");

graph.add_edge(a, b, 1);
graph.add_edge(b, c, 2);
graph.add_edge(c, d, 1);
graph.add_edge(a, d, 4);

let start = a;
let end = d;
let result = dijkstra(&graph, start, Some(end), |e| *e.weight());

println!("{:?}", result);
}
```

This example demonstrates how to create a graph, add nodes

and edges, and perform Dijkstra's algorithm to find the shortest path between nodes.

Practical Application: Portfolio Optimization with Advanced Data Structures

Advanced data structures are instrumental in implementing complex algorithms for portfolio optimization. For example, using a binary tree to store and search for optimal asset combinations can significantly speed up the optimization process.

```rust
use std::cmp::Ordering;

#[derive(Debug, Clone)]
struct Portfolio {
assets: Vec<f64>,
expected_return: f64,
}

impl Portfolio {
fn new(assets: Vec<f64>, expected_return: f64) -> Self {
Portfolio { assets, expected_return }
}
}

impl Ord for Portfolio {
fn cmp(&self, other: &Self) -> Ordering {
```

```
self.expected_return.partial_cmp(&other.expected_return).un
wrap()
}
}

impl PartialOrd for Portfolio {
fn partial_cmp(&self, other: &Self) -> Option<Ordering> {
Some(self.cmp(other))
}
}

impl Eq for Portfolio {}

impl PartialEq for Portfolio {
fn eq(&self, other: &Self) -> bool {
self.expected_return == other.expected_return
}
}

fn main() {
let portfolios = vec![
Portfolio::new(vec![0.1, 0.2, 0.3], 0.05),
Portfolio::new(vec![0.4, 0.3, 0.2], 0.06),
Portfolio::new(vec![0.3, 0.3, 0.2], 0.07),
];

let mut tree = std::collections::BinaryHeap::from(portfolios);
```

```
while let Some(portfolio) = tree.pop() {
println!("Optimized Portfolio: {:?}", portfolio);
}
}
` ` `
```

Here, a binary heap is used to maintain a priority queue of portfolios, facilitating efficient retrieval of the portfolio with the highest expected return.

Advanced data structures are indispensable in financial applications, enabling efficient data storage, retrieval, and processing. Rust's powerful type system and ownership model, combined with its rich standard library and ecosystem, provide the tools necessary to implement these data structures effectively. Whether you are managing large datasets, performing complex calculations, or optimizing portfolios, Rust ensures that your operations are both fast and safe. Embrace these advanced data structures to enhance the performance and reliability of your financial applications, and witness the transformative power of Rust in action.

Serialization and Deserialization of Financial Data

Serialization is the process of converting a data structure into a format that can be easily stored or transmitted, such as JSON, CSV, or binary. Deserialization is the reverse process, where the serialized data is converted back into a usable data structure. These processes are essential in financial applications for tasks such as saving historical price data, transmitting real-time market data, or interfacing with external APIs.

Why Serialization Matters in Finance

-Data Persistence: Serialization allows storing complex data structures in files or databases, ensuring data persistence between sessions.

-Data Transmission: Serialized data can be efficiently transmitted over networks, enabling real-time data sharing between trading systems.

-Interoperability: Serialization formats like JSON and CSV are widely supported, facilitating integration with various tools and platforms.

Implementing Serialization in Rust

Rust provides powerful libraries for serialization and deserialization, such as `serde`. The `serde` library is flexible and efficient, supporting various data formats and offering customizable serialization behavior. Here's how you can leverage `serde` for financial data serialization in Rust.

Setting Up `serde`

First, add `serde` and `serde_json` to your `Cargo.toml`:

```toml
[dependencies]
serde = { version = "1.0", features = ["derive"] }
serde_json = "1.0"
```

Next, import the necessary traits and derive macros in your Rust code:

```rust
use serde::{Serialize, Deserialize};
use serde_json;
```

Serializing Financial Data to JSON

Consider a struct representing a stock's data:

```rust
#[derive(Serialize, Deserialize)]
struct Stock {
symbol: String,
price: f64,
volume: u64,
}

fn main() {
let stock = Stock {
symbol: "AAPL".to_string(),
price: 150.0,
volume: 10000,
};
```

```rust
let serialized = serde_json::to_string(&stock).unwrap();
println!("Serialized JSON: {}", serialized);
}
```

In this example, the `Stock` struct is annotated with `#[derive(Serialize, Deserialize)]` to automatically implement the necessary traits. The `serde_json::to_string` function converts the `Stock` instance into a JSON string.

Deserializing JSON to Financial Data

Deserialization is equally straightforward:

```rust
fn main() {
let data = r#"{"symbol":"AAPL","price":150.0,"volume":10000}"#;
let stock: Stock = serde_json::from_str(data).unwrap();

println!("Deserialized Stock: {:?}", stock);
}
```

Here, `serde_json::from_str` parses the JSON string and reconstructs the `Stock` instance. Rust's type safety ensures that the deserialized data matches the expected structure, preventing runtime errors.

Handling CSV Data

CSV is another common format for financial data, especially for historical price data. Rust's `csv` crate, in conjunction with `serde`, makes it easy to serialize and deserialize CSV data.

First, add the `csv` crate to your `Cargo.toml`:

```toml
[dependencies]
csv = "1.1"
```

Serializing Financial Data to CSV

Here's how to serialize a collection of stocks to CSV:

```rust
use serde::Serialize;
use csv::Writer;

#[derive(Serialize)]
struct Stock {
symbol: String,
price: f64,
volume: u64,
```

```rust
}

fn main() {
let stocks = vec![
Stock {
symbol: "AAPL".to_string(),
price: 150.0,
volume: 10000,
},
Stock {
symbol: "MSFT".to_string(),
price: 250.0,
volume: 15000,
},
];

let mut wtr = Writer::from_writer(vec![]);
for stock in stocks {
wtr.serialize(stock).unwrap();
}
let data = String::from_utf8(wtr.into_inner().unwrap()).unwrap();
println!("Serialized CSV:\n{}", data);
}
```

In this code, the `Writer` from the `csv` crate serializes

each `Stock` to a CSV format, and `serialize` handles the conversion.

Deserializing CSV to Financial Data

Deserializing CSV data involves reading the data and reconstructing the Rust structs:

```rust
use serde::Deserialize;
use csv::Reader;

#[derive(Deserialize)]
struct Stock {
symbol: String,
price: f64,
volume: u64,
}

fn main() {
let data = "\
symbol,price,volume
AAPL,150.0,10000
MSFT,250.0,15000
";
let mut rdr = Reader::from_reader(data.as_bytes());
for result in rdr.deserialize() {
```

```rust
let stock: Stock = result.unwrap();
println!("Deserialized Stock: {:?}", stock);
}
}
```
```

Here, `Reader` reads the CSV data, and `deserialize` converts each record into a `Stock` instance. This approach ensures that financial data can be efficiently loaded from CSV files.

Custom Serialization and Deserialization

In some cases, you may need custom serialization behavior. For example, you might want to serialize dates in a specific format or handle optional fields differently. Rust's `serde` library allows for custom serialization logic using the `Serialize` and `Deserialize` traits.

# Custom Serialization Example

Consider a struct with a custom date format:

```rust
use serde::{Serialize, Serializer};
use chrono::{NaiveDate, DateTime, Utc};

#[derive(Debug)]
struct Trade {
symbol: String,
```
```

```rust
date: NaiveDate,
price: f64,
}

impl Serialize for Trade {
fn serialize<S>(&self, serializer: S) -> Result<S::Ok, S::Error>
where
S: Serializer,
{
let mut state = serializer.serialize_struct("Trade", 3)?;
state.serialize_field("symbol", &self.symbol)?;
state.serialize_field("date",        &self.date.format("%Y-%m-%d").to_string())?;
state.serialize_field("price", &self.price)?;
state.end()
}
}

fn main() {
let trade = Trade {
symbol: "AAPL".to_string(),
date: NaiveDate::from_ymd(2023, 1, 1),
price: 150.0,
};

let serialized = serde_json::to_string(&trade).unwrap();
println!("Serialized Trade: {}", serialized);
```

```
}
```
` ` `

In this example, the `Serialize` trait is manually implemented for the `Trade` struct to format the date as `YYYY-MM-DD`.

Custom Deserialization Example

Custom deserialization can be similarly implemented:

```rust
use serde::{Deserialize, Deserializer};
use chrono::NaiveDate;

#[derive(Debug)]
struct Trade {
symbol: String,
date: NaiveDate,
price: f64,
}

impl<'de> Deserialize<'de> for Trade {
fn deserialize<D>(deserializer: D) -> Result<Self, D::Error>
where
D: Deserializer<'de>,
{
let mut map = std::collections::HashMap::new();
```

```rust
map.insert("symbol", "");

map.insert("date", "");

map.insert("price", "");


let helper = map;

let symbol = helper.get("symbol").unwrap().to_string();

let date = NaiveDate::parse_from_str(helper.get("date").unwrap(), "%Y-%m-%d").unwrap();

let price = helper.get("price").unwrap().parse().unwrap();


Ok(Trade { symbol, date, price })
}
}


fn main() {

let data = r#"{"symbol":"AAPL","date":"2023-01-01","price":150.0}"#;

let trade: Trade = serde_json::from_str(data).unwrap();


println!("Deserialized Trade: {:?}", trade);

}
```
` ` `

This code demonstrates how to manually implement the `Deserialize` trait to parse a custom date format during deserialization.

Serialization and deserialization are indispensable processes in financial applications, enabling efficient data storage, transmission, and interoperability. Rust, with its powerful type system and robust libraries like `serde`, provides the tools necessary to handle these processes effectively. By mastering serialization and deserialization in Rust, you can ensure that your financial data is managed efficiently and safely, facilitating seamless data exchange and persistent storage. Embrace these techniques to enhance the reliability and performance of your financial applications, and harness the full potential of Rust in the world of high-stakes trading.

Introduction to Databases

Before immersing ourselves in the Rust ecosystem, it's crucial to understand the general landscape of databases. Databases can be broadly classified into two categories: relational (SQL-based) and non-relational (NoSQL-based). Relational databases such as PostgreSQL and MySQL are structured and utilize SQL for data manipulation, ensuring data integrity through ACID (Atomicity, Consistency, Isolation, Durability) properties. Conversely, NoSQL databases like MongoDB and Redis are schema-less, offering flexibility and scalability, often at the cost of some transactional guarantees.

Rust and Databases: The Perfect Union

Rust's performance, memory safety, and concurrency make it an ideal language for building robust database interactions. Rust's ecosystem offers several libraries, known as crates, for interfacing with both SQL and NoSQL databases. These crates provide abstractions and utilities that simplify database operations, ensuring that your code remains clean, efficient, and secure.

Setting Up a Database with Rust

To begin, let's explore setting up a PostgreSQL database, a common choice for financial applications due to its robustness and feature set. We'll use the `tokio-postgres` crate, providing asynchronous support for PostgreSQL, and the `sqlx` crate, an async, compile-time checked SQL framework for Rust.

First, add the necessary dependencies to your `Cargo.toml`:

```toml
[dependencies]
tokio = { version = "1", features = ["full"] }
tokio-postgres = "0.7"
sqlx = { version = "0.5", features = ["runtime-tokio", "postgres"] }
dotenv = "0.15"
```

The `tokio` crate is essential for asynchronous programming in Rust, while `dotenv` helps manage environment variables securely.

Connecting to the Database

Next, let's establish a connection to the PostgreSQL database. Create a `.env` file to store your database credentials:

```
```

DATABASE_URL=postgres://username:password@localhost/database_name

```
```

Now, in your `main.rs`, set up the connection using `tokio-postgres`:

```rust
use tokio_postgres::NoTls;
use dotenv::dotenv;
use std::env;

#[tokio::main]
async fn main() {
dotenv().ok();
let database_url = env::var("DATABASE_URL").expect("DATABASE_URL must be set");

let (client, connection) =
tokio_postgres::connect(&database_url,
NoTls).await.expect("Failed to connect to database");

// Spawn the connection to run in the background.
tokio::spawn(async move {
if let Err(e) = connection.await {
```

```
        eprintln!("connection error: {}", e);
    }
});

let rows = client.query("SELECT now()",
&[]).await.expect("Failed to execute query");
for row in rows {
let now: chrono::NaiveDateTime = row.get(0);
println!("Current time: {}", now);
}
}
```

Here, `tokio_postgres::connect` establishes a connection to the database using credentials from the `.env` file. The connection is then spawned in the background to handle asynchronous operations.

Performing CRUD Operations

CRUD (Create, Read, Update, Delete) operations are fundamental to interacting with any database. Let's walk through these operations using the `sqlx` crate, which provides a higher-level abstraction.

Creating a Table

First, create a table to store stock data:

```rust
use sqlx::PgPool;

#[tokio::main]
async fn main() -> Result<(), sqlx::Error> {
dotenv().ok();
let database_url = env::var("DATABASE_URL")?;
let pool = PgPool::connect(&database_url).await?;

sqlx::query(
"CREATE TABLE IF NOT EXISTS stocks (
id SERIAL PRIMARY KEY,
symbol VARCHAR NOT NULL,
price DOUBLE PRECISION NOT NULL,
volume BIGINT NOT NULL
)"
).execute(&pool).await?;

Ok(())
}
```

In this code, `PgPool::connect` creates a connection pool, and `sqlx::query` executes a SQL statement to create a `stocks` table if it doesn't already exist.

Inserting Data

To insert data into the table:

```rust
use sqlx::query;

async fn insert_stock(pool: &PgPool, symbol: &str, price: f64, volume: i64) -> Result<(), sqlx::Error> {
query("INSERT INTO stocks (symbol, price, volume) VALUES ($1, $2, $3)")
.bind(symbol)
.bind(price)
.bind(volume)
.execute(pool)
.await?;
Ok(())
}
```

This function uses `query` to insert a new stock record into the `stocks` table, with `bind` used to safely pass parameters to the query.

Reading Data

To read data from the table:

```rust
```

```rust
use sqlx::FromRow;

#[derive(FromRow, Debug)]
struct Stock {
id: i32,
symbol: String,
price: f64,
volume: i64,
}

async fn fetch_stocks(pool: &PgPool) -> Result<Vec<Stock>, sqlx::Error> {
let stocks = query_as!(Stock, "SELECT id, symbol, price, volume FROM stocks")
.fetch_all(pool)
.await?;
Ok(stocks)
}
```

Here, `query_as!` fetches all records from the `stocks` table and maps them to the `Stock` struct.

Updating Data

To update existing data in the table:

```rust
```

```rust
async fn update_stock_price(pool: &PgPool, symbol: &str,
new_price: f64) -> Result<(), sqlx::Error> {
query("UPDATE stocks SET price = $1 WHERE symbol = $2")
.bind(new_price)
.bind(symbol)
.execute(pool)
.await?;
Ok(())
}
```

This function updates the price of a stock identified by its symbol.

Deleting Data

To delete data from the table:

```rust
async fn delete_stock(pool: &PgPool, symbol: &str) ->
Result<(), sqlx::Error> {
query("DELETE FROM stocks WHERE symbol = $1")
.bind(symbol)
.execute(pool)
.await?;
Ok(())
}
```

```
```

This function deletes a stock record based on the given symbol.

Working with NoSQL Databases

Rust also excels in interacting with NoSQL databases. Let's explore working with MongoDB using the `mongodb` crate, a popular NoSQL database known for its flexibility and scalability.

Setting Up MongoDB

Add the `mongodb` crate to your `Cargo.toml`:

```toml
[dependencies]
mongodb = "2.1"
tokio = { version = "1", features = ["full"] }
```

Connecting to MongoDB

Initialize a connection to the MongoDB server:

```rust
use mongodb::{Client, options::ClientOptions};
use tokio;
use dotenv::dotenv;
```

```
use std::env;

#[tokio::main]
async fn main() -> Result<(), Box<dyn std::error::Error>> {
dotenv().ok();
let                database_url                =
env::var("DATABASE_URL").expect("DATABASE_URL must be
set");

let            mut            client_options            =
ClientOptions::parse(&database_url).await?;
client_options.app_name                            =
Some("RustMongoApp".to_string());

let client = Client::with_options(client_options)?;
let database = client.database("financial_data");
let collection = database.collection("stocks");

Ok(())
}
` ` `
```

Here, `ClientOptions::parse` configures the MongoDB client, and `Client::with_options` establishes the connection.

Performing CRUD Operations with MongoDB

Inserting Data

To insert a document into the collection:

```rust
use mongodb::bson::doc;
use mongodb::Collection;

async fn insert_stock(collection: &Collection, symbol: &str, price: f64, volume: i64) -> Result<(), Box<dyn std::error::Error>> {
let stock = doc! {
"symbol": symbol,
"price": price,
"volume": volume,
};
collection.insert_one(stock, None).await?;
Ok(())
}
```

This function creates a BSON document and inserts it into the MongoDB collection.

Reading Data

To read documents from the collection:

```rust
```

```rust
use mongodb::bson::Document;
use futures::stream::StreamExt;


async fn fetch_stocks(collection: &Collection) -> Result<Vec<Document>, Box<dyn std::error::Error>> {
let mut cursor = collection.find(None, None).await?;
let mut stocks = Vec::new();
while let Some(stock) = cursor.next().await {
stocks.push(stock?);
}
Ok(stocks)
}
```

This function fetches all documents from the collection and collects them into a vector.

Updating Data

To update a document in the collection:

```rust
async fn update_stock_price(collection: &Collection, symbol: &str, new_price: f64) -> Result<(), Box<dyn std::error::Error>> {
let filter = doc! { "symbol": symbol };
let update = doc! { "$set": { "price": new_price } };
collection.update_one(filter, update, None).await?;
```

```
Ok(())
}
```
` ` `

This function updates the price of a stock document identified by its symbol.

Deleting Data

To delete a document from the collection:

` ` `rust

```
async fn delete_stock(collection: &Collection, symbol: &str) -> Result<(), Box<dyn std::error::Error>> {
let filter = doc! { "symbol": symbol };
collection.delete_one(filter, None).await?;
Ok(())
}
```
` ` `

This function deletes a stock document based on the given symbol.

Working with databases in Rust allows for building high-performance, reliable financial applications. By leveraging Rust's powerful ecosystem of crates, you can easily interact with both SQL and NoSQL databases, ensuring that your data is stored, retrieved, and manipulated efficiently and securely. Mastering these techniques will enable you to develop robust trading systems that can handle the complexities and demands of modern financial markets. Embrace Rust's capabilities to enhance your database interactions, ensuring your financial applications are both performant and resilient.

Secure Coding Practices in Rust

Before delving into Rust-specific practices, it's crucial to understand the broader landscape of security in financial applications. Financial data is highly sensitive, and breaches can result in severe financial and reputational damage. Common threats include:

1.Data Breaches: Unauthorized access to sensitive data.

2.Injection Attacks: Exploiting vulnerabilities to inject malicious code.

3.Race Conditions: Concurrent processes leading to inconsistent states.

4.Unauthorized Transactions: Manipulation of trading algorithms to execute unapproved trades.

With these threats in mind, the goal is to build robust systems that can withstand and mitigate such risks.

Rust's Safety Guarantees

Rust's design philosophy inherently promotes safety and security. Its memory safety guarantees, enforced by the ownership system, prevent common vulnerabilities such as buffer overflows and use-after-free errors. Additionally, Rust's concurrency model minimizes the risk of data races, making it an ideal choice for secure financial applications.

Ownership and Borrowing

The cornerstone of Rust's safety is its ownership model, which ensures that each piece of data has a single owner, preventing dangling pointers and memory leaks. Borrowing and references provide a way to access data without transferring ownership, enforced at compile-time to avoid runtime errors.

Consider the following example where ownership and borrowing come into play:

```rust
fn main() {
let data = String::from("Financial Data");
process_data(&data); // Borrowing data
println!("{}", data); // Safe to use as ownership is retained
}

fn process_data(data: &String) {
println!("Processing: {}", data);
}
```

In this example, `data` is borrowed by `process_data` instead of transferring ownership, ensuring that the original variable remains valid for future use.

Memory Safety

Rust's strict compile-time checks eliminate many classes of memory-related vulnerabilities. For instance, double-free errors are impossible because Rust's ownership system ensures that each piece of memory is freed exactly once.

```rust
fn main() {
let mut data = vec![1, 2, 3];
{
let data_ref = &mut data; // Mutable borrow
data_ref.push(4);
} // `data_ref` goes out of scope here
println!("{:?}", data);
}
```

In this example, the mutable reference `data_ref` goes out of scope before `data` is used again, ensuring safe memory access.

Secure Coding Practices

While Rust's safety guarantees offer a strong foundation, secure coding practices further fortify your applications against sophisticated threats. Let's explore some key practices:

Input Validation

Unvalidated input is a common attack vector. Always validate and sanitize inputs to prevent injection attacks.

```rust
fn validate_input(input: &str) -> Result<(), &'static str> {
if input.chars().all(char::is_alphanumeric) {
Ok(())
} else {
Err("Invalid input")
}
}

fn main() {
let user_input = "stock123";
match validate_input(user_input) {
Ok(_) => println!("Valid input"),
Err(e) => println!("Error: {}", e),
}
}
```

In this example, `validate_input` ensures that only alphanumeric characters are accepted, mitigating the risk of injection attacks.

Secure Dependencies

Managing dependencies is crucial. Use tools like `cargo-audit` to scan for vulnerabilities in your dependencies.

```sh
cargo install cargo-audit
cargo audit
```

This command installs and runs `cargo-audit`, identifying known vulnerabilities and suggesting fixes.

Error Handling

Proper error handling prevents the exposure of sensitive information and ensures graceful degradation.

```rust
use std::fs::File;
use std::io::{self, Read};

fn read_file() -> Result<String, io::Error> {
let mut file = File::open("data.txt")?;
let mut contents = String::new();
file.read_to_string(&mut contents)?;
Ok(contents)
}
```

```
fn main() {
match read_file() {
Ok(contents) => println!("File contents: {}", contents),
Err(e) => eprintln!("Error reading file: {}", e),
}
}
```
` ` `

In this example, errors are handled using `Result`, ensuring that any file reading issues are reported appropriately without crashing the program.

Concurrency and Synchronization

Concurrency in Rust is managed through the `std::sync` library, which provides safe and efficient abstractions for multi-threaded programming.

Mutexes and Locks

Use `Mutex` to safely share data between threads, ensuring that only one thread accesses the data at a time.

` ` `rust
```
use std::sync::{Arc, Mutex};
use std::thread;

fn main() {
```

```
let data = Arc::new(Mutex::new(vec![1, 2, 3]));

let mut handles = vec![];
for _ in 0..3 {
let data = Arc::clone(&data);
let handle = thread::spawn(move || {
let mut data = data.lock().unwrap();
data.push(4);
});
handles.push(handle);
}

for handle in handles {
handle.join().unwrap();
}

println!("{:?}", *data.lock().unwrap());
}
```

In this example, `Mutex` ensures that modifications to `data` are synchronized across threads, preventing race conditions.

Atomic Operations

For simple shared-state scenarios, use atomic operations provided by the `std::sync::atomic` module.

```rust
use std::sync::atomic::{AtomicUsize, Ordering};
use std::thread;

fn main() {
let counter = AtomicUsize::new(0);

let mut handles = vec![];
for _ in 0..10 {
let counter = &counter;
let handle = thread::spawn(move || {
counter.fetch_add(1, Ordering::SeqCst);
});
handles.push(handle);
}

for handle in handles {
handle.join().unwrap();
}

println!("Counter: {}", counter.load(Ordering::SeqCst));
}
```

Atomic operations ensure that increments to `counter` are safe and free of race conditions.

Cryptography

Rust provides robust crates for cryptographic operations, essential for securing sensitive data and communications.

Using the `ring` Crate

The `ring` crate offers a comprehensive suite of cryptographic functions. Here's an example of generating a secure hash:

```rust
use ring::digest::{Context, Digest, SHA256};

fn sha256(data: &[u8]) -> Digest {
let mut context = Context::new(&SHA256);
context.update(data);
context.finish()
}

fn main() {
let data = b"important financial data";
let digest = sha256(data);
println!("SHA-256 hash: {:?}", digest);
}
```

This code computes the SHA-256 hash of the input data, ensuring its integrity.

Secure Communication

For secure communication, use the `rustls` crate to implement Transport Layer Security (TLS).

```rust
use rustls::{ClientConfig, ClientSession, StreamOwned};
use std::sync::Arc;
use std::net::TcpStream;

fn main() {
let mut config = ClientConfig::new();
config.root_store.add_server_trust_anchors(&webpki_roots::TLS_SERVER_ROOTS);

let rc_config = Arc::new(config);
let dns_name = webpki::DNSNameRef::try_from_ascii_str("example.com").unwrap();
let mut session = ClientSession::new(&rc_config, dns_name);

let mut socket = TcpStream::connect("example.com:443").unwrap();
let mut tls = StreamOwned::new(session, socket);
```

BLACK SCHOLES: ALGORITHMIC OPTIONS TRADING WITH RUST

```
tls.write_all(b"GET / HTTP/1.0\r\n\r\n").unwrap();
let mut plaintext = vec![];
tls.read_to_end(&mut plaintext).unwrap();
println!("{}", String::from_utf8_lossy(&plaintext));
}
```

This example establishes a secure TLS connection, ensuring encrypted communication with the server.

Rust's focus on safety, combined with robust secure coding practices, creates a formidable defense against security threats in financial applications. By leveraging Rust's ownership model, memory safety guarantees, and concurrency features, you can build secure, high-performance trading algorithms. Incorporating these practices into your development workflow will ensure that your financial systems remain resilient and robust, capable of withstanding the sophisticated threats present in today's digital landscape. Stay vigilant, keep your dependencies up to date, and continue to refine your security practices to maintain the integrity and reliability of your financial applications.

Profiling and Benchmarking Rust Code

To start, it's important to distinguish between profiling and benchmarking. Profiling involves analyzing a program to understand its behavior, focusing on aspects like CPU usage, memory consumption, and function call counts. Benchmarking, on the other hand, measures the performance of specific code segments, typically by running them repeatedly and reporting execution times.

Both practices are invaluable in the development of high-performance financial applications. By identifying and addressing performance bottlenecks, you can ensure that your trading algorithms are both efficient and responsive.

Tools for Profiling Rust Code

Several tools are available for profiling Rust code, each offering unique insights into your program's performance.

`cargo profiler`

`cargo profiler` is a convenient tool that integrates with the popular `perf` and `valgrind` profilers. It provides a straightforward way to profile your Rust applications without extensive setup.

To install `cargo profiler`, run:

```sh
cargo install cargo-profiler
```

Once installed, you can profile your application using `perf`:

```sh
cargo profiler callgrind
```

This command generates a call graph of your application, highlighting the functions that consume the most CPU cycles. You can visualize the results using tools like `kcachegrind` or `qcachegrind`.

`flamegraph`

Flamegraphs are a powerful visualization tool for understanding where your program spends its time. The `flamegraph` crate makes it easy to generate flamegraphs for Rust applications.

To install `flamegraph`, run:

```sh
cargo install flamegraph
```

You can then generate a flamegraph for your application:

```sh
cargo flamegraph
```

This command produces an interactive SVG file, where the width of each bar represents the amount of time spent in a function. This visualization helps you quickly identify performance hotspots.

`perf`

`perf` is a versatile performance analysis tool available on Linux. While `cargo profiler` wraps around `perf`, you can also use `perf` directly for more control over the profiling process.

To profile your application with `perf`, compile it with debug symbols:

```sh
cargo build --release
```

Then, run `perf` to collect performance data:

```sh
perf record -g ./target/release/your_application
```

Finally, generate a report:

```sh
perf report
```

The report includes a breakdown of CPU usage and call stacks, allowing you to pinpoint performance issues.

Benchmarking Rust Code

Benchmarking in Rust is typically done using the `criterion` crate, which provides a comprehensive suite of tools for measuring and comparing the performance of code segments.

Setting Up `criterion`

Add `criterion` to your `Cargo.toml` file:

```toml
[dependencies]
criterion = "0.3"
```

Create a new file in the `benches` directory (e.g., `benches/my_benchmark.rs`):

```rust
use criterion::{black_box, criterion_group, criterion_main, Criterion};

fn fibonacci(n: u64) -> u64 {
match n {
0 => 0,
1 => 1,
_ => fibonacci(n - 1) + fibonacci(n - 2),
}
```

```
}

fn criterion_benchmark(c: &mut Criterion) {
c.bench_function("fibonacci        20",        |b|        b.iter(||
fibonacci(black_box(20))));
}

criterion_group!(benches, criterion_benchmark);
criterion_main!(benches);
```

In this example, the `criterion_benchmark` function benchmarks the `fibonacci` function with an input of 20. The `black_box` function prevents the compiler from optimizing away the benchmarked code.

Running Benchmarks

To run the benchmarks, use:

```sh
cargo bench
```

`criterion` will execute the benchmarks multiple times, providing detailed statistics like mean execution time, standard deviation, and confidence intervals.

Analyzing Benchmark Results

`criterion` generates rich HTML reports that are easy to analyze. The reports include various visualizations, such as histograms and line plots, which provide insights into the performance characteristics of your code.

Practical Examples

Let's explore a practical example of profiling and benchmarking a Rust-based trading algorithm.

Profiling an Options Pricing Algorithm

Consider a Black-Scholes options pricing algorithm implemented in Rust. First, let's profile the algorithm using `cargo profiler` and `perf`.

```rust
use std::f64::consts::E;

fn black_scholes_call_price(s: f64, k: f64, t: f64, r: f64, sigma: f64) -> f64 {
let d1 = (s / k).ln() + (r + sigma.powi(2) / 2.0) * t / (sigma * t.sqrt());
let d2 = d1 - sigma * t.sqrt();
s * normal_cdf(d1) - k * E.powf(-r * t) * normal_cdf(d2)
}

fn normal_cdf(x: f64) -> f64 {
(1.0 + (x / (2.0f64).sqrt()).erf()) / 2.0
```

```
}

fn main() {
let s = 100.0;
let k = 100.0;
let t = 1.0;
let r = 0.05;
let sigma = 0.2;
let price = black_scholes_call_price(s, k, t, r, sigma);
println!("Call option price: {}", price);
}
```

Compile the code with debug symbols:

```sh
cargo build --release
```

Profile the application with `perf`:

```sh
perf record -g ./target/release/black_scholes
```

Generate a report:

```sh
perf report
```

Analyze the report to identify functions consuming the most CPU time. You might find that the `normal_cdf` function is a performance bottleneck.

Benchmarking the Algorithm

Next, let's benchmark the `black_scholes_call_price` function using `criterion`.

Create a new file in the `benches` directory (e.g., `benches/black_scholes.rs`):

```rust
use criterion::{black_box, criterion_group, criterion_main, Criterion};

fn black_scholes_call_price(s: f64, k: f64, t: f64, r: f64, sigma: f64) -> f64 {
let d1 = (s / k).ln() + (r + sigma.powi(2) / 2.0) * t / (sigma * t.sqrt());
let d2 = d1 - sigma * t.sqrt();
s * normal_cdf(d1) - k * E.powf(-r * t) * normal_cdf(d2)
}
```

```rust
fn normal_cdf(x: f64) -> f64 {
(1.0 + (x / (2.0f64).sqrt()).erf()) / 2.0
}

fn criterion_benchmark(c: &mut Criterion) {
c.bench_function("black_scholes_call_price", |b| {
b.iter(|| black_scholes_call_price(black_box(100.0),
black_box(100.0), black_box(1.0), black_box(0.05),
black_box(0.2)))
});
}

criterion_group!(benches, criterion_benchmark);
criterion_main!(benches);
```

Run the benchmarks:

```sh
cargo bench
```

Analyze the generated HTML report to understand the performance characteristics of the `black_scholes_call_price` function.

Optimizing Performance

With profiling and benchmarking data in hand, you can now focus on optimizing your code. Potential optimization strategies include:

1.Algorithmic Improvements: Investigate more efficient algorithms or mathematical techniques.

2.Parallelism: Leverage Rust's concurrency features to parallelize computations.

3.Memory Management: Optimize memory usage to reduce cache misses and improve data locality.

4.Inlining and Unrolling: Use compiler hints to inline small functions and unroll loops.

By iteratively profiling, benchmarking, and optimizing, you can achieve significant performance gains, ensuring your Rust-based financial applications are both efficient and competitive.

Profiling and benchmarking are essential practices in the development of high-performance Rust applications, particularly in the realm of algorithmic trading. By leveraging tools like `cargo profiler`, `flamegraph`, `perf`, and `criterion`, you can gain deep insights into your program's performance, identify bottlenecks, and implement targeted optimizations. This meticulous approach to performance tuning will enable you to build robust, efficient trading algorithms capable of thriving in the fast-paced financial markets.

Developing Custom Financial Libraries

Before diving into the development of your custom financial

library, it's crucial to define the scope and requirements. This involves identifying the specific financial instruments and calculations your library will handle, such as options pricing, risk metrics, or stochastic processes. Understanding these requirements ensures that the library is tailored to meet the precise needs of your trading strategies.

Designing the Architecture

The architecture of your financial library should be modular and extensible, allowing for easy integration and future enhancements. Begin with a high-level design that outlines the core components and their interactions. In Rust, this typically involves defining modules and structs that encapsulate the various functionalities.

For instance, a module for options pricing might include structs for different types of options (e.g., European, American) and traits that define common behaviors. Here's a simplified example:

```rust
pub mod options_pricing {
pub trait Option {
fn price(&self) -> f64;
}

pub struct EuropeanOption {
pub strike_price: f64,
pub maturity: f64,
```

```
pub volatility: f64,

pub risk_free_rate: f64,

pub underlying_price: f64,
}


impl Option for EuropeanOption {
fn price(&self) -> f64 {
// Implement the Black-Scholes formula
let d1 = (self.underlying_price / self.strike_price).ln()
+ (self.risk_free_rate + self.volatility.powi(2) / 2.0) *
self.maturity;
let d1 = d1 / (self.volatility * self.maturity.sqrt());
let d2 = d1 - self.volatility * self.maturity.sqrt();
self.underlying_price * d1 - self.strike_price * (-
self.risk_free_rate * self.maturity).exp() * d2
}
}
}
` ` `
```

This snippet outlines a basic structure for pricing a European option using the Black-Scholes formula. The use of traits ensures that different types of options can implement their pricing logic.

Implementing Core Functionalities

With the architecture in place, proceed to implement

the core functionalities. This involves writing efficient, well-documented code that adheres to Rust's idiomatic practices. Pay special attention to performance considerations, particularly in computationally intensive tasks like numerical methods and simulations.

For example, you might implement a Monte Carlo simulation for option pricing, leveraging Rust's concurrency features to parallelize the computation:

```rust
use rand::prelude::*;
use rayon::prelude::*;

pub fn monte_carlo_pricing(num_simulations: usize, option: &options_pricing::EuropeanOption) -> f64 {
let mut rng = thread_rng();
let simulations: Vec<f64> = (0..num_simulations)
.into_par_iter()
.map(|_| {
let z: f64 = rng.sample(StandardNormal);
let st = option.underlying_price * ((option.risk_free_rate - 0.5 * option.volatility.powi(2)) * option.maturity
+ option.volatility * (option.maturity.sqrt()) * z).exp();
(st - option.strike_price).max(0.0) // Payoff for a call option
})
.collect();
simulations.iter().sum::<f64>() / num_simulations as f64 * (-option.risk_free_rate * option.maturity).exp()
```

```
}
` ` `
```

This code demonstrates a parallelized Monte Carlo simulation to price a European call option, showcasing Rust's powerful concurrency capabilities through the `rayon` crate.

Testing and Validation

Testing is a critical step in developing any financial library. Implement unit tests to validate the correctness of your functions and structures. Rust's built-in testing framework makes it straightforward to write and run tests:

```rust
#[cfg(test)]
mod tests {
use super::*;

#[test]
fn test_european_option_pricing() {
let option = options_pricing::EuropeanOption {
strike_price: 100.0,
maturity: 1.0,
volatility: 0.2,
risk_free_rate: 0.05,
underlying_price: 100.0,
};
```

```
let price = option.price();
assert!((price - 10.4506).abs() < 0.0001);
}

#[test]
fn test_monte_carlo_pricing() {
let option = options_pricing::EuropeanOption {
strike_price: 100.0,
maturity: 1.0,
volatility: 0.2,
risk_free_rate: 0.05,
underlying_price: 100.0,
};
let price = monte_carlo_pricing(10000, &option);
assert!((price - 10.45).abs() < 0.5);
}
}
` ` `
```

These tests ensure that the Black-Scholes pricing function and the Monte Carlo simulation produce results within acceptable error margins.

Documentation and Maintenance

Comprehensive documentation is essential for any financial library. Use Rust's documentation comments to describe the functionality and usage of each module, struct, and function.

This not only enhances the usability of the library but also aids in maintenance and future development.

```rust
/// A European option struct.
pub struct EuropeanOption {
/// The strike price of the option.
pub strike_price: f64,
/// The time to maturity in years.
pub maturity: f64,
/// The volatility of the underlying asset.
pub volatility: f64,
/// The risk-free interest rate.
pub risk_free_rate: f64,
/// The current price of the underlying asset.
pub underlying_price: f64,
}
```

Developing custom financial libraries in Rust involves meticulous planning, efficient implementation, and rigorous testing. By adhering to best practices and leveraging Rust's powerful features, you can create libraries that are not only performant and reliable but also maintainable and scalable. These libraries will serve as the foundation for advanced algorithmic trading systems, providing you with a significant edge in the competitive world of finance.

Deployment and Maintenance of Trading Applications

A well-thought-out deployment strategy is essential for minimizing downtime and ensuring the seamless operation of your trading application. Here are the key steps:

1.Continuous Integration and Continuous Deployment (CI/CD) Pipelines:

- Implement CI/CD pipelines to automate the process of building, testing, and deploying your application. Tools like Jenkins, GitLab CI, and GitHub Actions can help streamline this process.

- Ensure that each code commit triggers automated tests to catch issues early. After passing all tests, the code can be deployed to a staging environment for further validation before going live.

2.Containerization:

- Use containerization technologies like Docker to package your application along with its dependencies. This ensures consistency across different environments and simplifies the deployment process.

- Containers can be orchestrated using tools like Kubernetes, which provide scalability and fault tolerance.

3.Environment Configuration:

- Manage environment-specific configurations (e.g., API keys, database credentials) using environment variables or configuration management tools like Ansible or Terraform.

- Ensure that sensitive information is securely stored and accessed, using tools like HashiCorp Vault.

4.Zero-Downtime Deployments:

- Implement zero-downtime deployment techniques, such as blue-green deployments or rolling updates, to minimize the impact on live trading operations.

- These techniques involve deploying new versions of the application alongside the old ones and gradually transitioning traffic to the new version.

Monitoring and Logging

Effective monitoring and logging are crucial for detecting and resolving issues promptly. They provide insights into the performance and behavior of your trading application, enabling you to take corrective actions swiftly.

1.Real-Time Monitoring:

- Use monitoring tools like Prometheus, Grafana, or Datadog to collect and visualize real-time metrics from your trading application.

- Monitor key performance indicators (KPIs) such as trade execution times, latency, memory usage, and CPU utilization.

2.Alerting:

- Set up alerting mechanisms to notify you of any anomalies or issues. These can include email alerts, SMS notifications, or integration with incident management tools like PagerDuty.

- Define thresholds and conditions for critical metrics, ensuring that alerts are triggered only when necessary to avoid alert fatigue.

3.Logging:

- Implement comprehensive logging using tools like ELK Stack (Elasticsearch, Logstash, Kibana) or Fluentd. Logs should capture detailed information about trade executions, errors, and system events.

- Use structured logging formats (e.g., JSON) to facilitate easier parsing and analysis of log data.

Maintenance and Updates

Maintaining and updating your trading application is an ongoing process. Regular maintenance ensures that the application remains secure, performant, and aligned with evolving market conditions.

1.Security Updates:

- Regularly apply security patches and updates to your application and its dependencies. This includes the Rust compiler, libraries, and any third-party tools.

- Conduct periodic security audits and vulnerability assessments to identify and mitigate potential risks.

2.Performance Optimization:

- Continuously profile and benchmark your application to identify performance bottlenecks. Use profiling tools like `perf`, `valgrind`, or Rust's built-in `cargo bench` to analyze performance.

- Optimize critical sections of code, leveraging Rust's concurrency features and efficient data structures to improve execution speed and reduce latency.

3.Code Refactoring:

- Refactor code periodically to improve readability, maintainability, and extensibility. This involves simplifying complex logic, removing redundant code, and adhering to best practices.

- Use code review processes to ensure that changes are thoroughly vetted by team members, promoting code quality and knowledge sharing.

4.Feature Enhancements:

- Stay abreast of new developments in the algorithmic trading and Rust ecosystems. Incorporate new features and improvements that can enhance the functionality and performance of your trading application.

- Engage with the Rust community to leverage open-source libraries and tools that can accelerate development and innovation.

Backup and Recovery

Ensuring data integrity and availability is paramount in trading applications. Implement robust backup and recovery strategies to protect against data loss and system failures.

1.Data Backups:

- Regularly backup critical data, including trade logs, configuration files, and database snapshots. Use automated backup solutions to schedule and manage backups.

- Store backups in multiple locations (e.g., cloud storage, offsite servers) to ensure redundancy and availability in case of a disaster.

2.Disaster Recovery Plan:

- Develop and test a comprehensive disaster recovery plan that outlines the steps to be taken in the event of a system failure or data loss. This plan should include procedures for data restoration, system reconfiguration, and service resumption.

- Conduct regular disaster recovery drills to ensure that the team is familiar with the procedures and can execute them efficiently under pressure.

Example: Deploying a Rust-Based Trading Application

To illustrate the deployment process, let's consider an example of deploying a Rust-based trading application using Docker and Kubernetes.

1.Dockerfile:

- Create a Dockerfile to containerize the application:

```dockerfile
FROM rust:latest AS builder

WORKDIR /app

COPY . .

RUN cargo build --release

FROM debian:buster-slim

COPY --from=builder /app/target/release/trading_app /usr/local/bin/trading_app

CMD ["trading_app"]
```

` ` `

2.Kubernetes Deployment:

- Define a Kubernetes deployment manifest:

```yaml
apiVersion: apps/v1
kind: Deployment
metadata:
name: trading-app
spec:
replicas: 3
selector:
matchLabels:
app: trading-app
template:
metadata:
labels:
app: trading-app
spec:
containers:
- name: trading-app
image: your-docker-repo/trading_app:latest
ports:
- containerPort: 8080
```

3.CI/CD Pipeline:

- Configure a CI/CD pipeline in GitHub Actions:

```yaml
name: CI/CD Pipeline

on: [push]

jobs:
  build:
    runs-on: ubuntu-latest

    steps:
    - uses: actions/checkout@v2
    - name: Build
      run: cargo build --release
    - name: Docker Build
      run: docker build -t your-docker-repo/trading_app:latest .
    - name: Docker Push
      run: docker push your-docker-repo/trading_app:latest
    - name: Deploy to Kubernetes
      run: kubectl apply -f k8s/deployment.yaml
```

This example demonstrates a streamlined deployment process using Docker and Kubernetes, integrated with a CI/CD pipeline for automated builds, tests, and deployments.

Deploying and maintaining trading applications require meticulous planning, robust infrastructure, and continuous monitoring. By leveraging modern tools and best practices, you can ensure that your Rust-based trading applications are reliable, performant, and secure. This proactive approach to deployment and maintenance will provide a solid foundation for your trading operations, enabling you to capitalize on market opportunities with confidence.

CHAPTER 6: CASE STUDIES AND REAL-WORLD APPLICATIONS

B efore diving into the implementation, let's revisit the concept of hedging. At its core, hedging involves taking an offsetting position in a related security to reduce the risk of adverse price movements. Options, due to their flexibility and leverage, are particularly effective for hedging purposes.

1.Types of Hedges:

-Protective Puts: Buying put options to guard against a decline in the value of an asset.

-Covered Calls: Selling call options against a held asset to generate income, which can offset potential losses.

-Collars: Combining a protective put and a covered call to create a cost-effective hedge.

2.Determining Hedge Ratios:

- The hedge ratio, often derived using the option's delta, determines the proportion of the position to be hedged. For instance, a delta of 0.5 suggests that 50% of the position is hedged.

Setting Up the Rust Environment

Before we proceed with coding, ensure that the Rust environment is properly configured. This includes installing Rust and setting up a new project.

```sh
$ curl --proto '=https' --tlsv1.2 -sSf https://sh.rustup.rs | sh
$ rustup update
$ cargo new hedging_with_options --bin
$ cd hedging_with_options
```

Implementing a Protective Put Hedge in Rust

We will implement a protective put strategy. This involves buying put options to hedge against a decline in the value of a stock.

1.Define the Option Struct:

- Start by defining a struct to represent an option contract.

```rust
#[derive(Debug)]
```

```rust
struct OptionContract {
strike_price: f64,
premium: f64,
expiry: String,
option_type: String, // "Call" or "Put"
delta: f64,
}
```

2.Calculate the Hedge Ratio:

- Implement a function to calculate the hedge ratio based on the option's delta.

```rust
impl OptionContract {
fn hedge_ratio(&self, position_size: f64) -> f64 {
position_size * self.delta
}
}
```

3.Simulate a Hedged Portfolio:

- Create a function to simulate the performance of a hedged portfolio.

```rust
fn    simulate_hedged_portfolio(stock_price:    f64,    options:
```

```rust
&Vec<OptionContract>, position_size: f64) -> f64 {
let mut hedged_value = stock_price * position_size;
for option in options {
let hedge = option.hedge_ratio(position_size);
if option.option_type == "Put" {
hedged_value    -=    hedge    *    (stock_price    -
option.strike_price).max(0.0);
}
}
hedged_value
}
```

4.Example Usage:

- Demonstrate the usage of the above functions with an example.

```rust
fn main() {
let stock_price = 100.0;
let position_size = 50.0;

let put_option = OptionContract {
strike_price: 95.0,
premium: 2.0,
expiry: "2023-12-31".to_string(),
option_type: "Put".to_string(),
```

```rust
delta: -0.5,
};

let options = vec![put_option];

let hedged_value = simulate_hedged_portfolio(stock_price,
&options, position_size);
println!("Hedged Portfolio Value: ${:.2}", hedged_value);
}
```

Analyzing the Hedge

To evaluate the effectiveness of the hedge, it's crucial to analyze the performance of the hedged portfolio under various market conditions.

1.Scenario Analysis:
- Test the hedged portfolio against different stock prices to see how well the hedge performs.

```rust
fn main() {
let stock_prices = vec![90.0, 95.0, 100.0, 105.0, 110.0];
let position_size = 50.0;

let put_option = OptionContract {
strike_price: 95.0,
```

```rust
premium: 2.0,

expiry: "2023-12-31".to_string(),

option_type: "Put".to_string(),

delta: -0.5,

};


let options = vec![put_option];


for price in stock_prices {

let hedged_value = simulate_hedged_portfolio(price, &options, position_size);

println!("Stock Price: ${:.2}, Hedged Portfolio Value: ${:.2}", price, hedged_value);

}

}
```

2. Real-World Data Analysis:

- Integrate real stock price data to analyze the hedge's performance over actual market movements. For this, you might use a library like `reqwest` to fetch historical data.

```rust
use reqwest;

use serde::Deserialize;


#[derive(Deserialize)]

struct StockData {
```

```rust
    date: String,
    close: f64,
}

async fn fetch_stock_data(symbol: &str) -> Result<Vec<StockData>, reqwest::Error> {
    let url = format!("https://api.example.com/stocks/{}", symbol);
    let response = reqwest::get(&url).await?;
    let stock_data: Vec<StockData> = response.json().await?;
    Ok(stock_data)
}

#[tokio::main]
async fn main() {
    let position_size = 50.0;

    let put_option = OptionContract {
        strike_price: 95.0,
        premium: 2.0,
        expiry: "2023-12-31".to_string(),
        option_type: "Put".to_string(),
        delta: -0.5,
    };

    let options = vec![put_option];

    match fetch_stock_data("AAPL").await {
```

```
Ok(stock_data) => {

for data in stock_data {

let hedged_value = simulate_hedged_portfolio(data.close,
&options, position_size);

println!("Date: {}, Stock Price: ${:.2}, Hedged Portfolio Value: $
{:.2}", data.date, data.close, hedged_value);

}

}

Err(e) => println!("Error fetching stock data: {:?}", e),

}

}
```
` ` `

In this case study, we have explored the intricacies of hedging with options, implemented a protective put strategy using Rust, and analyzed its performance under various market conditions. By leveraging Rust's performance and safety features, we can create robust and efficient trading applications that stand up to the demands of real-world financial markets.

This hands-on approach not only reinforces the theoretical concepts of hedging but also provides practical skills in implementing these strategies using Rust. As you continue to develop your expertise, consider experimenting with different types of hedges and market scenarios to further enhance your understanding and proficiency in algorithmic options trading.

Case Study: Arbitrage Strategies in Rust

Arbitrage opportunities arise when there is a price difference between two or more markets or financial instruments. Traders can capitalize on these discrepancies by buying low in one market and selling high in another. Arbitrage can be broadly categorized into several types:

1.Spatial Arbitrage:

- This involves taking advantage of price differences for the same asset in different locations or exchanges.

2.Temporal Arbitrage:

- This involves exploiting price differences over time, such as between spot and futures markets.

3.Statistical Arbitrage:

- This relies on quantitative models to identify temporary mispricings in related financial instruments.

Setting Up the Rust Environment

Before implementing an arbitrage trading strategy, ensure that your Rust environment is configured correctly. This includes installing Rust and setting up a new project.

```sh
$ curl --proto '=https' --tlsv1.2 -sSf https://sh.rustup.rs | sh
$ rustup update
$ cargo new arbitrage_strategy --bin
$ cd arbitrage_strategy
```

```
` ` `
```

Implementing a Spatial Arbitrage Strategy in Rust

We will focus on spatial arbitrage, where we exploit price differences of the same asset on two different exchanges.

1.Define the Asset Struct:

- Start by defining a struct to represent the asset and its price on different exchanges.

```rust
#[derive(Debug)]
struct Asset {
name: String,
exchange_a_price: f64,
exchange_b_price: f64,
}
```

2.Identify Arbitrage Opportunities:

- Implement a function to identify arbitrage opportunities based on the price difference.

```rust
impl Asset {
fn arbitrage_opportunity(&self) -> bool {
(self.exchange_a_price - self.exchange_b_price).abs() > 0.01
```

```
}
}
```
` ` `

3.Simulate an Arbitrage Trade:

- Create a function to simulate the execution and profit calculation of an arbitrage trade.

` ` `rust

```
fn simulate_arbitrage_trade(asset: &Asset, trade_size: f64) -> f64 {

if asset.arbitrage_opportunity() {

if asset.exchange_a_price < asset.exchange_b_price {

return trade_size * (asset.exchange_b_price - asset.exchange_a_price);

} else {

return trade_size * (asset.exchange_a_price - asset.exchange_b_price);

}
}
0.0
}
```
` ` `

4.Example Usage:

- Demonstrate the usage of the above functions with an example.

```rust
fn main() {
let asset = Asset {
name: "BTC".to_string(),
exchange_a_price: 45000.0,
exchange_b_price: 45200.0,
};

let trade_size = 1.0; // 1 BTC
let profit = simulate_arbitrage_trade(&asset, trade_size);
if profit > 0.0 {
println!("Arbitrage opportunity detected! Potential profit: ${:.2}", profit);
} else {
println!("No arbitrage opportunity detected.");
}
}
```

Analyzing the Arbitrage Strategy

To evaluate the effectiveness of the arbitrage strategy, it is crucial to analyze its performance using historical data. This involves fetching real-world data and testing the strategy's robustness under various market conditions.

1.Fetching Historical Data:

- Use a library like `reqwest` to fetch historical price data for the asset from two different exchanges.

```rust
use reqwest;
use serde::Deserialize;

#[derive(Deserialize)]
struct PriceData {
timestamp: String,
price: f64,
}

async fn fetch_price_data(exchange: &str, symbol: &str) -> Result<Vec<PriceData>, reqwest::Error> {
let url = format!("https://api.example.com/{}/prices?symbol={}", exchange, symbol);
let response = reqwest::get(&url).await?;
let price_data: Vec<PriceData> = response.json().await?;
Ok(price_data)
}
```

2.Simulating Arbitrage Across Historical Data:

- Implement a function to simulate the arbitrage strategy over historical data.

```rust
```

```
#[tokio::main]
async fn main() {
let symbol = "BTC";

let exchange_a_data = fetch_price_data("exchange_a", symbol).await.unwrap();
let exchange_b_data = fetch_price_data("exchange_b", symbol).await.unwrap();

let trade_size = 1.0; // 1 BTC
let mut total_profit = 0.0;

in exchange_a_data.iter().zip(exchange_b_data.iter()) {
let asset = Asset {
name: symbol.to_string(),
exchange_a_price: a.price,
exchange_b_price: b.price,
};

total_profit += simulate_arbitrage_trade(&asset, trade_size);
}

println!("Total profit from arbitrage: ${:.2}", total_profit);
}
```
` ` `

3.Performance Metrics:

- Evaluate the strategy using key performance metrics such as total profit, number of trades executed, and average profit per trade.

```rust
fn main() {
let symbol = "BTC";

let exchange_a_data = fetch_price_data("exchange_a", symbol).await.unwrap();
let exchange_b_data = fetch_price_data("exchange_b", symbol).await.unwrap();

let trade_size = 1.0; // 1 BTC
let mut total_profit = 0.0;
let mut trade_count = 0;

in exchange_a_data.iter().zip(exchange_b_data.iter()) {
let asset = Asset {
name: symbol.to_string(),
exchange_a_price: a.price,
exchange_b_price: b.price,
};

let profit = simulate_arbitrage_trade(&asset, trade_size);
if profit > 0.0 {
total_profit += profit;
trade_count += 1;
}
```

```
}

let average_profit_per_trade = if trade_count > 0 {
total_profit / trade_count as f64
} else {
0.0
};

println!("Total profit from arbitrage: ${:.2}", total_profit);
println!("Number of trades executed: {}", trade_count);
println!("Average      profit      per      trade:      ${:.2}",
average_profit_per_trade);
}
```
` ` `

In this case study, we have explored the concept of arbitrage, implemented a spatial arbitrage strategy using Rust, and analyzed its performance using historical data. By leveraging Rust's concurrency and performance features, we can create efficient and robust trading applications capable of identifying and executing arbitrage opportunities in real-time.

Real-World Application: Portfolio Optimization

Portfolio optimization involves selecting the best mix of assets to achieve specific investment goals. The most common objective is to maximize the expected return for a given level of risk, often measured by variance or standard deviation. This approach is rooted in Modern Portfolio Theory (MPT), introduced by Harry Markowitz in the 1950s.

1.Risk and Return:

- The foundation of portfolio optimization lies in understanding the trade-off between risk and return. Expected return is the weighted sum of individual asset returns, while risk is typically quantified by the portfolio's variance.

2.Efficient Frontier:

- The efficient frontier represents the set of optimal portfolios that offer the highest expected return for a given level of risk. Portfolios on the efficient frontier are considered well-diversified and optimized.

3.Sharpe Ratio:

- The Sharpe Ratio measures the performance of an investment compared to a risk-free asset, adjusted for its risk. It is a crucial metric in portfolio optimization, helping investors understand the return of an investment per unit of risk.

Setting Up the Rust Environment

Before diving into the implementation, ensure your Rust environment is set up correctly. This includes installing Rust and creating a new project.

```sh
$ curl --proto '=https' --tlsv1.2 -sSf https://sh.rustup.rs | sh
$ rustup update
```

```
$ cargo new portfolio_optimization --bin
$ cd portfolio_optimization
```

Implementing Portfolio Optimization in Rust

We'll implement a simple mean-variance optimization algorithm. This involves calculating the expected returns, variances, and covariances of the assets, and then determining the optimal weights that maximize the Sharpe Ratio.

1.Define the Asset Struct:

- Start by defining a struct to represent the asset, including its expected return and standard deviation.

```rust
#[derive(Debug)]
struct Asset {
name: String,
expected_return: f64,
std_dev: f64,
}
```

2.Calculate Portfolio Metrics:

- Implement functions to calculate the portfolio's expected return and variance.

```rust
fn portfolio_return(assets: &[Asset], weights: &[f64]) -> f64 {
    assets.iter().zip(weights).map(|(asset,          &weight)|
    asset.expected_return * weight).sum()
}


fn portfolio_variance(cov_matrix: &[Vec<f64>], weights:
&[f64]) -> f64 {
let mut variance = 0.0;
for i in 0..weights.len() {
for j in 0..weights.len() {
variance += weights[i] * weights[j] * cov_matrix[i][j];
}
}
variance
}
```


3.Optimize Weights:

- Use an optimization library like `nalgebra` to find the weights that maximize the Sharpe Ratio.

```rust
use nalgebra::{DMatrix, DVector};

fn optimize_portfolio(assets: &[Asset], cov_matrix:
&[Vec<f64>], risk_free_rate: f64) -> Vec<f64> {
```

```rust
let n = assets.len();

let returns: DVector<f64> = DVector::from_iterator(n, assets.iter().map(|a| a.expected_return - risk_free_rate));

let cov_matrix: DMatrix<f64> = DMatrix::from_fn(n, n, |i, j| cov_matrix[i][j]);


let weights = cov_matrix.try_inverse().unwrap() * returns;

let sum_weights: f64 = weights.iter().sum();

weights.iter().map(|&w| w / sum_weights).collect()
}
```

4.Example Usage:

- Demonstrate the usage of the above functions with an example.

```rust
fn main() {

let assets = vec![

Asset { name: "Asset A".to_string(), expected_return: 0.10, std_dev: 0.15 },

Asset { name: "Asset B".to_string(), expected_return: 0.12, std_dev: 0.20 },

Asset { name: "Asset C".to_string(), expected_return: 0.14, std_dev: 0.25 },

];


let cov_matrix = vec![
```

```rust
    vec![0.0225, 0.0027, 0.0039],
    vec![0.0027, 0.04, 0.0048],
    vec![0.0039, 0.0048, 0.0625],
    ];

    let risk_free_rate = 0.03;
    let optimal_weights = optimize_portfolio(&assets, &cov_matrix, risk_free_rate);

    println!("Optimal weights: {:?}", optimal_weights);
}
```

Analyzing the Optimized Portfolio

To evaluate the effectiveness of the portfolio optimization, we need to analyze the performance of the optimized portfolio using historical data. This involves fetching real-world data, calculating realized returns and risks, and comparing them with the expected metrics.

1.Fetching Historical Data:

- Use a library like `reqwest` to fetch historical price data for the assets.

```rust
use reqwest;
use serde::Deserialize;
```

```rust
#[derive(Deserialize)]
struct PriceData {
timestamp: String,
price: f64,
}

async fn fetch_price_data(asset: &str) -> Result<Vec<PriceData>, reqwest::Error> {
let url = format!("https://api.example.com/{}?interval=daily", asset);
let response = reqwest::get(&url).await?;
let price_data: Vec<PriceData> = response.json().await?;
Ok(price_data)
}
```

2.Simulating Portfolio Performance:

- Implement a function to simulate the performance of the optimized portfolio over historical data.

```rust
#[tokio::main]
async fn main() {
let assets = vec!["Asset A", "Asset B", "Asset C"];
let mut historical_data = Vec::new();

for asset in &assets {
```

```rust
        let data = fetch_price_data(asset).await.unwrap();
        historical_data.push(data);
    }

    // Calculate realized returns and risk...

    let optimal_weights = optimize_portfolio(&assets,
&cov_matrix, risk_free_rate);

    // Calculate realized portfolio metrics...

    println!("Realized portfolio performance: ...");
    }
```

3.Performance Metrics:

- Evaluate the optimized portfolio using key performance metrics such as realized return, risk, and Sharpe Ratio.

```rust
fn                    calculate_realized_metrics(historical_data:
&[Vec<PriceData>], weights: &[f64]) -> (f64, f64) {
    // Calculate realized returns and risk based on historical data...
    // Return realized return and realized risk
    (realized_return, realized_risk)
}

#[tokio::main]
```

```rust
async fn main() {
// Fetch historical data...

let (realized_return, realized_risk) = calculate_realized_metrics(&historical_data, &optimal_weights);

let realized_sharpe_ratio = (realized_return - risk_free_rate) / realized_risk;

println!("Realized return: {:.2}%", realized_return * 100.0);

println!("Realized risk: {:.2}%", realized_risk * 100.0);

println!("Realized Sharpe Ratio: {:.2}", realized_sharpe_ratio);
}
```

This hands-on approach not only reinforces the theoretical concepts of portfolio optimization but also provides practical skills in implementing these strategies using Rust. As you continue to develop your expertise, consider exploring more advanced optimization techniques, such as robust optimization and multi-objective optimization, to further enhance your understanding and proficiency in quantitative finance.

Mastering the implementation of portfolio optimization strategies in Rust, you position yourself at the forefront of modern finance, equipped with the tools and knowledge to construct optimal portfolios and achieve superior investment performance.

Using Rust for Predictive Analytics in Trading

Predictive analytics involves using historical data, statistical algorithms, and machine learning techniques to identify the likelihood of future outcomes. In trading, it helps forecast price movements, identify trends, and make informed trading decisions.

1.Historical Data Analysis:

- Analyzing past market performance to identify patterns and trends that can predict future movements.

2.Statistical Methods:

- Employing techniques such as linear regression, time series analysis, and ARIMA models to forecast prices.

3.Machine Learning:

- Utilizing machine learning algorithms like Random Forest, Support Vector Machines (SVM), and Neural Networks for more complex and accurate predictions.

Setting Up the Rust Environment

Ensure your Rust environment is set up correctly. Install necessary libraries for data manipulation, statistical analysis, and machine learning.

```sh
$ cargo new predictive_analytics --bin
```

$ cd predictive_analytics

$ cargo add csv serde serde_json reqwest nalgebra ndarray rand

` ` `

Implementing Predictive Analytics in Rust

We'll implement a simple predictive model using linear regression to forecast stock prices. This involves data preprocessing, model training, and prediction.

1.Fetching Historical Data:

- Use `reqwest` to fetch historical price data.

``` rust
use reqwest;
use serde::Deserialize;

#[derive(Deserialize)]
struct PriceData {
timestamp: String,
close: f64,
}

async fn fetch_price_data(symbol: &str) -> Result<Vec<PriceData>, reqwest::Error> {
let url = format!("https://api.example.com/{}?interval=daily", symbol);
```

```rust
let response = reqwest::get(&url).await?;

let price_data: Vec<PriceData> = response.json().await?;

Ok(price_data)

}
```

2.Data Preprocessing:

- Clean and prepare the data for analysis.

```rust
fn preprocess_data(price_data: Vec<PriceData>) -> (Vec<f64>,
Vec<f64>) {

let mut dates = Vec::new();

let mut prices = Vec::new();

for data in price_data {

dates.push(data.timestamp);

prices.push(data.close);

}

// Convert dates to numerical values if necessary

(dates, prices)

}
```

3.Implementing Linear Regression:

- Use `nalgebra` to implement linear regression.

```rust
use nalgebra::DMatrix;

fn linear_regression(dates: &[f64], prices: &[f64]) -> (f64, f64) {
let n = dates.len();
let x = DMatrix::from_column_slice(n, 1, dates);
let y = DMatrix::from_column_slice(n, 1, prices);

let x_t = x.transpose();
let x_t_x = x_t.clone() * &x;
let x_t_y = x_t * y;

let beta = x_t_x.try_inverse().unwrap() * x_t_y;

(beta[(0, 0)], beta[(1, 0)])
}
```

4.Making Predictions:
- Use the trained model to make predictions.

```rust
fn predict_price(date: f64, intercept: f64, slope: f64) -> f64 {
intercept + slope * date
}
```

5.Example Usage:

- Demonstrate the usage of the above functions with an example.

```rust
#[tokio::main]
async fn main() {
let symbol = "AAPL";
let price_data = fetch_price_data(symbol).await.unwrap();
let (dates, prices) = preprocess_data(price_data);

let (intercept, slope) = linear_regression(&dates, &prices);

let prediction_date = dates.last().unwrap() + 1.0; // Predicting the next day's price
let predicted_price = predict_price(prediction_date, intercept, slope);

println!("Predicted price for {}: ${:.2}", symbol, predicted_price);
}
```

Evaluating Predictive Models

To validate the effectiveness of our predictive model, we need to backtest it using historical data. This involves comparing the model's predictions with actual market performance and calculating performance metrics.

1.Backtesting the Model:

- Implement a function to backtest the predictive model.

```rust
fn backtest_model(dates: &[f64], prices: &[f64], intercept: f64,
slope: f64) -> (f64, f64) {
let mut predictions = Vec::new();

for &date in dates {
let predicted_price = predict_price(date, intercept, slope);
predictions.push(predicted_price);
}

// Calculate performance metrics...

(mean_squared_error, r_squared)
}
```

2.Performance Metrics:

- Evaluate the model using metrics such as Mean Squared Error
(MSE) and R-squared.

```rust
fn calculate_performance_metrics(actual: &[f64], predicted:
&[f64]) -> (f64, f64) {
```

```rust
let n = actual.len();
let mean_actual = actual.iter().sum::<f64>() / n as f64;

let mut ss_total = 0.0;
let mut ss_residual = 0.0;

for i in 0..n {
ss_total += (actual[i] - mean_actual).powi(2);
ss_residual += (actual[i] - predicted[i]).powi(2);
}

let mse = ss_residual / n as f64;
let r_squared = 1.0 - (ss_residual / ss_total);

(mse, r_squared)
}

#[tokio::main]
async fn main() {
// Fetch and preprocess data...

let (intercept, slope) = linear_regression(&dates, &prices);
let (mse, r_squared) = backtest_model(&dates, &prices,
intercept, slope);

println!("Model Performance:");
println!("Mean Squared Error: {:.2}", mse);
```

```
println!("R-squared: {:.2}", r_squared);
}
```

\` \` \`

Advanced Predictive Analytics Techniques

While linear regression is a good starting point, more advanced techniques can significantly improve predictive accuracy. Consider exploring the following methods:

1.Time Series Analysis:

- Techniques like ARIMA, GARCH, and LSTM (Long Short-Term Memory networks) are well-suited for modeling time-dependent data.

2.Machine Learning Algorithms:

- Utilize algorithms such as Random Forest, Gradient Boosting, and Support Vector Machines to capture complex relationships in the data.

3.Deep Learning:

- Implement deep learning models using frameworks like `tch-rs` (Rust bindings for PyTorch) for highly accurate predictions.

This hands-on approach not only reinforces the theoretical concepts of predictive analytics but also provides practical skills in implementing these strategies using Rust. As you continue to develop your expertise, consider exploring more advanced techniques and algorithms to further enhance your predictive models and achieve superior trading performance.

Low Latency Trading Systems

Low latency trading, often synonymous with high-frequency trading (HFT), involves executing a large number of orders at extremely high speeds. The goal is to capitalize on minute price discrepancies that exist for mere milliseconds. Achieving low latency involves optimizing every aspect of the trading system, from data acquisition to order execution.

1.Market Data Feed Handling:

- Efficiently receiving and processing market data in real-time.

2.Order Management:

- Quickly generating and sending orders to the exchange.

3.Network Optimization:

- Minimizing the time data takes to travel between the trading system and the exchange.

4.Hardware and Software Optimization:

- Using specialized hardware and finely-tuned software to reduce processing times.

Setting Up the Rust Environment

Before diving into the implementation, ensure your Rust environment is configured for optimal performance. Install the necessary libraries for network communication, data parsing, and concurrency handling.

```sh
$ cargo new low_latency_trading --bin
```

```
$ cd low_latency_trading
$ cargo add tokio tokio-tungstenite serde serde_json
` ` `
```

Architecture of a Low Latency Trading System

Designing a low latency trading system involves several key components:

1.Market Data Feed Handlers:

- These components connect to market data sources, receive data packets, and process them in real-time.

2.Order Management System (OMS):

- The OMS generates, manages, and sends orders to the exchange with minimal delay.

3.Decision-Making Algorithms:

- These algorithms analyze market data and make trading decisions based on predefined strategies.

4.Network Interface:

- Optimized network interfaces reduce latency in data transmission between the system and the exchange.

Implementing Market Data Feed Handlers in Rust

The first step is to handle incoming market data efficiently. We'll use `tokio` and `tokio-tungstenite` for asynchronous networking and WebSocket communication.

1.Connecting to Market Data Feed:

- Establish a WebSocket connection to receive real-time market data.

```rust
use tokio_tungstenite::connect_async;
use tokio_tungstenite::tungstenite::Message;
use futures_util::stream::StreamExt;

async fn connect_to_market_data_feed(url: &str) -> tokio_tungstenite::tungstenite::Result<()> {
let (ws_stream, _) = connect_async(url).await?;
let (mut write, mut read) = ws_stream.split();

// Listen for incoming messages
while let Some(message) = read.next().await {
let message = message?;
if let Message::Text(text) = message {
handle_market_data(text).await;
}
}

Ok(())
}

async fn handle_market_data(data: String) {
// Parse and process market data
println!("Received market data: {}", data);
```

```
}
```
` ` `

2.Parsing Market Data:

- Use `serde` for efficient data serialization and deserialization.

```rust
use serde::Deserialize;

#[derive(Deserialize)]
struct MarketData {
symbol: String,
price: f64,
volume: f64,
timestamp: u64,
}

async fn handle_market_data(data: String) {
let market_data: MarketData = serde_json::from_str(&data).unwrap();
println!("Parsed market data: {:?}", market_data);

// Further processing...
}
```

Implementing the Order Management System (OMS)

The OMS is responsible for quickly generating and sending orders to the exchange. This requires efficient data structures and network communication.

1.Order Generation:

- Create and manage orders based on market conditions.

```rust
struct Order {
symbol: String,
side: String,
quantity: f64,
price: f64,
timestamp: u64,
}

impl Order {
fn new(symbol: &str, side: &str, quantity: f64, price: f64, timestamp: u64) -> Self {
Order {
symbol: symbol.to_string(),
side: side.to_string(),
quantity,
price,
timestamp,
}
```

```
}
}
```
` ` `

2.Sending Orders to the Exchange:

- Use `tokio` for asynchronous order submission.

` ` `rust
```rust
async fn send_order(order: Order) -> tokio_tungstenite::tungstenite::Result<()> {
let url = "wss://exchange.example.com/orders";
let (ws_stream, _) = connect_async(url).await?;
let (mut write, _) = ws_stream.split();

let order_json = serde_json::to_string(&order).unwrap();
write.send(Message::Text(order_json)).await?;

Ok(())
}
```
` ` `

Optimizing Network Communication

Network latency can be a significant bottleneck in a low latency trading system. Optimizing network communication involves:

1.Minimizing Data Transmission Time:

- Using direct and efficient network protocols.

2.Reducing Network Hops:

- Placing trading servers closer to the exchange's servers.

3.Using High-Speed Network Interfaces:

- Leveraging technologies like InfiniBand or 10-Gigabit Ethernet.

Hardware and Software Optimization

1.Specialized Hardware:

- Use FPGA (Field-Programmable Gate Array) or GPU (Graphics Processing Unit) for accelerating specific tasks.

2.Efficient Data Structures:

- Implement lock-free data structures to avoid contention and improve concurrency.

3.Code Optimization:

- Profile and optimize Rust code to minimize execution time.

```rust
fn optimized_function(data: &[f64]) -> f64 {
data.iter().sum()
}
```

Example Usage

Let's put everything together in a simplified example that demonstrates connecting to a market data feed, processing data, and sending orders.

```rust
#[tokio::main]
async fn main() {
let market_data_url = "wss://api.example.com/marketdata";
tokio::spawn(async move {
connect_to_market_data_feed(market_data_url).await.unwrap();
});

// Simulate generating and sending an order
let order = Order::new("AAPL", "buy", 100.0, 150.0, 1625269200);
send_order(order).await.unwrap();
}
```

Low latency trading requires continuous optimization and fine-tuning. As you develop your trading systems, consider exploring advanced techniques and technologies to further reduce latency and improve performance. By mastering the implementation of low latency trading systems in Rust, you position yourself at the cutting edge of algorithmic trading, equipped with the tools and knowledge to execute trades with unparalleled speed and precision.

Development of Automated Market Making Algorithms

Automated market making involves the use of algorithms to provide liquidity by continuously posting buy and sell orders for a particular asset. Market makers earn the bid-ask spread as their profit, and their primary objective is to balance inventory while minimizing risk. The key components of an AMM algorithm include:

1.Quoting Engine:

- Generates bid and ask quotes based on market conditions.

2.Inventory Management:

- Maintains a balance of assets to avoid excessive exposure.

3.Risk Management:

- Implements strategies to mitigate potential losses.

4.Execution Logic:

- Handles order placement and execution at the exchange.

Key Considerations for AMM Algorithms

When designing AMM algorithms, several factors must be taken into account to ensure optimal performance and profitability:

1.Latency:

- Minimize the time between receiving market data and updating quotes.

2.Spread Management:

- Dynamically adjust the bid-ask spread based on market volatility and competition.

3.Inventory Control:

- Monitor and manage inventory levels to avoid significant imbalances.

4.Risk Mitigation:

- Implement hedging strategies to protect against adverse market movements.

5.Regulatory Compliance:

- Ensure adherence to market regulations and trading rules.

Setting Up the Rust Environment

To begin, set up your Rust environment with the necessary libraries for networking, data handling, and concurrency:

```sh
$ cargo new market_making --bin
$ cd market_making
$ cargo add tokio tokio-tungstenite serde serde_json
```

Architecture of an Automated Market Making Algorithm

The architecture of an AMM algorithm can be broken down into several key components:

1.Market Data Feed:

- Receives real-time market data and updates quotes accordingly.

2.Quoting Engine:

- Generates bid and ask prices based on predefined strategies.

3.Order Management System (OMS):

- Manages order placement, modification, and cancellation.

4.Risk Management Module:

- Monitors risk exposure and implements hedging strategies.

5.Inventory Management Module:

- Tracks asset holdings and adjusts quoting behaviour to maintain balance.

Implementing the Quoting Engine in Rust

The quoting engine is responsible for generating bid and ask quotes. It must respond quickly to market changes and adjust quotes dynamically.

1.Connecting to Market Data Feed:

- Establish a WebSocket connection to receive real-time market data.

```rust
use tokio_tungstenite::connect_async;

use tokio_tungstenite::tungstenite::Message;

use futures_util::stream::StreamExt;


async fn connect_to_market_data_feed(url: &str) -> tokio_tungstenite::tungstenite::Result<()> {

let (ws_stream, _) = connect_async(url).await?;
```

```rust
let (mut write, mut read) = ws_stream.split();

while let Some(message) = read.next().await {
let message = message?;
if let Message::Text(text) = message {
handle_market_data(text).await;
}
}

Ok(())
}

async fn handle_market_data(data: String) {
// Parse and process market data
println!("Received market data: {}", data);
}
```

2.Generating Quotes:

- Generate bid and ask quotes based on the received market data.

```rust
struct Quote {
symbol: String,
bid_price: f64,
ask_price: f64,
```

```
timestamp: u64,

}


impl Quote {

fn new(symbol: &str, bid_price: f64, ask_price: f64,
timestamp: u64) -> Self {

Quote {

symbol: symbol.to_string(),

bid_price,

ask_price,

timestamp,

}

}

}


async fn handle_market_data(data: String) {

let         market_data:         MarketData         =
serde_json::from_str(&data).unwrap();

let bid_price = market_data.price - 0.01; // Example logic for
bid price

let ask_price = market_data.price + 0.01; // Example logic for
ask price

let quote = Quote::new(&market_data.symbol, bid_price,
ask_price, market_data.timestamp);


println!("Generated quote: {:?}", quote);


// Further processing...
```

```
}
```
` ` `

Implementing the Order Management System (OMS)

The OMS is responsible for placing, modifying, and cancelling orders based on the generated quotes.

1.Order Placement:

- Place buy and sell orders at the generated bid and ask prices.

` ` `rust

```rust
struct Order {
symbol: String,
side: String,
quantity: f64,
price: f64,
timestamp: u64,
}

impl Order {
fn new(symbol: &str, side: &str, quantity: f64, price: f64,
timestamp: u64) -> Self {
Order {
symbol: symbol.to_string(),
side: side.to_string(),
quantity,
```

```rust
price,
timestamp,
    }
  }
}

async fn send_order(order: Order) -> tokio_tungstenite::tungstenite::Result<()> {
let url = "wss://exchange.example.com/orders";
let (ws_stream, _) = connect_async(url).await?;
let (mut write, _) = ws_stream.split();

let order_json = serde_json::to_string(&order).unwrap();
write.send(Message::Text(order_json)).await?;

Ok(())
}
```

2.Order Modification and Cancellation:

- Modify or cancel existing orders based on market conditions.

```rust
async fn modify_order(order_id: &str, new_price: f64) -> tokio_tungstenite::tungstenite::Result<()> {
let url = format!("wss://exchange.example.com/orders/{}", order_id);
let (ws_stream, _) = connect_async(&url).await?;
```

```rust
let (mut write, _) = ws_stream.split();

let modify_order_json = serde_json::json!({
"action": "modify",
"new_price": new_price
});
write.send(Message::Text(modify_order_json.to_string())).await?;

Ok(())
}


async fn cancel_order(order_id: &str) -> tokio_tungstenite::tungstenite::Result<()> {
let url = format!("wss://exchange.example.com/orders/{}", order_id);
let (ws_stream, _) = connect_async(&url).await?;
let (mut write, _) = ws_stream.split();

let cancel_order_json = serde_json::json!({
"action": "cancel"
});
write.send(Message::Text(cancel_order_json.to_string())).await?;

Ok(())
}
```

Implementing Risk and Inventory Management

Risk and inventory management are critical to the success of an AMM algorithm. Implement strategies to monitor and adjust positions to minimize risk.

1.Inventory Management:

- Track and adjust asset holdings to maintain balance.

```rust
struct Inventory {
symbol: String,
quantity: f64,
}

impl Inventory {
fn new(symbol: &str, quantity: f64) -> Self {
Inventory {
symbol: symbol.to_string(),
quantity,
}
}

fn adjust(&mut self, quantity: f64) {
self.quantity += quantity;
}
}
```

` ` `

2.Risk Management:

- Implement hedging strategies to protect against adverse market movements.

```rust
struct RiskManager {
max_position: f64,
current_position: f64,
}

impl RiskManager {
fn new(max_position: f64) -> Self {
RiskManager {
max_position,
current_position: 0.0,
}
}

fn evaluate_risk(&self, potential_position: f64) -> bool {
(self.current_position + potential_position).abs() <= self.max_position
}

fn adjust_position(&mut self, position_change: f64) {
self.current_position += position_change;
```

```
}

}
` ` `
```

Example Usage

Let's combine the components into a simplified example that demonstrates connecting to a market data feed, generating quotes, and managing orders.

```rust
#[tokio::main]
async fn main() {
let market_data_url = "wss://api.example.com/marketdata";
tokio::spawn(async move {
connect_to_market_data_feed(market_data_url).await.unwrap();
});

// Simulate generating and sending an order
let order = Order::new("AAPL", "buy", 100.0, 150.0, 1625269200);
send_order(order).await.unwrap();
}
```

Automated market making is a complex and dynamic field that requires continuous optimization and innovation. As you develop your AMM algorithms, consider exploring advanced strategies and technologies to enhance performance and profitability. With Rust as your tool of choice, you are well-equipped to navigate the challenges and opportunities in the world of automated market making.

Application in Cryptocurrency Options

Cryptocurrency options are derivative contracts that give the holder the right, but not the obligation, to buy or sell a cryptocurrency at a predetermined price before a specified expiration date. These are similar to traditional financial options but come with additional challenges and opportunities due to the volatile nature of cryptocurrencies.

Volatility and Pricing Models

The first step in developing robust cryptocurrency options trading algorithms is understanding the underlying volatility. Unlike traditional assets, cryptocurrencies exhibit extreme volatility, which can significantly impact the pricing of options. Traditional models like Black-Scholes must be adapted to account for these nuances.

In Rust, you can implement modified versions of the Black-Scholes model or other models such as the Heston model, which incorporates stochastic volatility. Here's a simplified Rust example to get you started:

```rust
extern crate rand;

extern crate statrs;
```

```rust
use rand::Rng;
use statrs::distribution::{Normal, Continuous};

pub fn heston_model(
s0: f64, // Initial asset price
k: f64,  // Strike price
r: f64,  // Risk-free rate
q: f64,  // Dividend yield
v0: f64, // Initial volatility
kappa: f64, // Mean reversion rate
theta: f64, // Long-term variance
sigma: f64, // Volatility of volatility
rho: f64, // Correlation
t: f64, // Time to maturity
steps: u32 // Number of simulation steps
) -> f64 {
let mut rng = rand::thread_rng();
let dt = t / steps as f64;
let mut v = v0;
let mut s = s0;

for _ in 0..steps {
let z1: f64 = rng.gen();
let z2: f64 = rng.gen();
let norm_inv1 = Normal::new(0.0, 1.0).unwrap().inverse_cdf(z1);
```

```rust
let        norm_inv2        =        Normal::new(0.0,
1.0).unwrap().inverse_cdf(z2);


let dw1 = norm_inv1 * dt.sqrt();

let dw2 = rho * dw1 + (1.0 - rho.powi(2)).sqrt() * norm_inv2 *
dt.sqrt();


v += kappa * (theta - v) * dt + sigma * (v.sqrt()) * dw2;

s += (r - q - 0.5 * v) * dt + v.sqrt() * dw1;
}


(s - k).max(0.0) * (-r * t).exp()
}


fn main() {

let option_price = heston_model(100.0, 110.0, 0.05, 0.02, 0.04,
1.0, 0.04, 0.5, -0.7, 1.0, 1000);

println!("Option Price: {}", option_price);

}
```
` ` `

This Rust code snippet demonstrates a simplified implementation of the Heston model. It simulates the underlying asset price and its volatility path using correlated Brownian motions. This model is more suited for the high volatility observed in cryptocurrencies compared to the traditional Black-Scholes model.

Implementing Cryptocurrency Options Trading Algorithms

Once you have a reliable pricing model, the next step is to develop trading algorithms. These algorithms can range from simple moving average crossovers to more complex machine learning-based strategies. Rust's performance capabilities make it ideal for processing large datasets and executing high-frequency trades.

Here's an example of a simple momentum-based trading algorithm using Rust:

```rust
extern crate chrono;
extern crate csv;

use chrono::prelude::*;
use csv::ReaderBuilder;
use std::error::Error;

#[derive(Debug)]
struct Trade {
date: DateTime<Utc>,
price: f64,
signal: i8,
}

fn main() -> Result<(), Box<dyn Error>> {
let mut rdr = ReaderBuilder::new().from_path("crypto_data.csv")?;
```

```rust
let mut trades: Vec<Trade> = Vec::new();
let mut prices: Vec<f64> = Vec::new();

for result in rdr.records() {
let record = result?;
let date = DateTime::parse_from_rfc3339(&record[0])?.with_timezone(&Utc);
let price: f64 = record[1].parse()?;
prices.push(price);

if prices.len() > 20 {
let short_avg = prices.iter().rev().take(5).sum::<f64>() / 5.0;
let long_avg = prices.iter().rev().take(20).sum::<f64>() / 20.0;
let signal = if short_avg > long_avg { 1 } else { -1 };

trades.push(Trade { date, price, signal });
}
}

for trade in trades {
println!("{:?}", trade);
}

Ok(())
}
```

In this example, we read historical cryptocurrency price data from a CSV file and implement a simple moving average crossover strategy. When the short-term average crosses above the long-term average, it generates a buy signal, and vice versa.

Risk Management and Performance Optimization

Effective trading isn't just about identifying opportunities but also managing risks efficiently. With the inherent volatility of cryptocurrencies, risk management becomes paramount. Rust's safety features, such as its strong type system and ownership model, help prevent common programming errors that could lead to significant financial losses.

Additionally, Rust's concurrency and parallelism capabilities allow for the development of high-performance trading systems. By leveraging these features, you can execute multiple trading strategies simultaneously, backtest them against extensive datasets, and optimize them for maximum efficiency.

Real-World Example: Hedging with Cryptocurrency Options

To illustrate the application of these concepts, consider a scenario where you wish to hedge a large Bitcoin position using options. By implementing a delta-neutral strategy, you can mitigate the risk of adverse price movements.

Here's a simplified Rust code snippet for calculating the delta and adjusting the hedge:

```rust
extern crate statrs;

use statrs::distribution::{Normal, Continuous};

fn calculate_delta(s: f64, k: f64, t: f64, r: f64, sigma: f64) -> f64
{
let d1 = (s.ln() - k.ln() + (r + sigma.powi(2) / 2.0) * t) / (sigma *
t.sqrt());
Normal::new(0.0, 1.0).unwrap().cdf(d1)
}

fn adjust_hedge(position: f64, delta: f64, option_contracts:
f64) -> f64 {
position - (delta * option_contracts)
}

fn main() {
let spot_price = 30000.0;
let strike_price = 32000.0;
let time_to_maturity = 0.5;
let risk_free_rate = 0.01;
let volatility = 0.6;
let position = 10.0; // Long 10 Bitcoins
let option_contracts = 100.0; // Each contract represents 0.1
Bitcoin
```

```
let    delta    =    calculate_delta(spot_price,    strike_price,
time_to_maturity, risk_free_rate, volatility);

let    hedge_adjustment    =    adjust_hedge(position,    delta,
option_contracts);

println!("Delta: {}", delta);

println!("Hedge Adjustment: {}", hedge_adjustment);
}
` ` `
```

This example calculates the delta of a Bitcoin option and adjusts the hedge accordingly. By continuously monitoring the delta and rebalancing the hedge, you can effectively manage the risk associated with holding a large cryptocurrency position.

Implementing cryptocurrency options trading algorithms in Rust combines the best of both worlds: the flexibility and power of advanced financial models and the performance and safety of a modern programming language. By leveraging Rust's capabilities, you can build robust, efficient, and secure trading systems that capitalize on the unique opportunities presented by the cryptocurrency market. As the landscape continues to evolve, staying ahead of the curve with cutting-edge technology and innovative strategies will be crucial for sustained success in this exciting domain.

Integrating Machine Learning with Rust Trading Systems

Before diving into machine learning models, acquiring and preprocessing high-quality data is crucial. Data forms the backbone of any ML system, and the quality of your data preprocessing directly impacts the model's performance. Let's begin with an example of sourcing and preprocessing financial data using Rust crates.

```rust
extern crate csv;
extern crate chrono;

use csv::ReaderBuilder;
use chrono::prelude::*;
use std::error::Error;

#[derive(Debug)]
struct MarketData {
date: DateTime<Utc>,
open: f64,
high: f64,
low: f64,
close: f64,
volume: f64,
}

fn        read_market_data(file_path:        &str)        ->
Result<Vec<MarketData>, Box<dyn Error>> {
```

```rust
let mut rdr = ReaderBuilder::new().from_path(file_path)?;
let mut data: Vec<MarketData> = Vec::new();

for result in rdr.records() {
let record = result?;
let date = DateTime::parse_from_rfc3339(&record[0])?.with_timezone(&Utc);
let open: f64 = record[1].parse()?;
let high: f64 = record[2].parse()?;
let low: f64 = record[3].parse()?;
let close: f64 = record[4].parse()?;
let volume: f64 = record[5].parse()?;

data.push(MarketData { date, open, high, low, close, volume });
}
Ok(data)
}

fn main() -> Result<(), Box<dyn Error>> {
let market_data = read_market_data("market_data.csv")?;
for data in market_data {
println!("{:?}", data);
}
Ok(())
}
```

This code snippet demonstrates how to read and parse market data from a CSV file in Rust, ensuring the data is in a structured format suitable for further analysis.

Feature Engineering

Feature engineering involves transforming raw data into meaningful features that enhance the predictive power of machine learning models. In the context of financial data, common features include moving averages, volatility measures, and momentum indicators. Here's an example of calculating the Simple Moving Average (SMA) in Rust:

```rust
fn calculate_sma(prices: &Vec<f64>, window: usize) -> Vec<f64> {
prices.windows(window)
.map(|window_slice|  window_slice.iter().sum::<f64>()  / window as f64)
.collect()
}

fn main() {
let prices = vec![100.0, 102.0, 104.0, 106.0, 108.0, 110.0];
let sma = calculate_sma(&prices, 3);
println!("SMA: {:?}", sma);
}
```

This function computes the SMA over a specified window, a fundamental feature used in many trading algorithms.

Implementing Machine Learning Models

To integrate machine learning models with Rust, leveraging existing ML libraries like TensorFlow or PyTorch can be beneficial. Although these libraries are primarily used with Python, Rust provides bindings that allow you to utilize their capabilities. For instance, the `tensorflow` crate in Rust enables you to build and execute TensorFlow models seamlessly.

Training a Model in Python

First, train an ML model using Python and save the model. Here's a simple example of training a logistic regression model using scikit-learn:

```python
import pandas as pd
from sklearn.linear_model import LogisticRegression
import joblib

# Load dataset
data = pd.read_csv('market_data.csv')
X = data[['feature1', 'feature2', 'feature3']]
y = data['target']
```

```python
# Train model
model = LogisticRegression()
model.fit(X, y)

# Save model
joblib.dump(model, 'model.pkl')
```

Loading and Using the Model in Rust

Next, use Rust to load and make predictions with the trained model. The `joblib` library and the `serde` crate facilitate this process.

```rust
extern crate joblib;

use joblib::JoblibError;

fn load_model(file_path: &str) -> Result<joblib::Joblib, JoblibError> {
joblib::load(file_path)
}

fn make_prediction(model: &joblib::Joblib, features: Vec<f64>) -> f64 {
model.predict(&features)
}
```

```rust
fn main() {
let model_path = "model.pkl";
let model = load_model(model_path).expect("Failed to load model");

let features = vec![1.0, 0.5, 0.2];
let prediction = make_prediction(&model, features);
println!("Prediction: {}", prediction);
}
```

This code illustrates loading a pre-trained model and making predictions in Rust, leveraging the power of machine learning without leaving the Rust ecosystem.

Backtesting and Performance Evaluation

Backtesting involves testing trading strategies on historical data to evaluate their performance. Rust's performance strengths are invaluable here, allowing you to run extensive backtests efficiently. Here's a simple backtesting framework in Rust:

```rust
#[derive(Debug)]
struct Trade {
entry_date: DateTime<Utc>,
exit_date: DateTime<Utc>,
```

```rust
    profit: f64,
}


fn backtest_strategy(data: &Vec<MarketData>, signals:
&Vec<i8>) -> Vec<Trade> {
    let mut trades: Vec<Trade> = Vec::new();
    let mut entry_date = None;
    let mut entry_price = 0.0;

    for (i, signal) in signals.iter().enumerate() {
        if *signal == 1 && entry_date.is_none() {
            entry_date = Some(data[i].date);
            entry_price = data[i].close;
        } else if *signal == -1 && entry_date.is_some() {
            let exit_date = data[i].date;
            let exit_price = data[i].close;
            trades.push(Trade {
                entry_date: entry_date.unwrap(),
                exit_date,
                profit: exit_price - entry_price,
            });
            entry_date = None;
        }
    }

    trades
}
```

```
fn main() -> Result<(), Box<dyn Error>> {
let market_data = read_market_data("market_data.csv")?;
let signals = vec![1, 0, 0, -1, 1, -1]; // Example signals
let trades = backtest_strategy(&market_data, &signals);

for trade in trades {
println!("{:?}", trade);
}
Ok(())
}
```

This example demonstrates a basic backtesting framework that evaluates a simple trading strategy, recording trades and their profits.

Real-World Application: Predictive Analytics with Machine Learning

Predictive analytics involves using historical data to predict future market movements. By integrating machine learning models with Rust, you can develop highly accurate predictive analytics systems. Consider a scenario where you predict the next day's closing price of a cryptocurrency based on historical data and other features.

Training the Predictive Model in Python

```python
import pandas as pd
from sklearn.ensemble import RandomForestRegressor
import joblib

# Load dataset
data = pd.read_csv('crypto_data.csv')
X = data[['feature1', 'feature2', 'feature3']]
y = data['next_day_close']

# Train model
model = RandomForestRegressor()
model.fit(X, y)

# Save model
joblib.dump(model, 'predictive_model.pkl')
```

Using the Predictive Model in Rust

```rust
extern crate joblib;

use joblib::JoblibError;

fn load_predictive_model(file_path: &str) -> Result<joblib::Joblib, JoblibError> {
```

```
joblib::load(file_path)
}

fn predict_next_day_close(model: &joblib::Joblib, features:
Vec<f64>) -> f64 {
model.predict(&features)
}

fn main() {
let model_path = "predictive_model.pkl";
let model =
load_predictive_model(model_path).expect("Failed to load
model");

let features = vec![1.0, 0.5, 0.2];
let predicted_close = predict_next_day_close(&model,
features);
println!("Predicted Next Day Close: {}", predicted_close);
}
` ` `
```

Integrating machine learning with Rust trading systems, you can build robust, efficient, and highly predictive trading strategies. This powerful combination enables you to stay ahead of market trends, manage risks effectively, and optimize trading performance.

Handling Big Data with Rust

The first step in handling big data is efficient data ingestion and storage. In Rust, several crates can help with this, such as `tokio` for asynchronous operations and `csv` for handling CSV files. Let's start by examining how to ingest large financial datasets asynchronously.

```rust
extern crate tokio;
extern crate csv;

use tokio::fs::File;
use tokio::io::{self, AsyncBufReadExt, BufReader};
use csv::StringRecord;
use std::error::Error;

#[tokio::main]
async fn main() -> Result<(), Box<dyn Error>> {
let file = File::open("large_market_data.csv").await?;
let reader = BufReader::new(file);
let mut csv_reader = csv::ReaderBuilder::new().from_reader(reader);

while let Some(result) = csv_reader.records().next() {
let record: StringRecord = result?;
// Process each record
println!("{:?}", record);
}
```

```rust
Ok(())
}
```

This example illustrates how to read a large CSV file asynchronously, ensuring that your system remains responsive while processing massive amounts of data.

In-Memory Data Processing with Arrow

Apache Arrow is a cross-language development platform for in-memory data that enables high-performance data processing. Rust has a robust `arrow` crate that can be utilized to handle columnar data efficiently, which is particularly useful for the types of operations common in financial analytics.

```rust
extern crate arrow;

use arrow::array::{Float64Array, StringArray};
use arrow::record_batch::RecordBatch;
use arrow::datatypes::{DataType, Field, Schema};
use std::sync::Arc;

fn main() -> Result<(), Box<dyn std::error::Error>> {
// Create an array for each field
let date_array = StringArray::from(vec!["2023-01-01", "2023-01-02", "2023-01-03"]);
```

```rust
let close_array = Float64Array::from(vec![100.0, 101.0,
102.0]);

// Define the schema
let schema = Arc::new(Schema::new(vec![
Field::new("date", DataType::Utf8, false),
Field::new("close", DataType::Float64, false),
]));

// Create a RecordBatch
let record_batch = RecordBatch::try_new(
schema,
vec![
Arc::new(date_array) as Arc<dyn arrow::array::Array>,
Arc::new(close_array) as Arc<dyn arrow::array::Array>,
],
)?;

// Process the record batch
println!("{:?}", record_batch);

Ok(())
}
```
` ` `

This code demonstrates how to create and process in-memory columnar data using Apache Arrow in Rust, providing a foundation for high-performance data manipulation.

Distributed Data Processing with DataFusion

For even larger datasets that cannot fit into memory, distributed data processing frameworks become necessary. DataFusion is a Rust-based query engine that leverages Apache Arrow for in-memory processing. It allows you to perform complex queries on large datasets in a distributed manner.

```rust
extern crate datafusion;

use datafusion::prelude::*;
use arrow::datatypes::{DataType, Field, Schema};
use std::sync::Arc;

#[tokio::main]
async fn main() -> Result<()> {
let schema = Arc::new(Schema::new(vec![
Field::new("date", DataType::Utf8, false),
Field::new("close", DataType::Float64, false),
]));

let csv_config = CsvReadOptions::new()
.schema(&schema)
.delimiter(b',')
.has_header(true);
```

```
let mut ctx = ExecutionContext::new();
let df = ctx.read_csv("large_market_data.csv", csv_config)?;

let results = df
.filter(col("close").gt_eq(lit(100.0)))?
.collect()
.await?;

results.iter().for_each(|batch| {
println!("{:?}", batch);
});

Ok(())
}
```

This example demonstrates how to use DataFusion to perform a distributed query on a large CSV file, filtering records where the closing price is greater than or equal to 100.0. DataFusion's ability to handle large datasets distributed across multiple nodes makes it a powerful tool for big data processing in Rust.

Real-Time Data Streaming with Kafka

In financial markets, real-time data streaming is critical for making timely decisions. Apache Kafka is a popular platform for building real-time data pipelines, and the `rdkafka` crate in Rust offers bindings to interact with Kafka.

```rust
extern crate rdkafka;

use rdkafka::config::ClientConfig;
use rdkafka::consumer::{Consumer, StreamConsumer};
use rdkafka::message::Message;
use rdkafka::error::KafkaResult;

#[tokio::main]
async fn main() -> KafkaResult<()> {
let consumer: StreamConsumer = ClientConfig::new()
.set("group.id", "example_group")
.set("bootstrap.servers", "localhost:9092")
.create()?;

consumer.subscribe(&["financial_data"])?;

while let Some(message) = consumer.recv().await {
match message {
Ok(m) => {
if let Some(payload) = m.payload() {
println!("Received: {:?}", String::from_utf8_lossy(payload));
}
}
Err(e) => eprintln!("Kafka error: {:?}", e),
}
```

```
}

Ok(())
}
```

This code snippet shows how to consume real-time financial data from a Kafka topic using Rust, enabling your trading systems to react quickly to market changes.

Parallel and Concurrent Data Processing

Rust's strong support for concurrency and parallelism is another advantage for handling big data. The `rayon` crate provides a simple and efficient way to perform data processing in parallel.

```rust
extern crate rayon;

use rayon::prelude::*;
use std::time::Instant;

fn main() {
let data: Vec<i32> = (1..1_000_000).collect();
let start = Instant::now();

let sum: i32 = data.par_iter().map(|&x| x * 2).sum();
```

```rust
    println!("Sum: {}", sum);
    println!("Time elapsed: {:?}", start.elapsed());
}
```

This example demonstrates how to use the `rayon` crate to perform parallel processing, doubling each element in a large vector and computing their sum. By leveraging parallelism, you can significantly reduce the time required for data processing tasks.

Optimizing Performance and Memory Usage

Handling big data efficiently requires optimizing both performance and memory usage. Rust's ownership model and zero-cost abstractions help to minimize overhead and maximize performance. Additionally, using efficient data structures and algorithms is crucial.

Consider using memory-mapped files for fast data access without loading the entire file into memory. The `memmap` crate allows you to create memory-mapped file objects in Rust.

```rust
extern crate memmap;

use memmap::MmapOptions;
use std::fs::File;
use std::io::Error;
```

```
fn main() -> Result<(), Error> {
let file = File::open("large_file.dat")?;
let mmap = unsafe { MmapOptions::new().map(&file)? };

for byte in mmap.iter() {
println!("{}", byte);
}

Ok(())
}
```

This example shows how to use memory-mapped files to access large datasets efficiently, avoiding the overhead of loading the entire file into memory.

Case Study: High-Frequency Trading with Real-Time Data Analysis

To illustrate the practical application of these techniques, consider a high-frequency trading (HFT) system that processes real-time market data to execute trades. The system must ingest data from multiple sources, preprocess and analyze it in real-time, and make trading decisions within milliseconds.

1.Data Ingestion: Use Kafka or similar real-time data streaming platforms to ingest market data.

2.Data Preprocessing: Apply feature engineering techniques

such as calculating moving averages, volatility, and other indicators using Apache Arrow for in-memory processing.

3.Real-Time Analysis: Implement parallel and concurrent data processing using the `rayon` crate to ensure low-latency analysis.

4.Decision Making: Deploy machine learning models trained offline using libraries like TensorFlow, and integrate them with Rust for real-time predictions.

5.Execution: Execute trades based on the analysis and predictions, ensuring ultra-low latency using Rust's performance-optimized code.

Combining these elements, you can create a robust HFT system capable of handling and processing big data efficiently in real-time, ultimately gaining a competitive edge in the financial markets.

Rust's capabilities in handling big data make it an excellent choice for developing high-performance financial applications. From efficient data ingestion and in-memory processing to distributed querying and real-time data streaming, Rust provides the tools you need to manage and analyze large datasets effectively. By leveraging these techniques and tools, you can build powerful, scalable, and efficient trading systems that handle the complexities of modern financial markets with ease.

The Rise of Machine Learning and AI in Trading

One of the most significant trends in algorithmic trading is the increasing integration of machine learning (ML) and artificial intelligence (AI) techniques. ML models can analyze vast amounts of historical data to identify patterns and make predictions, while AI systems can automate trading strategies and decision-making processes. Rust's performance capabilities make it an ideal language for implementing these advanced models.

Implementing ML Models in Rust

Although Rust is not traditionally associated with machine learning, its ecosystem is growing rapidly. Libraries like `smartcore` and bindings to popular ML frameworks like TensorFlow and PyTorch allow you to implement sophisticated ML models in Rust.

```rust
extern crate smartcore;

use smartcore::linalg::naive::dense_matrix::DenseMatrix;
use smartcore::linear::linear_regression::LinearRegression;

fn main() {
let x = DenseMatrix::from_2d_array(&[
&[1.0, 2.0],
&[2.0, 3.0],
&[3.0, 4.0],
&[4.0, 5.0],
]);
let y = vec![1.0, 2.0, 3.0, 4.0];
```

```
let        lr       =          LinearRegression::fit(&x,         &y,
Default::default()).unwrap();

println!("{:?}", lr.predict(&x).unwrap());
}
```
```

This example demonstrates how to implement a simple linear regression model in Rust using the `smartcore` library. As the ML ecosystem in Rust matures, expect more sophisticated models and tools to become available.

Distributed Computing and Cloud Integration

Another trend is the move towards distributed computing and cloud-based solutions. These technologies enable the processing of massive datasets and the execution of complex algorithms with minimal latency. Rust's concurrency and performance features make it well-suited for distributed computing environments.

# Rust and Distributed Systems

Rust's `tokio` and `async-std` libraries facilitate the creation of asynchronous applications that can efficiently manage resources in a distributed system. Moreover, Rust's strong compile-time guarantees ensure that distributed applications are reliable and safe.

```rust
extern crate tokio;
```
```

```
use tokio::sync::mpsc;

#[tokio::main]
async fn main() {
let (tx, mut rx) = mpsc::channel(32);

tokio::spawn(async move {
for i in 0..10 {
tx.send(i).await.unwrap();
}
});

while let Some(value) = rx.recv().await {
println!("Got: {}", value);
}
}
```

This example shows how to use `tokio` for asynchronous message passing, a common pattern in distributed systems. As cloud computing and distributed architectures become more prevalent, Rust's capabilities in these areas will become increasingly valuable.

High-Frequency Trading (HFT) and Latency Optimization

High-frequency trading relies on ultra-low latency to gain a competitive edge. The need for speed is paramount, and Rust's performance characteristics make it a strong candidate for HFT applications.

Optimizing Latency with Rust

Rust's zero-cost abstractions and fine-grained control over memory management allow developers to optimize code for minimal latency. Techniques such as lock-free data structures and efficient use of hardware resources are crucial.

```rust
extern crate crossbeam;

use crossbeam::channel::unbounded;
use std::thread;

fn main() {
let (sender, receiver) = unbounded();

let handle = thread::spawn(move || {
for _ in 0..10 {
sender.send(1).unwrap();
}
});

for _ in 0..10 {
let msg = receiver.recv().unwrap();
println!("Received: {}", msg);
```

```
}
```

```
handle.join().unwrap();
```

```
}
```

` ` `

This example demonstrates how to use the `crossbeam` crate to implement lock-free channels, which are essential for reducing latency in HFT systems.

Regulatory Compliance and Risk Management

With the increasing complexity of financial markets, regulatory compliance and risk management are becoming more critical. Rust's safety guarantees and deterministic behavior make it a suitable choice for developing systems that adhere to strict regulatory requirements.

Risk Management with Rust

Rust's type system and ownership model help prevent many common programming errors, leading to more robust and compliant systems. Additionally, Rust's ability to perform static analysis at compile time can be leveraged to enforce compliance rules.

` ` `rust

```
fn calculate_risk(position: f64, market_price: f64) -> f64 {
if position < 0.0 {
panic!("Negative position not allowed!");
```

```
}
position * market_price
}

fn main() {
let risk = calculate_risk(100.0, 50.0);
println!("Risk: {}", risk);
}
` ` `
```

This simple example demonstrates how Rust's type system can be used to enforce rules and prevent erroneous inputs, a crucial aspect of risk management.

The Role of Quantum Computing

Quantum computing is an emerging field that promises to revolutionize algorithmic trading by solving complex problems at unprecedented speeds. While still in its infancy, the integration of quantum computing with traditional systems is a trend to watch.

Quantum Computing and Rust

Although Rust is not yet a primary language for quantum computing, its performance and safety features make it a candidate for hybrid systems that combine classical and quantum computing. Libraries like `qrusty` are beginning to explore this space.

```rust
extern crate qrysty;

use qrysty::qvm::QuantumState;

fn main() {
let mut state = QuantumState::new(1);
state.h(0);
println!("{:?}", state.measure());
}
```

This example illustrates a basic quantum computing operation using the `qrysty` library. As quantum computing evolves, Rust could play a significant role in developing hybrid systems.

The Future of Rust in Algorithmic Trading

The trends discussed above highlight the growing role of Rust in the future of algorithmic trading. Its performance, safety, and concurrency features make it well-suited for the demands of modern trading systems. As the Rust ecosystem continues to evolve, expect to see more libraries and tools tailored specifically for financial applications.

Moreover, the community around Rust is vibrant and rapidly growing, contributing to its robust ecosystem. This growth, combined with Rust's technical advantages, positions it as a key player in the future of algorithmic trading.

The future of algorithmic trading is set to be defined by advancements in machine learning, distributed computing, high-frequency trading, regulatory compliance, and quantum computing. Rust, with its unique combination of performance, safety, and concurrency, is ideally positioned to be at the forefront of these developments. By staying abreast of these trends and leveraging Rust's capabilities, you can ensure that your trading systems remain cutting-edge and competitive in the ever-evolving financial markets.